# Beginner's Guide to SolidWorks 2011 – Level II

**Alejandro Reyes, MSME**
**Certified SolidWorks Professional**

ISBN: 978-1-58503-651-6

PUBLICATIONS

Schroff Development Corporation

www.SDCpublications.com

**Schroff Development Corporation**
P.O. Box 1334
Mission KS 66222
(913) 262-2664
www.SDCpublications.com

Publisher: Stephen Schroff

## Trademarks and Disclaimer

SolidWorks and its family of products are registered trademarks of Dassault Systemes. Microsoft Windows and its family products are registered trademarks of the Microsoft Corporation.

Every effort has been made to provide an accurate text. The author and the manufacturers shall not be held liable for any parts developed with this book or held responsible for any inaccuracies or errors that appear in the book.

## Examination Copies:

Books received as examination copies are for review purposes only and may not be made available for student use. Resale of examination copies is prohibited.

## Electronic Files:

Any electronic files associated with this book are licensed to the original user only. These files may not be transferred to any other party.

# *Acknowledgements*

The first release of *Beginner's Guide to SolidWorks 2011 – Level II* is dedicated to the love of my life, my wife Patricia and my kids Liz, Ale and Hector, who have given me the time, support and patience to write this book. To you, all my love.

Also, I wish to thank the hundreds of students, users, professors and engineers whose great ideas and words of encouragement helped me to make this second SolidWorks training book.

Special thanks to Larry Dixon who sparked the idea to start writing the second volume of Beginner's Guide to SolidWorks.

# *About the Author*

Alejandro Reyes holds a BSME from the Instituto Tecnológico de Ciudad Juárez, Mexico in electro-mechanical engineering and a Masters Degree from the University of Texas at El Paso in mechanical design, with strong focus in Materials Science and Finite Element Analysis.

Alejandro spent more than 8 years as a SolidWorks Value Added Reseller. During this time he was a Certified SolidWorks Instructor and Support Technician, CosmosWorks Support Technician, and a Certified SolidWorks Professional, credentials that he still maintains. Alejandro has over 17 years of experience using CAD/CAM/FEA software and is currently the President of MechaniCAD Inc.

His professional interests include finding alternatives and improvements to existing products, FEA analyses and new technologies. On a personal level, he enjoys spending time with his family and friends.

**Notes:**

# *Table of Contents*

List of commands introduced in each chapter. Note that many commands are used extensively in following chapters after been presented.

### Multi Body Parts
Multi Body
Local Operations
Hide/Show Body
Merge
Feature Scope
Delete Body
Body Pattern
Combine Bodies
  Add
  Subtract
  Common
Bodies to keep

### Contour Selection
Regions available
Contour Selection
Shared Sketch
Start From: Condition

### Part Editing
What's Wrong
Parent/Child relations
Sketch Editing
Dangling Relations
Delete Absorbed
  Features
Sketch Relations
Over Defined Sketch
Not Solved Sketch
SketchXpert
View Sketch Relations

### Equations
Rename Dimensions
Pattern Seed Only
Add Equations
Edit Equations
Delete Equations
Link Values

### Top Down Design
New Part
Edit In Context
Assembly Transparency
Internal Part
Externalize Part
Edit Assembly
External References
  In Context
  Out of Context
  Locked
  Broken
List External References

### Sheet Metal and Top Down Design
Base Flange
Sheet Metal Thickness
Bend Radius
Bend Allowance
Bend Deduction
K-Factor
Auto-Relief
  Rectangular
  Obround
  Tear
Flat Pattern
Forming Tools
Modify Sketch
Link to Thickness
Normal Cut
3D Content Central
Vent feature
Miter Flange
Unfold/Fold Bend
Edge Flange
Build Library Features
Library Parts
Mate Reference
Break Corners
Jog bend
Flat Pattern Drawing
Bend Notes

Convert to Sheet Metal
Closed Corners
Selection Filters
Sketch Pattern
Feature Driven Pattern
Hem Feature
Creating Forming Tools
Component Pattern
Collision Detection
Flexible Sub Assemblies
Assembly Features

### 3D Sketch
3D Sketch
3D Sketch Relations
Derived Sketch
Projected Curve

### Weldments
3D Sketch review
Cut list
Weldment feature
Structural Member
Corner Treatment
  End Miter
  End Butt
Locate Profile
Rotate Profile
Trim/Extend
Gusset
End Cap
Weld Beads
Weldment Cut List
Weldment Drawings
Cut List Table
Weld Table
Weld Symbols
Save Bodies to
  Assembly
Structural Member
  Libraries

**Surfacing**
Revolved Surface
Lofted Surface
Extruded Surface
Direction of Extrusion
Extrude with Draft
Trim Surface
Mutual Trim
Planar Surface
Filled Surface
Knit Surface
Constant Width Fillet
Thicken
Body Split

Face Fillet
Extend Surface
Extrude From
Mirror Bodies
Swept Surface
Twist Along Path
Sweep Cut

**Mold Tools**
Draft Analysis
Direction of Pull
Positive Draft
Negative Draft
Draft

Neutral Plane
Rollback/Roll Forward
Scale
Parting Line
Parting Surface
Tooling Split
Shut Off Surfaces
Move/Copy body
Delete Face
Face Classification
Manual Parting Line
  Selection
Select Open Loop
Side Core

**Notes:**

# *Introduction*

*Beginner's Guide to SolidWorks 2011 – Level II* starts where *Beginner's Guide – Level I* ends, following the same easy to read style, but this time covering advanced topics and techniques.

The purpose of this book is to teach advanced techniques including sheet metal, surfacing, how to create components in the context of an assembly and reference other components (Top-down design), propagate design changes with SolidWorks' parametric capabilities, mold design, welded structures, and more while explaining the basic concepts of each trade to allow the reader to understand the how and why of each operation.

We'll use simple examples to allow the reader to better understand each command and environment, as well as to make it easier to explain the purpose of each step, maximizing the learning time by focusing on one task at a time. Keep in mind that this is a SolidWorks learning book, and the specific details of some of the topics that will be covered go far beyond the scope of this book; entire books have been written about sheet metal processes, mold design, welded structures, and such; with that in mind, please remember that this book will teach you how to use SolidWorks' tools for those trades, and at no time will attempt to teach the trade itself.

At the end of this book, the reader will have acquired enough skills to be highly competitive when it comes to designing with SolidWorks, and while there are many less frequently used commands and options available that will not be covered in this book, rest assured that those covered are most of the commands used every day by SolidWorks designers.

Files required to complete some of the exercises will be available for download on our website (***http://www.mechanicad.com/download.html***) as well as the completed files made throughout the book to help you practice and enhance your skills. We hope you learn many new things and enjoy reading this book as much as we enjoyed making it. We love to hear ideas and comments from our readers. If you have any, please share them with us and our readers; we'll try our best to accommodate any suggestions to improve and expand the content of this book, and while we cannot guarantee that any will make it to the next edition, we can assure you that we reply to all email messages.

areyes@mechanicad.com

## *Prerequisites*

This book has been written assuming the reader has knowledge of the following topics:

- Familiarity with the Windows operating system;
- General knowledge of mechanical design and drafting;
- Previous experience with SolidWorks.
- A general understanding of sheet metal, structural and molding processes will help to better understand these topics.

# *Multi Body Parts, Sketch Editing and Other Tools*

SolidWorks offers a number of tools to help us model components easier and faster with powerful options like multi body parts and contour selection. Multi body parts means that we can have more than one "solid" in a part. Up until now we have been modeling parts as single body parts, meaning that each feature either added or removed material to the part, but always resulted in a single solid body. Designing with multi body parts allows us to do things that are not possible with a single body component like, among other things, combine bodies, remove one body from another or calculate their common volume. Multi body operations are particularly useful when working with mold design and is the essence of the weldments environment (both are covered in this book).

So far we have worked with single and multiple contour open or closed sketches. In this section we'll cover how to use Contour selection to work with sketches with multiple entities sharing an endpoint and/or having self-intersecting lines. We'll learn how to take advantage of these situations and make the best of them.

Another topic that is very important to modeling in SolidWorks is editing parts to fix errors or change components. After all, when we are designing, most likely we'll have to make changes along the way, and sometimes those changes can cause trouble down the road. In the Editing section we'll cover different options available when editing parts, as well as fixing and recovering from errors.

One last topic we'll cover in this section deals with maintaining design intent; we'll learn how to add, edit and delete equations in a part.

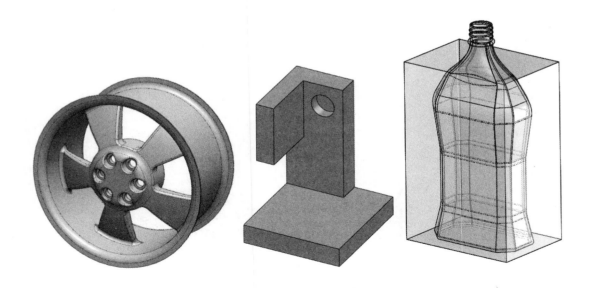

**Notes:**

## *Multi Body Parts*

As we stated earlier, multi body parts allow us to do certain operations that would be difficult to accomplish with a single body part. First, we'll talk about how to make multi body parts, and after that how to use them.

**1. –** Multi body parts are made by adding material that is not connected to the current solid, that is purposely <u>not</u> merged to it, or by splitting an existing body. To show this, make a new part, and add a sketch to the Front plane as shown. We will not worry about dimensions here as we are just illustrating the concept of how multi bodies work.

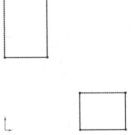

**2. –** Select the "Boss Extrude" command. Notice that we are not given a warning about having two separate bodies; it just works. Extrude any size that looks similar to the following image (dimensions are not important at this time) and click **OK** to finish. (Making two or more extruded/revolved/swept/lofted features would work just the same.)

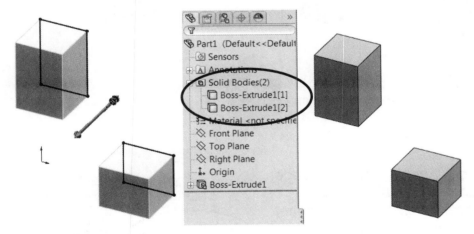

The first thing we notice is a new folder in the FeatureManager called "**Solid Bodies(2)**". This folder is automatically added when SolidWorks detects multiple disjointed bodies in a part and lists the number of bodies found in the part (in this case, 2). If we expand the folder, we can see the two bodies in our part listed under it. The important thing to know and remember is that **multi body parts are not to be confused or used as an assembly**; parts and assemblies have significant differences and each serves a different purpose. A multi body part is used mostly as a means to an end.

**3.** – The next step is to add a new feature. When working in a multi body part we can make 'local' operations; for example, a shell feature affecting only one body. Select the "Shell" command from the Features toolbar, and shell the bottom body as indicated.

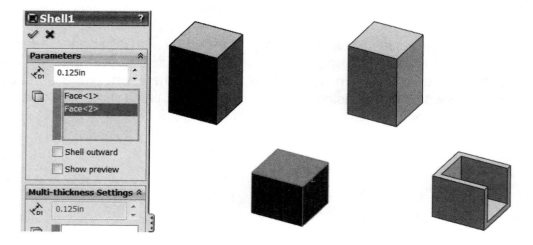

**4.** – Select the **Fillet** command and round two corners to the top body as shown.

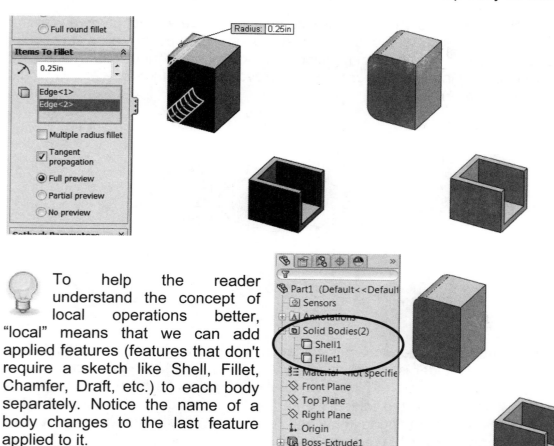

To help the reader understand the concept of local operations better, "local" means that we can add applied features (features that don't require a sketch like Shell, Fillet, Chamfer, Draft, etc.) to each body separately. Notice the name of a body changes to the last feature applied to it.

**5.** – When working with multi body parts, adding more features automatically selects existing bodies to modify; this is the default behavior. Optionally, we can select which bodies to "merge" (or fuse with) to make a single body, or select which bodies to cut. Here we'll make a new boss and explore the option to merge two existing bodies. Select the front face of a body and make the following sketch.

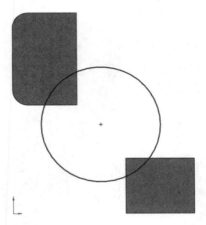

**6.** – Extrude the sketch *into* the existing bodies. Notice the "**Merge result**" option in the Extrude command. It's always been there (except when there are no existing bodies), and by default is always checked. A new option at the bottom of the Extrude command is "**Feature Scope**". This is where we can select which bodies to affect, either "All bodies" or "Selected bodies" and either is automatically or manually selected. By default Feature Scope is set to "**Selected bodies**" and "**Auto-select**". These two options mean that by default the new feature will merge with any body it intersects. Uncheck "**Merge result**" and click **OK** to finish (when unchecked, "**Feature Scope**" is automatically removed.)

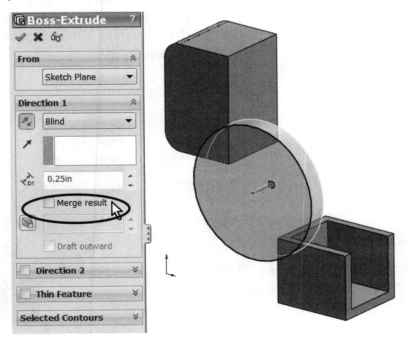

**7. –** The result is three bodies in our part. See how the different bodies' edges intersect each other. If we had left the "**Merge result**" option checked, we would not see these edges overlapping as they would have merged into a single body. Edit the definition of the last extrusion to explore the effect of different "**Merge Result**" and "**Feature Scope**" combinations.

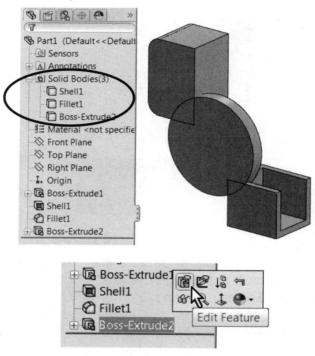

| Combination: | Result: |
|---|---|
| **Merge Result**: Checked<br>**Feature Scope**: Auto-Select<br><br>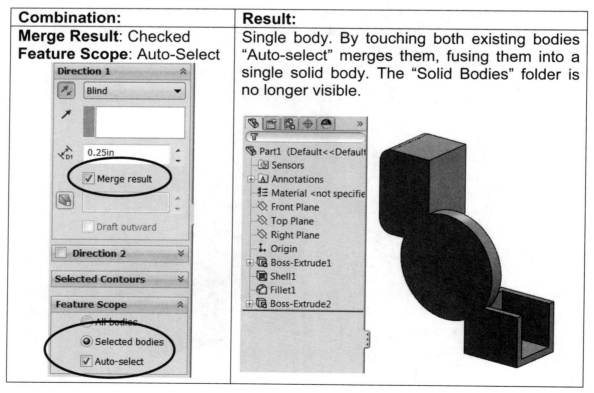 | Single body. By touching both existing bodies "Auto-select" merges them, fusing them into a single solid body. The "Solid Bodies" folder is no longer visible. |

| **Merge result:** Checked<br>**Auto-select**: Unchecked<br>Add shell body to selection box<br><br>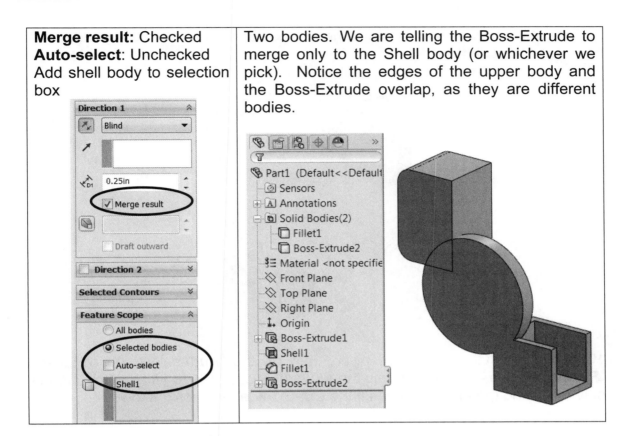 | Two bodies. We are telling the Boss-Extrude to merge only to the Shell body (or whichever we pick). Notice the edges of the upper body and the Boss-Extrude overlap, as they are different bodies. |
|---|---|

**8.** –The "**Merge result**" option works the same way with any feature that adds material to the part, including revolved boss, sweep, loft, etc. Now we'll see how it works when we remove material. Delete the Boss-Extrude feature and keep the sketch. Select the sketch and click in Cut-Extrude using the "Through All" option. In this case the only difference from a boss extrude is that we only have the "**Feature Scope**" option at the bottom with the same selection options: "All bodies" or "Selected Bodies," and with the "Auto-select" or manually selected bodies. Leave the "Auto-select" option on and click **OK** to finish.

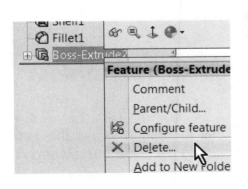

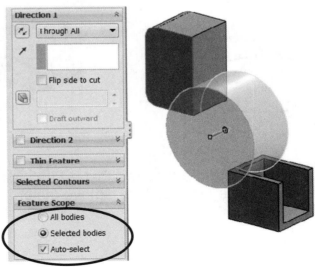

**9. –** What we end up with is the same two bodies we had before, but now they have a cut through them.

**10. –** Edit the Cut-Extrude definition, turn off the "Auto-select" option in the **"Feature Scope,"** and select only the top body. Click **OK** to finish. Now we are only modifying the top solid, even if the Cut-Extrude overlaps the lower body.

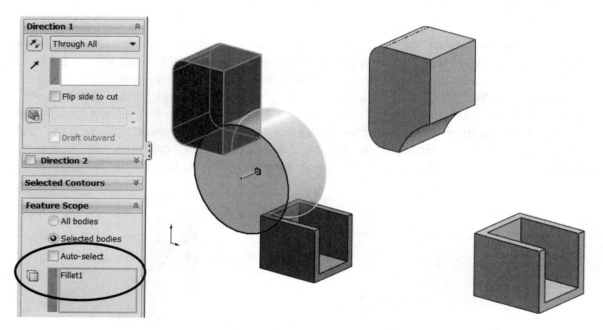

And just as with the features that add material, this technique works the same way with all the features that remove material including revolved cut, sweep cut, loft cut, etc.

**11.** – Modeling with multi bodies is a powerful technique to model parts that would otherwise be difficult to complete. One frequently used technique is called "bridging"; this means to connect two or more bodies by adding material between them to merge into a single solid body.  Reasons to use this technique may include a model where we know what opposite sides/ends of a part look like, but we may not know what the middle (the "bridge") should be like. For our example we'll assume that we need to design a car's wheel. We know what the actual tire and hub dimensions should be, but we don't know yet what the spokes will look like; we just know it has to look great ☺.

We'll assume the dimensions for the wheel are as shown in the following sketches. The first part of the wheel will be the hub or mounting pad.  Draw the following sketch in the Right plane and make a 360° Boss-Revolve.  Tire dimensions are usually in millimeters. Since the sketch dimensions are given in millimeters, be sure to change your part's dimensions accordingly (**Tools, Options, Document Options, Units**). Pay attention to the diameter dimensions (doubled about the horizontal centerline).

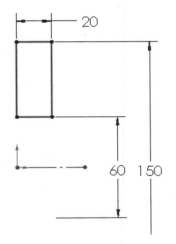
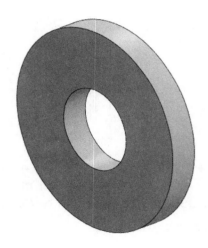

**12.** – Make a pattern of 5 holes to mount the wheel to the car.

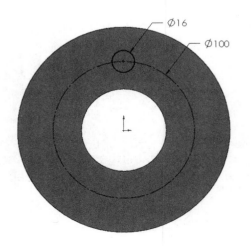
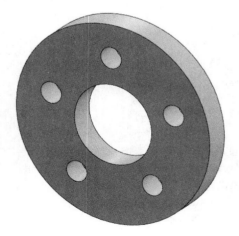

**13.** – Now we'll make the wheel's rim that matches the tire. Draw the following sketch also in the Right plane. (The 330 mm diameter dimension is doubled about the horizontal centerline as diameter.)

> **TIP:** Make the two short lines on the sides equal, and the two lines connected to the 12mm horizontal line also equal.

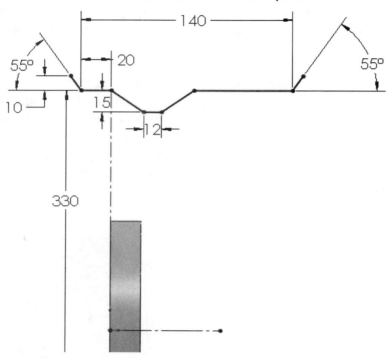

**14.** – After finishing the sketch, make a Revolved-Boss. Since this is an open sketch we will be warned about closing it if we don't want a thin feature. Select NO when asked. Make a thin revolved feature 5mm thick going inside.

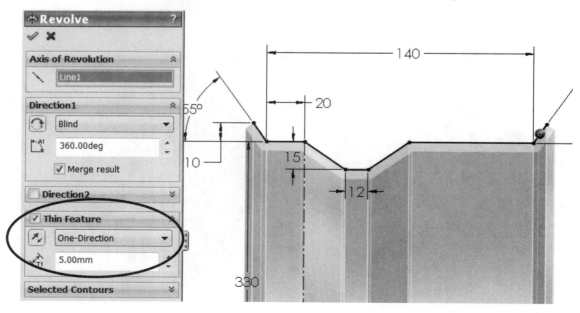

After finishing the revolved feature, we can see that now we have two bodies.

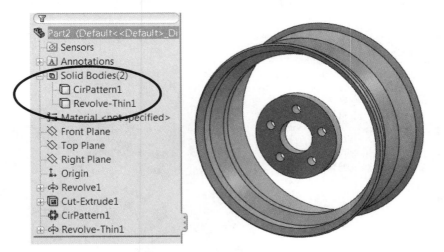

**15. –** Now we need to make the spoke in the wheel; this is the part where we can get creative. We'll assume our limitations are defined by the hub and the actual rim where the tire mounts. We'll design the first spoke and will not merge it to any other body; we'll have to make a couple of local operations on the spoke and show how to make a body pattern later on. Switch to a Right view and add a sketch in the Right plane. Change to "Hidden Lines Visible" mode for visibility. A shaded model is shown for sketch clarity. Make arcs tangent to both lines and each other, and with equal radii. The vertical lines are coincident to the first hole in the hub and the rim's outside edge. This will be the path for a sweep.

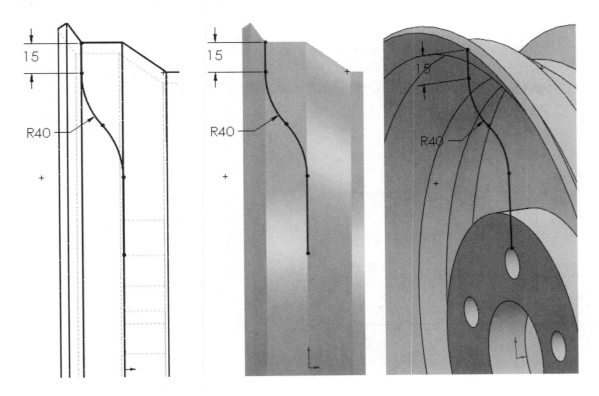

**16.** – Exit the sketch and make a new plane parallel to the Top plane coincident to the top endpoint of the previous sketch on which to draw the profile.

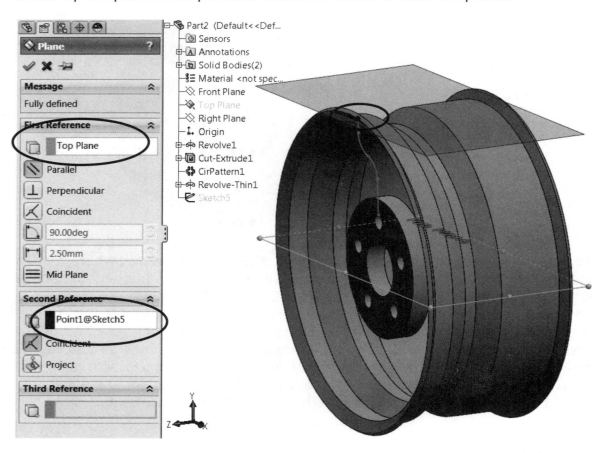

**17.** – Switch to a Top view, add a new sketch to the new plane and draw the following sketch. This sketch will be the Profile for the sweep. The arc is tangent to the edge where the path starts. Exit the sketch when done.

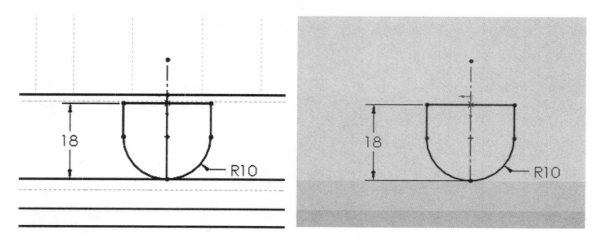

**18. –** Select the **Sweep** command; pick the second sketch for the profile and the first one as the path. In the Options, uncheck "**Merge Result**" as we still need to make a couple more operations before merging all bodies. Click **OK** to finish.

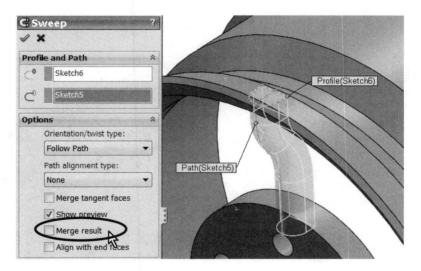

**19. –** Now we have three bodies. To continue, we'll hide the first two and only leave the Sweep body visible. Select each of the other two bodies and hide them.

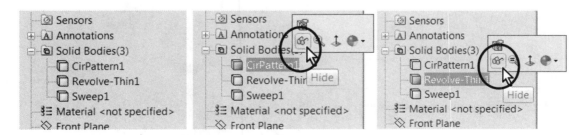

**20. –** After we are left with only the Sweep body, select the **Shell** command and remove the ends and back of the body. Make the shell 3mm thick.

**21. –** We need to make a cylindrical cut to the top; otherwise we'll have a part of the Sweep coming through the top. Show the Revolve-Thin body to see it.

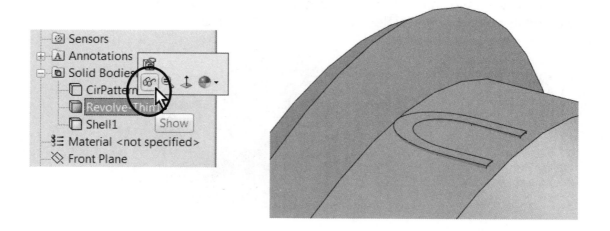

**22.** – Hide the Revolve-Thin feature again and switch to a Right view. Add a new sketch in the Right plane as shown. We are making the cut just under the top to make sure the Sweep body (now named Shell1) will not go through the top. Add a horizontal centerline at the origin to make the Revolved Cut about it.

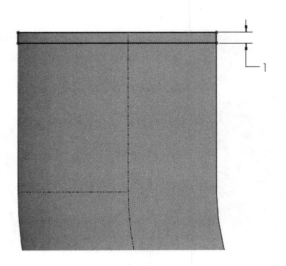

**23.** – Select the **Revolved Cut** command. What we want to do is to cut only the spoke body, and nothing else. Under "**Feature Scope**" uncheck "Auto-select" and select the spoke body only.

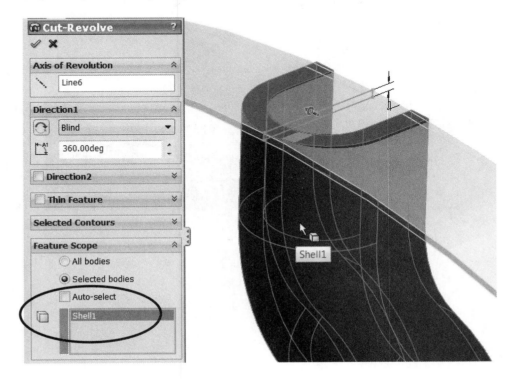

**24.** – After clicking **OK** we get a new dialog box asking us which bodies we want to keep, since the cut we are making divides the spoke in three pieces. Pick the "**Selected bodies**" option, and check the box for the spoke's largest piece which we are interested in keeping. Click **OK** to complete. In this case we still have our three original bodies and discard the two smaller ones.

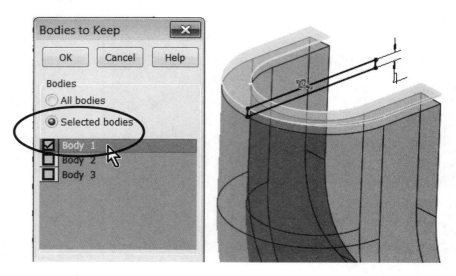

**25.** – If we had opted to keep all three bodies after the Revolved Cut, we would have five bodies in our part. To eliminate the two extra bodies we don't want, we have to delete them. Select the two bodies, right mouse click and select "**Delete Bodies**". Make sure the correct bodies are selected and click **OK** to finish.

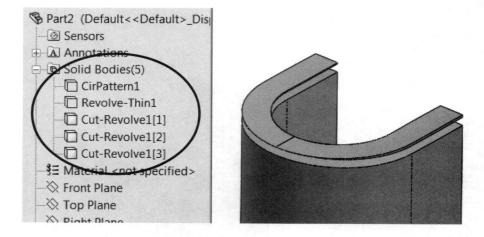

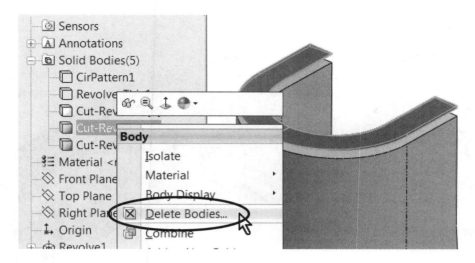

A new feature "**Body-Delete**" is added to the FeatureManager.

For our example we'll use the approach to select the bodies to keep at the time of making the Cut-Revolve instead of deleting the remaining bodies with an additional operation.

**26. –** Now add a Full Round Fillet to each of the sides of the Spoke. Select the **Fillet** command with the **Full Round** option. Select both side and center faces to round both sides of the spoke. Two fillets will be added.

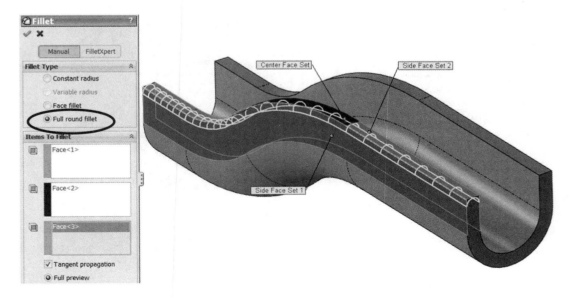

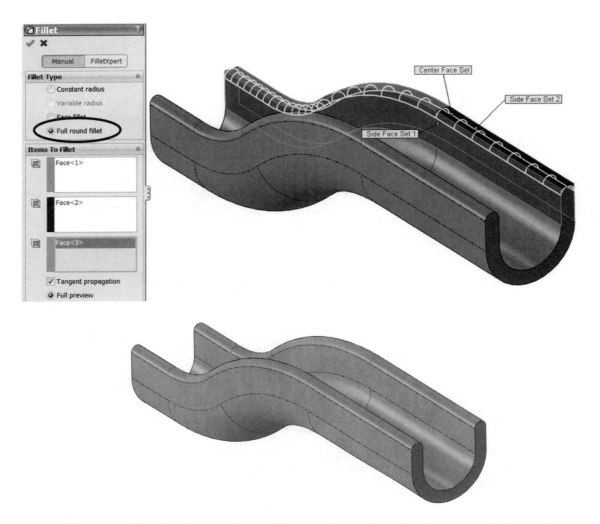

**27. –** We are now ready to pattern the spoke body. To show the hidden bodies, select them in the "**Solid Bodies**" folder and click in the **Show** command.

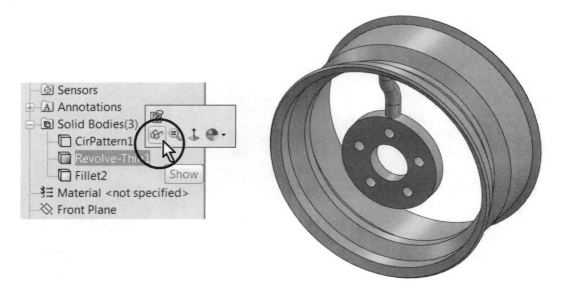

**28. –** Select the **Circular Pattern** command, but instead of making a pattern of features, we'll make a pattern of bodies. Select a circular edge to define the pattern's axis and expand the "**Bodies to Pattern**" selection box. In the graphics area, select the Spoke and make 7 copies equally spaced in 360 degrees. Click **OK** to finish.

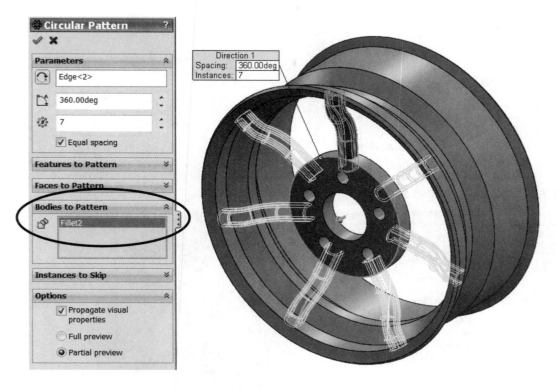

**29. –** Now we have nine solid bodies in our part.

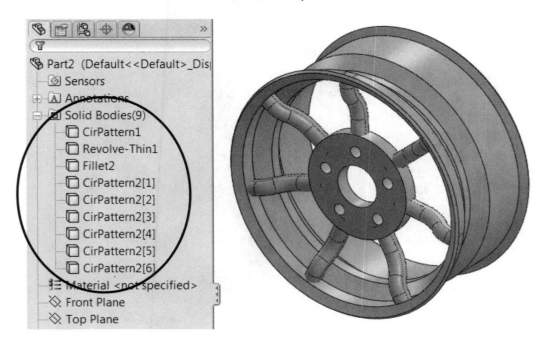

**30. –** We are ready to combine all solids into a single body. Select all bodies in the FeatureManager, right mouse click on them, and select "**Combine Bodies**" from the pop-up menu, or from the menu "**Insert, Features, Combine**," and select all the bodies in the graphics area.

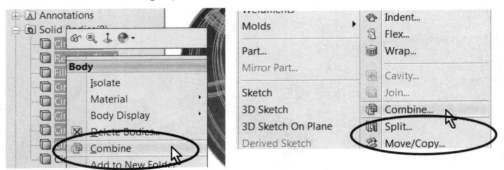

**31. –** Select the "**Add**" option and click **OK** to finish. All bodies are now combined into a single solid.

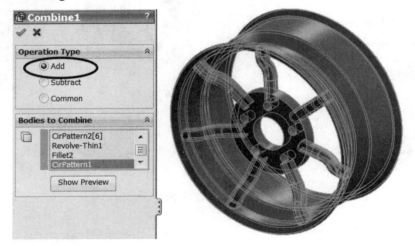

**32. –** Add a 5mm fillet to the faces indicated.

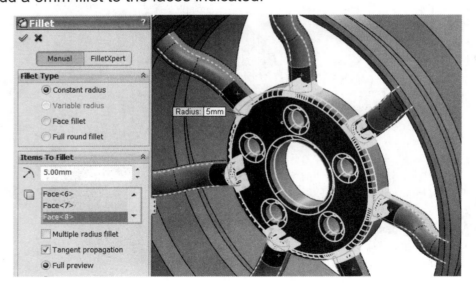

**33. –** To add a similar fillet to the other side of the Spokes, first we need to add a fillet to the Rim's body.  If we try to add the fillet after the bodies are combined, the fillet will fail. Drag the Rollback bar from the bottom of the FeatureManager before the "Combine1" feature and add a 20mm fillet to the indicated edge.

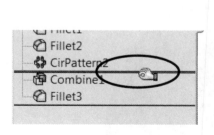

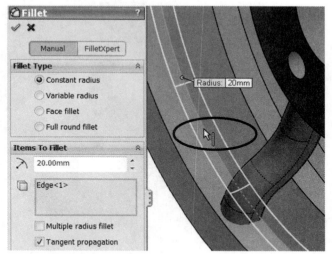

**34. –** Drag the Rollback bar down to the bottom when finished.

**35. –** Add a 5 mm fillet to the face of the previous fillet to propagate it to all Spokes at the same time.

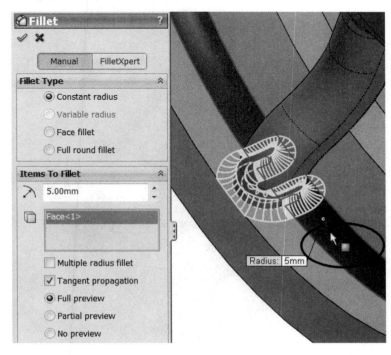

**36.** – Your finished wheel should now look like this:

I know this is not a good-looking wheel, but it's a good example to show how to work with multi body parts and perform local operations. We'd love to see the designs from our readers; please email us a picture to areyes@mechanicad.com.

**37. –** Now we'll learn more about combining bodies. What we did with the wheel was to add bodies, in essence merging or fusing them. The other two operations we can do when combining bodies is to subtract one or more bodies from another, or get the common volume between them. To obtain the common volume between bodies, first we need two bodies that intersect. Open a new part and draw the following sketch in the Right plane.

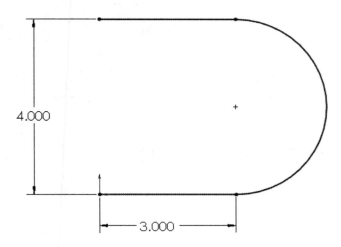

**38. –** Make a Boss-Extrude as a Thin Feature. The extrusion's depth will be 3″ and the thickness of the part 0.5″ inside.

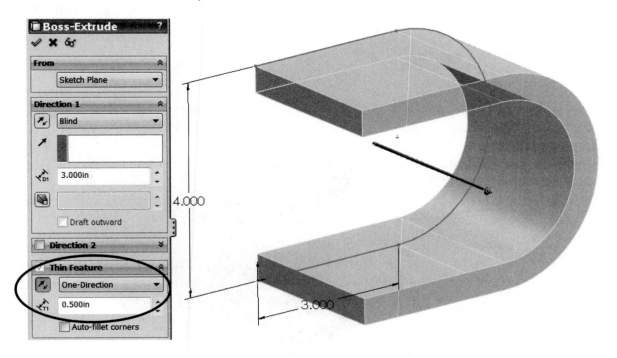

**39. –** For the next feature, add a sketch in the Top face of the first feature. Looking at it from a Top view should look like this:

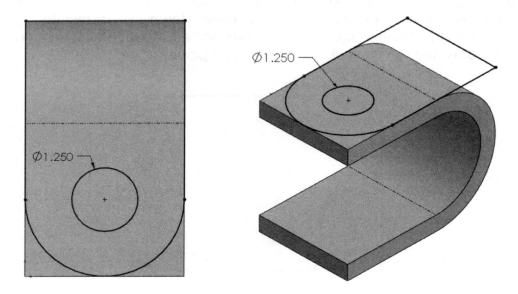

Notice the only dimension we need to add is the hole's diameter; everything else is defined with geometric relations.

**40. –** Extrude the second sketch downwards with the "**Through All**" end condition, and be sure to uncheck the "**Merge result**" checkbox. We want to have two separate bodies.

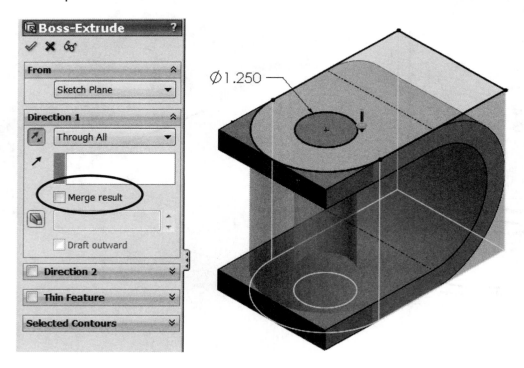

**41. –** Now that we have two separate bodies, we can combine them to get the common volume. Select the menu "**Insert, Features, Combine**; " or from the "**Solid Bodies**" folder in the FeatureManager select BOTH bodies, right mouse click in either one and select "**Combine**" from the pop-up menu.

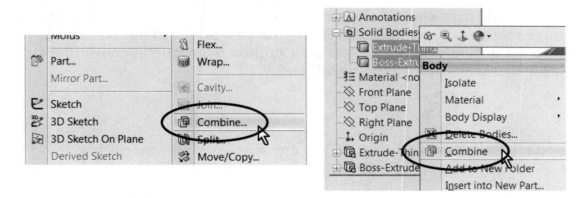

**42. –** In the Combine operation select the "**Common**" option under "**Operation Type**". Click on the "**Preview**" button to see what the resulting body will look like and click **OK** to finish.

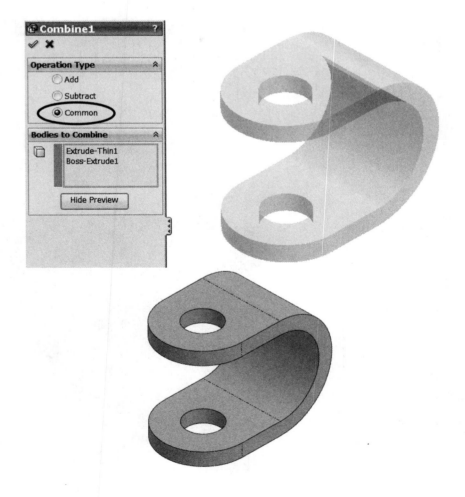

**43. –** The next operation to cover is the difference between bodies. One common use for a body difference is to obtain a mold's core and/or cavity (which we'll cover later in the book), but here we'll show how to obtain the volume capacity of an irregularly shaped bottle.  Download the part *Bottle.sldprt* from our website (www.mechanicad.com/download.html) and open it.  In order to obtain a volume with the inside capacity of the bottle, we need to make a new solid body that will enclose the bottle up to the fill level. Make a new sketch in the Front plane and draw a rectangle as shown.  Make the extrusion big enough to cover the entire bottle and uncheck the "**Merge result**" option.

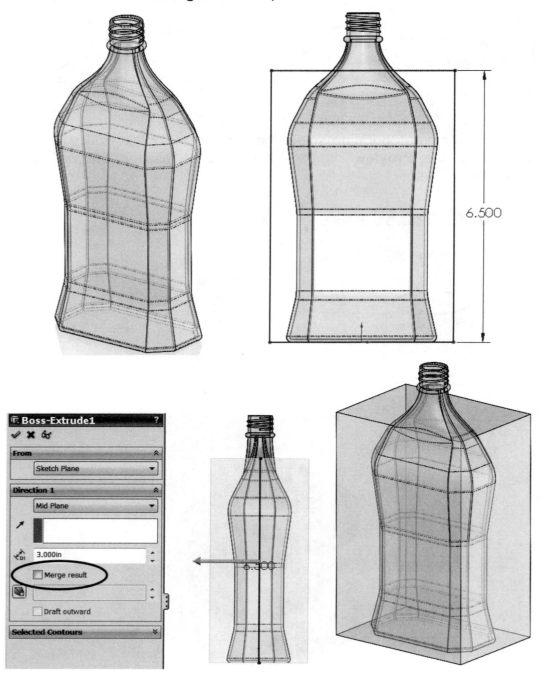

**44.** – Now that we have the two solid bodies, select the menu "**Insert, Features, Combine**". Select the "**Subtract**" option under "**Operation Type**". In order to get a difference, we need to select the body that we want to remove material from (Main Body) and the body(ies) that we want to remove from it. In the "**Main Body**" selection box, select the body just created, and under "**Bodies to Subtract**" select the Bottle. Click **OK** when done selecting.

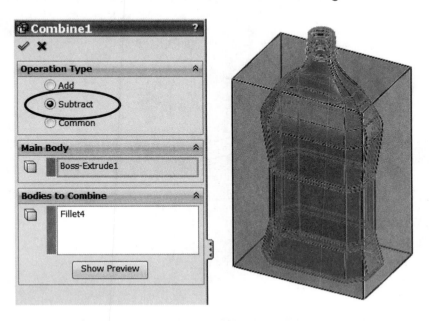

**45.** – We are immediately presented with the "**Bodies to Keep**" dialog. There are two bodies resulting from the operation, but we are interested only in the inside body. Select the inside body and click **OK** to finish.

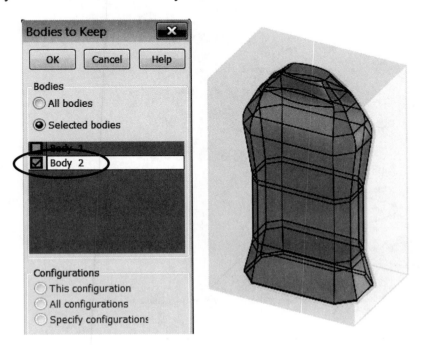

**46. –** Now we have the actual volume of the bottle up to the fill line.  Notice that when we subtract one body from another, the original bodies are consumed and we are left with only the resulting difference.  After running a "**Mass Properties**" analysis, we can see that the volume of liquid inside the bottle up to the fill line is 25.1 cubic inches.  Save and close the part.

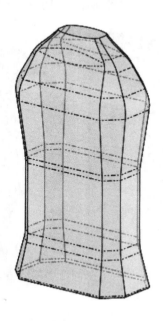

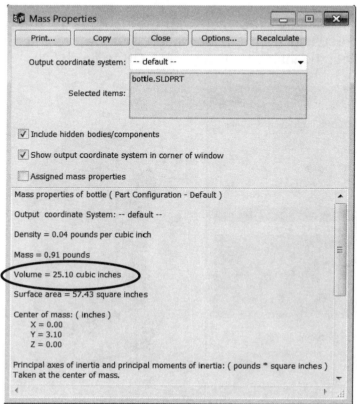

## *Contour Selection*

Contour Selection is a way to work with a sketch that has intersecting entities, endpoints shared by multiple entities and many of the common problems that prevent us from using a sketch for a feature. We'll also learn how to reuse a sketch for multiple features and a previously unused Extrude/Cut option.

**47. –** Make a new part and add a sketch to the Front plane as shown. In this example we will not worry about dimensions to simplify the explanation and concentrate on how contour selection works.

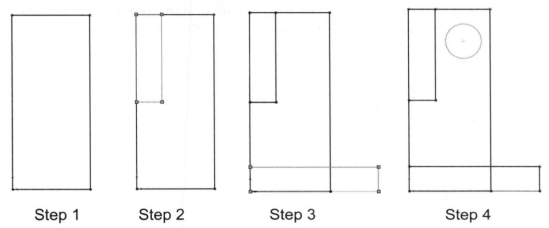

| Step 1 | Step 2 | Step 3 | Step 4 |

In this sketch we are drawing three rectangles and one circle. Note that the rectangles are overlapping and sharing endpoints.

**48. –** When we try to create a feature using this sketch, the Contour Selection tool is automatically activated and the "**Selected Contours**" selection box is open. Also notice we don't get an Extrusion/Cut preview until we select the region(s) or contour(s) that we want to use in the feature. Select the Boss-Extrude icon. In the graphics area move the mouse pointer around and see the different regions available for selection. We can select single or multiple regions *and/or* closed contours.

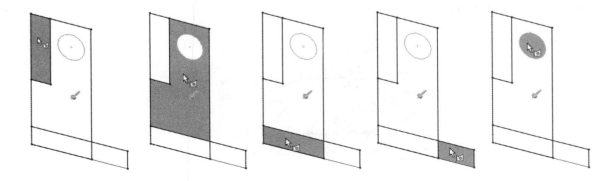

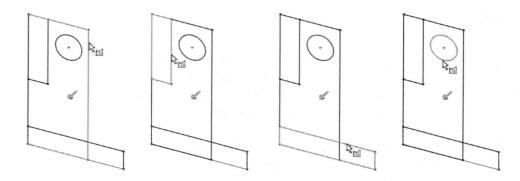

**49.** – Select the bottom square profile (or both bottom regions) and extrude *approximately* as shown. Just like with any other feature the sketch is automatically hidden.

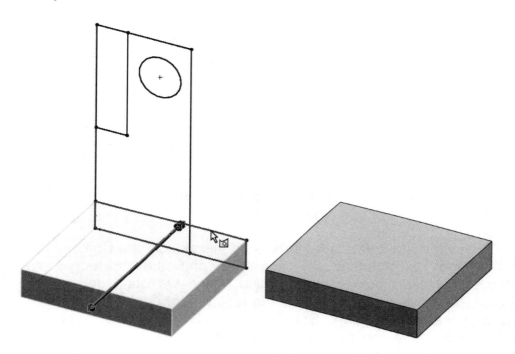

**50.** – To re-use the sketch for more features, select the sketch in the Feature-Manager and click "**Show**" in the pop-up menu. Note the "**Contours**" icon next to the sketch's name.

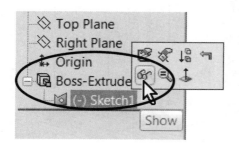

**51.** – We will now use the same sketch again for a new feature. To activate the Contour Selection tool we have to make a right mouse click in the graphics area (or the sketch itself). Be aware that by default the "**Contour Select Tool**" option is not available in the pop-up menu; you have to expand the menu at the bottom to make this option visible.

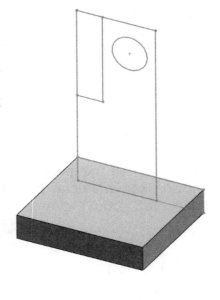

**52.** – After selecting the "**Contour Select Tool**" option select the regions indicated and extrude *approximately* as shown. You may have to click in the sketch to enable (activate) selection of regions, and either: hold down the Ctrl key to pre-select all three regions and then extrude, OR select the Extruded Base command *and then* select the regions. Either one works the same.

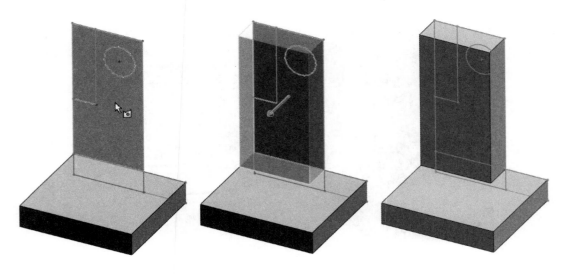

After using the same sketch for two or more features we can see a slightly different icon next to the sketch name with a little hand under it. This means the sketch is "shared" by more than one feature, and the sketch name is the same.

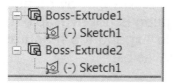

**53. –** Repeat the previous process to select the next contour and extrude as shown. Remember at this time we are only showing how it works and are not concerned about the dimensions.

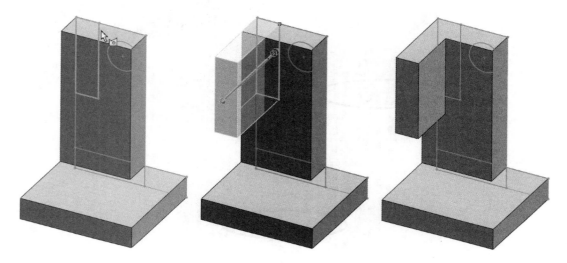

**54. –** For the final feature select the "**Contour Select Tool**" and select the circle. What we have done up until now is to make features starting in the sketch plane. SolidWorks has a powerful (yet sometimes under used feature) that allows us to start the feature somewhere *other* than the sketch plane. After selecting the circle, click in the **Extruded Cut** command; in the "**From**" start condition's drop-down menu select "**Surface/Face/Plane**" (we can also use a vertex or offset).

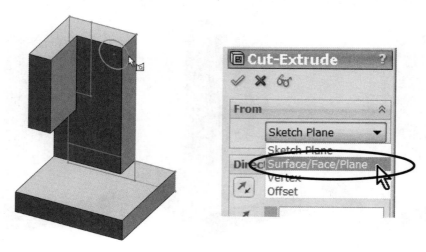

**55. –** Now select the front face of the second boss as indicated. Our Cut feature will start here. Make the feature's depth *about* half way deep, and click **OK** to finish. By using the "**Start Condition**" option for feature creation we can easily save time by not having to create auxiliary planes or geometry.

**56. –** Now that we have made four features from the same multiple contour and self-intersecting sketch, we can hide it.

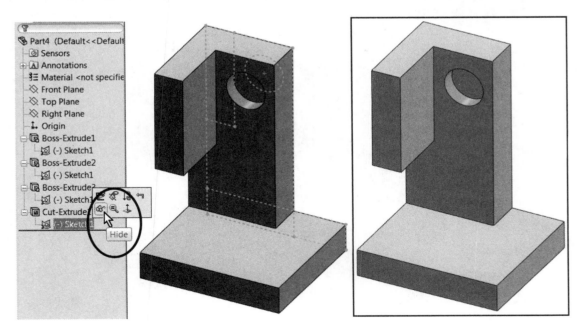

## Contour Selection Review

Make the following sketch and make all four features off of it using contour selection.

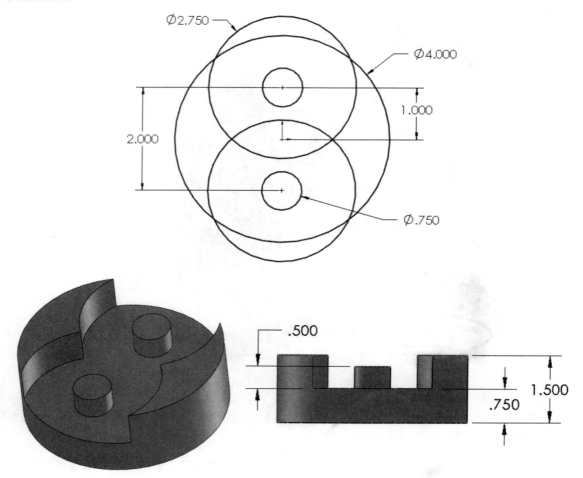

## Part Editing

A very important skill to have when modeling in SolidWorks (or any CAD package for that matter) is to be able to change a model and fix errors. Let's face it: the only constant in design is change, and when we make changes to our model, chances are we may cause an error down the road, that is, the Feature-Manager. For example, if we have a part with round edges (fillets) and we change a previous feature and eliminate an edge, the fillet will give us an error because it cannot find it. That's the type of error we are talking about.

**57.** – To practice editing and fixing errors, please download the part *Repair.sldprt* from www.mechanicad.com/download.html. The part should look like this when we are done.

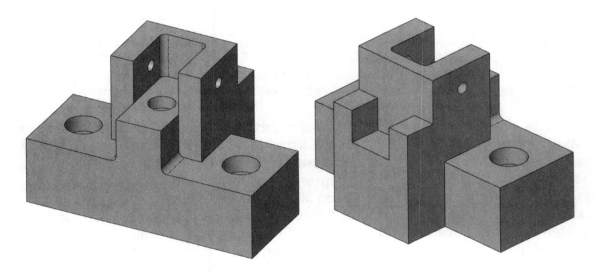

**58.** – When we open the file we are asked if we want to rebuild it. Select **"Rebuild"** from the dialog.

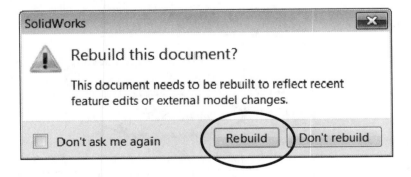

**59.** – When rebuilt, we get a list of error messages and no geometry at all.

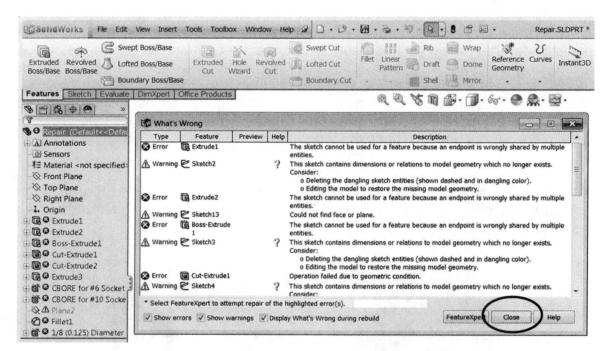

**60.** – This part has so many errors that no geometry can be generated, and the "**What's Wrong**" dialog contains the full list of things that need to be fixed. Click the "Close" button for now. Since features are added chronologically starting at the top, the logical order to start fixing errors is from the top and work your way down the FeatureManager. The reason is if a 'parent' feature has an error, it may cause problems in a 'child' feature, therefore the dependency between features is referred to as "**Parent/Child**" relations. For example, if a sketch is added to a face of another feature, or a dimension references another feature's geometry, a Parent/Child relation is generated. To identify these relations, click in the "**Boss-Extrude1**" feature with the right mouse button and select "**Parent/Child**."

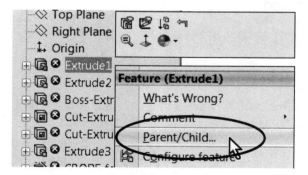

 There are two types or errors: a red X means the feature failed to build; the yellow warning triangle means the feature has an error, but SolidWorks was able to build it.

**61. –** Here we can see which features affect "Boss-Extrude1" and which features it affects. The higher we go in the FeatureManager, the more Children a feature has. Click "Close" to continue.

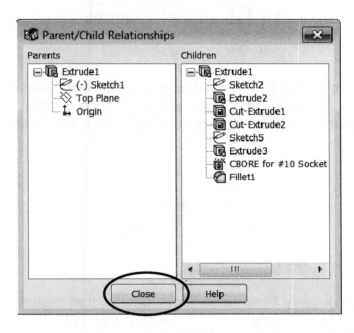

**62. –** To start fixing errors, we'll check what the error at the "Extrude1" feature is. Right mouse click on it and select "**What's Wrong?**"

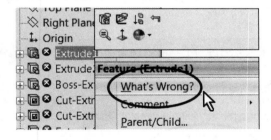

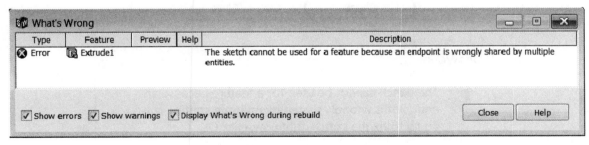

This error means that the sketch has intersecting lines or more than 2 lines connected to the same endpoint. One common cause of this problem is when sketching we accidentally add overlapping lines. Close the "**What's Wrong**" dialog, expand the "Extrude1" feature and edit the sketch.

**63.** – Sometimes it's easy to see the geometric elements causing the problem in a sketch and we can correct them, but sometimes it's not that obvious. To help us identify the problem, select the menu "**Tools, Sketch Tools, Check Sketch for Feature**."

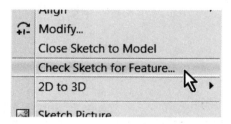

If this sketch has already been used for a feature, that feature type will be pre-selected in the drop-down menu. If the sketch has not been used, we have to select the type of feature that we intend to use it for. In our case "Base Extrude" is already selected. Click on "**Check**" to analyze the sketch. Immediately we see the same error message that we got using "**What's Wrong**." Click **OK** to dismiss it and continue.

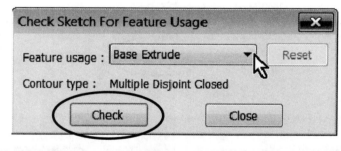

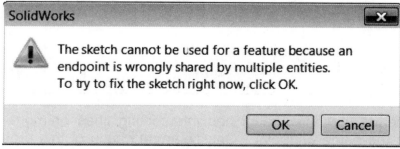

**64.** – SolidWorks immediately reorients the sketch and places the magnifying glass on top of the geometric element suspected of causing the problem. We are given two areas of concern: the first one is that we have overlapping entities, and the second one multiple (more than 2) elements sharing the same endpoint.

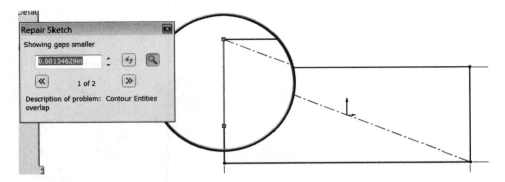

The advantage of using this tool is that we can quickly identify where the problem is and correct it, instead of hunting down small line segments in a sketch. Now that we know where the problem is, window-select the overlapping line and delete it. Click "**Refresh**" to confirm that we don't have any more problems and close the "Repair Sketch" window.

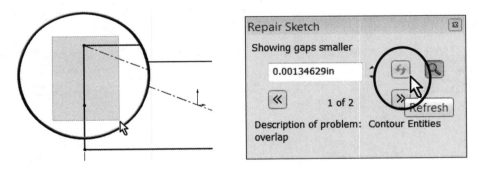

**65.** – Exit the sketch (or rebuild the model) to continue. We are notified that a subsequent feature has an error and we are asked if we wish to repair it now or continue with the error. Click on "**Continue (Ignore Error)**" and close the "What's Wrong?" message.

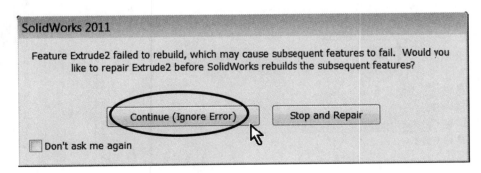

Now we can see some features and (more importantly) the error from the first feature is gone.

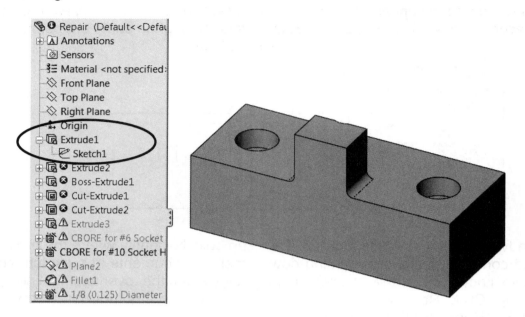

**66.** – Select the "Extrude2" feature, right mouse click and select "**What's Wrong?**" to continue. Essentially we have the same problem as the first feature. Edit the "Extrude2" sketch to fix it.

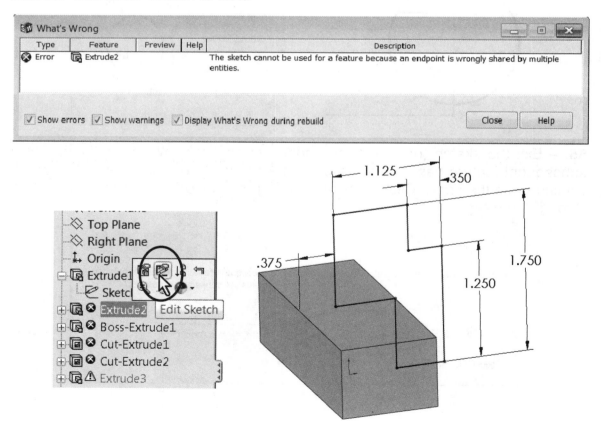

**67.** – Once we are editing the sketch, select the menu "**Tools, Sketch Tools, Check Sketch for Feature**" to find out what the problem is. Close the error message when it comes up. In this case, looking at all three problems (one overlapping entity and two with more than two entities at an endpoint), we can tell that we have two identical lines overlapping. Close the dialog and delete one.

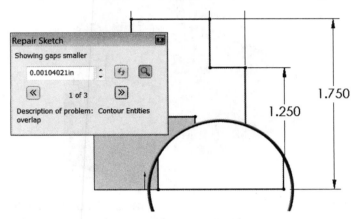

If we use window-selection we'll delete both lines; if we click to select one, only one is selected.

**68.** – After selecting one of the overlapping lines and deleting it, we may be warned that other entities will also be deleted, most likely dimensions.

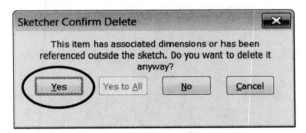

**69.** – If this is the case click "Yes" to continue. Notice the top horizontal line's dimension is also deleted. This is because that dimension was referencing the line we deleted. Add the missing dimension again and exit the sketch. Select "Continue (Ignore Error)" and close the "What's Wrong?" message.

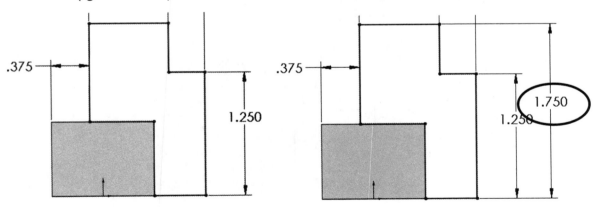

**70.** – Now our model is starting to look better. Notice that we have fixed only two features and we have cleared many errors.

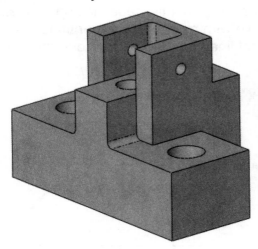

**71.** – After reviewing the next error with "**What's Wrong?**" we see that it's the same error as the two previous features. After editing the sketch we can see an extra diagonal line. We can either delete it, or convert it to **Construction Geometry**. The second option is usually safer, as we could lose dimensions and/or relations if we delete it, and we can always revert it if needed. Select the diagonal line and convert it to construction geometry from the pop-up toolbar.

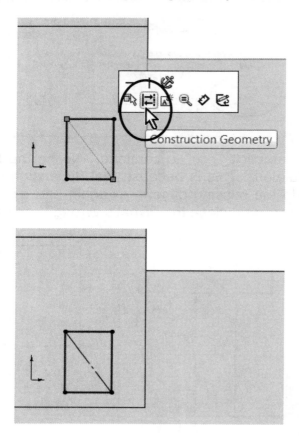

**72.** – Exit the sketch to rebuild the part. The newly created feature does not seem to be part of the original design, so the logical step would be to delete it. Select the feature and after selecting "**Delete**" we get the confirmation dialog:

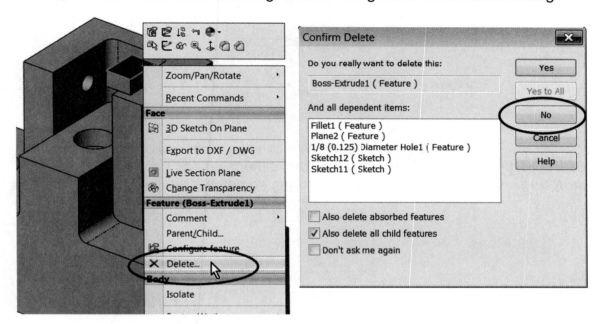

**73.** – In the confirmation we can see that if we delete this feature we'll also delete its dependent features, but we need to have them in our part. The reason those features would also be deleted is because they are "children" features of "Boss-Extrude1." Select "**Cancel**." We don't want to delete anything at this time; we'll edit those features to remove the dependencies *and then* delete this feature. Select the extrusion's "**Parent/Child**" relationships.

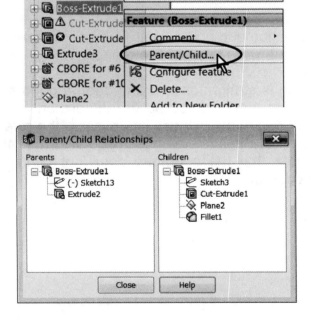

**74. –** We can see that the first dependant feature is "Sketch3" from "Cut-Extrude1." Select it in the FeatureManager and edit it.

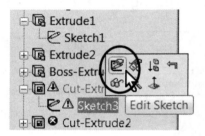

**75. –** Change to a Top view for clarity. We can see a dimension colored in brown (0.603). The brown color means that the dimension (or geometric relation) is '***dangling***,' which means that it is referencing something that no longer exists.

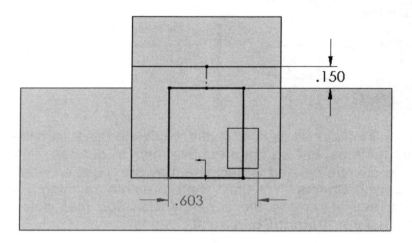

Here we can do one of two things:

    a) Delete the dimension and add it again to a valid reference, or
    b) Re-attach the dimension to a valid reference.

Deleting the dimension is straightforward and often a good solution, so we'll talk about the second option. After selecting the dimension, we see a witness line ending with a red dot; this is the witness line missing the reference. To re-attach it, <u>drag the red dot</u> onto a valid reference. Here we'll use the right side edge. After re-attaching, note that the geometry does not change; the value of the dimension is what updates.

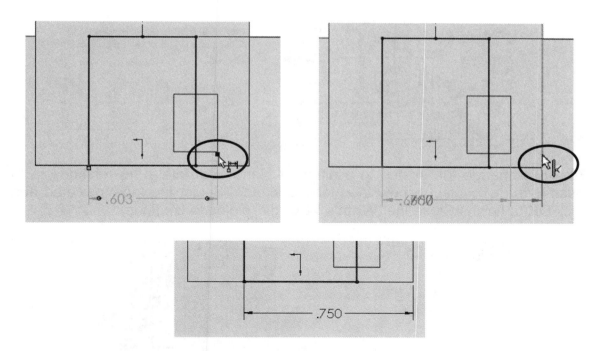

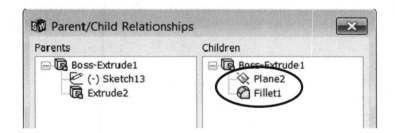

**76.** – Exit the sketch and review the "**Parent/Child**" relationships again (dismiss the "**What's Wrong**" dialog). Now Sketch3 and Cut-Extrude1 are no longer listed.

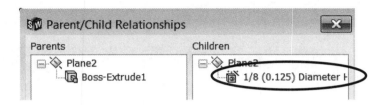

**77.** – From the relationships dialog we can see that the only children are Plane2 and Fillet1. If we check the Parent/Child relations for Plane2, we see that the only child feature is the "1/8 (0.125) Diameter Hole". A Hole Wizard feature has two sketches; the first one is the hole's location.

To find out if the hole is located in Plane2, expand the Hole feature and edit the first sketch's **plane**. As we can see, the sketch is located in Plane2.

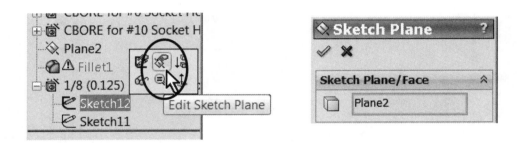

**78. –** To change the sketch to a different plane and delete the relationship to Boss-Extrude1, select a new face for the sketch. Select the face indicated and click **OK** to finish. Close the "**What's Wrong?**" dialog to continue.

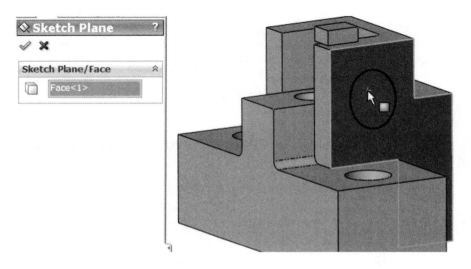

**79. –** Review the Parent/Child relationships again. Now the only children of Boss-Extrude1 are Plane2 and Fillet1, and Plane2 has no children. Close the dialog to continue.

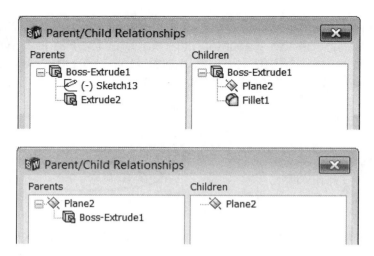

**80.** – Select Fillet1 and check "**What's Wrong**?" This error is a warning; the Fillet was built but it's missing an edge.  Close the dialog and edit the Fillet feature.

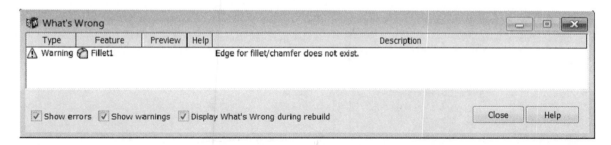

**81.** – The selection box is listing a missing edge in the same 'dangling' brown color, and the missing edge is shown with a faint red phantom line.  Since we no longer need the fillet in that missing edge, delete it from the selection list and click **OK** to finish.

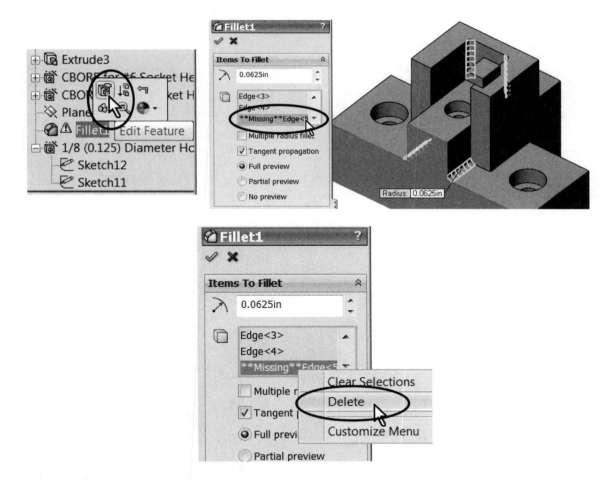

**82.** – After fixing Fillet1 we can delete the Boss-Extrude1 feature. Select it in the FeatureManager and delete it.  This time the confirmation only lists Plane2, which we don't want and it's OK to delete. Be sure to click on the option "**Also delete absorbed features**" to delete the sketch, too.

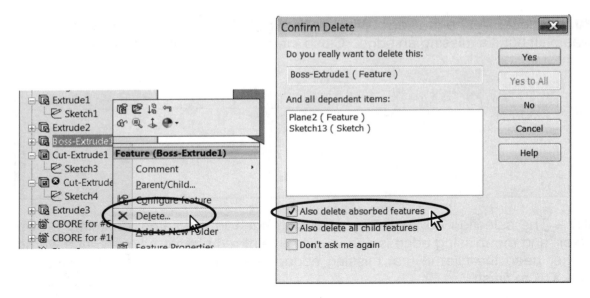

**83.** – Now we have one error left to fix. This error means that the cut is not cutting through the model.

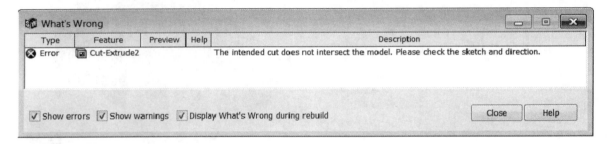

**84.** – Close the "**What's Wrong**" dialog and edit the Cut-Extrude2 feature. We can see the preview is not going deep enough and we want it to be 0.375″ deep into the lower step.

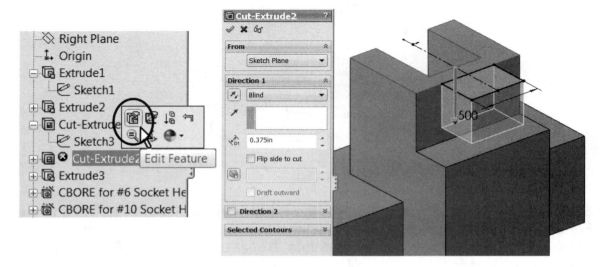

**85. –** Change the cut's end condition to "**Offset from Surface**" and select the lower step's face as indicated. The offset can be to either side of the selected face; if needed, turn on the "**Reverse offset**" checkbox. Click **OK** to finish.

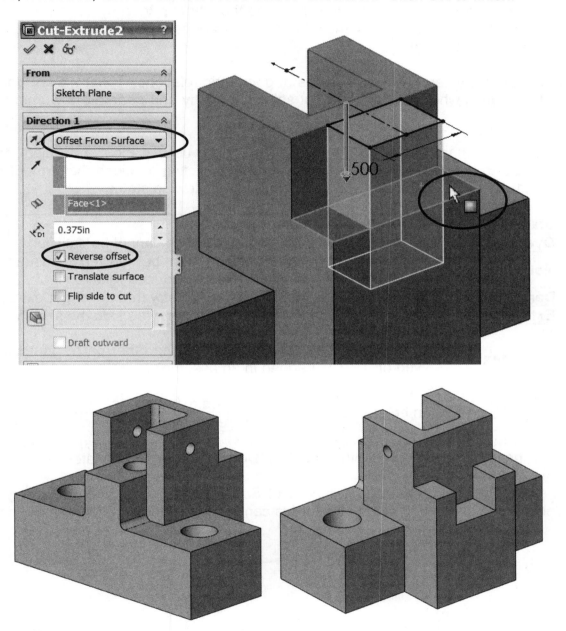

**86. –** When working in a sketch we can have different errors, so we decided to show them with a different part. Download the part *Sketch Relations.sldprt* from www.mechanicad.com/download.html. Just like the part before, we have a number of errors in this part's sketch. Close the "**What's Wrong**" dialog and edit the sketch in the part. We'll show the use of diagnostic tools to help us correct the errors.

In a sketch we can have many types of geometric relations. What we are going to focus on is when relations are not solved correctly and generate a warning or error.

An Under Defined or Fully Defined sketch can be used without a problem, the latter being the desired state. When we add conflicting relations that cannot be solved, a sketch's geometry can be in one of the following states:

| State | Color | Description |
|---|---|---|
| **Over defined** | Red | Conflicting relations cannot be satisfied. |
| **Not Solved** | Yellow | Relations cannot be solved; geometry cannot meet the required relations. |
| **Dangling** | Brown/Gold | Relations to geometry that no longer exists. |
| **External** | Can be under, | Relations to geometry outside the sketch; |
| **In Context \*** | fully or over defined, not solved or dangling. | Relations referencing other part's geometry added in an assembly. |
| **Locked \*** | Can be any color | *'Frozen'* in context relations. |
| **Broken \*** | | In context relations to other parts broken. |

\* Will be covered more in depth in the **Top Down Design** section later.

A sketch can become Over Defined, Not Solved or Dangling when geometry is deleted, modified, or when the user adds conflicting relations and/or dimensions.

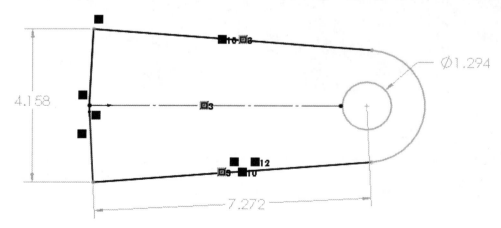

**87. –** After editing the sketch we see red and yellow entities. There are two ways we can approach this: we can manually sort through the relations and delete the conflicting ones, or we can use the **SketchXpert** to resolve them. We'll try the manual mode first. Select the "**Display/Delete Relations**" icon from the Sketch toolbar, or the menu "**Tools, Sketch Relations, Display/Delete.**"

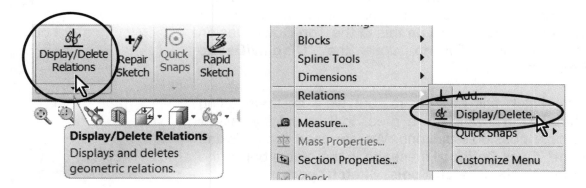

**88. –** In the PropertyManager we can see the list of existing relations in the sketch. We can see the relations highlighted with different colors, and their state listed under the list. At the top of the list we can filter the relations displayed by state, or if we select an entity, its relations will be listed.

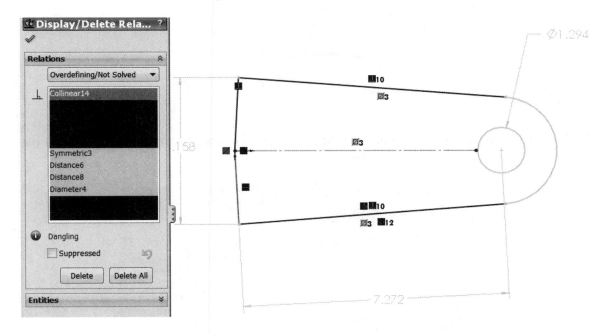

As the user can see, having a large number of conflicting relations can be difficult to sort manually. This is a good diagnostic option when we have problems with a few relations. On the other hand, this is a good tool to identify and/or delete relations, especially External, In context, Locked or Broken, if needed.

**89.** – Using this tool we'll remove the "**In Context**" relations. Select the drop down filter menu and select "**Defined In Context**." In our sketch we only have a Parallel relation and its status is "Out of Context." Click the "Delete" button at the bottom or select the relation and press "Delete" on the keyboard. By deleting this relation, our part is no longer referencing geometry outside the part (more on this in the Top Down Design section). Click **OK** to close the "**Display/Delete Relations**" dialog.

Our sketch still has errors, but we'll fix them using **SketchXpert**, which is a great tool to quickly review multiple possible solutions. We can load it by clicking in the "**Over Defined**" message in the status bar or the menu "**Tools, Sketch Tools, SketchXpert**."

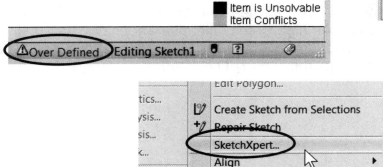

**90.** – In the **SketchXpert** dialog select "**Diagnose**" to automatically analyze the sketch and evaluate possible solutions.

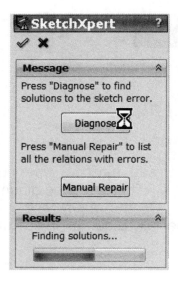

**91. – SketchXpert** quickly diagnoses the sketch and offers possible solutions. We can view each option by advancing in the "Results" box. In the "More Information/Options" box we are shown the relations and/or dimensions that would be deleted if we accept the solution displayed. Scroll until you see the following solution and click "**Accept**" when done.

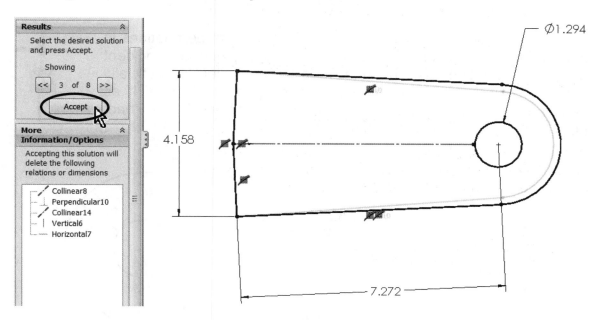

We see the message "The sketch can now find a valid solution" with a green background. Click **OK** to finish.

**92. –** We want to make the lines on the left to be collinear and horizontal (along the short origin arrow; the sketch is shown sideways to save space). What we need to do is to find what relations are keeping the lines fully defined, and then make the lines horizontal. Turn on the display of sketch relations using the menu "**View, Sketch Relations**" if not already activated; this way we can see all the relations in every geometric element.

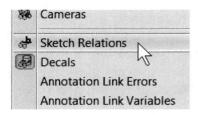

**93.** – We can see immediately that there are only three relations in the two lines that we are interested in: a perpendicular, a coincident and a "**Fix**" relation.  The Fix relation is the equivalent of artificially and arbitrarily constraining an element in space.  Think of it as putting a nail in a geometric element and hammering it in.  Read: brute force.  Select this Fix relation and delete it.

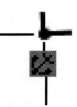

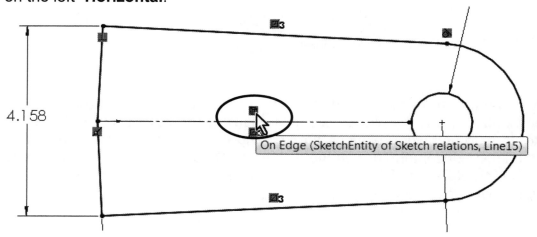

**94.** – If we pay attention, we'll see that we have a brown relation in the centerline. This relation is "**On Edge**," and is the type of relation created when we use "**Convert Entities**" in a sketch. Delete this relation as well, and make both lines on the left "**Horizontal**."

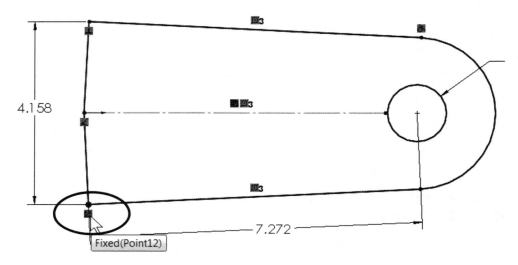

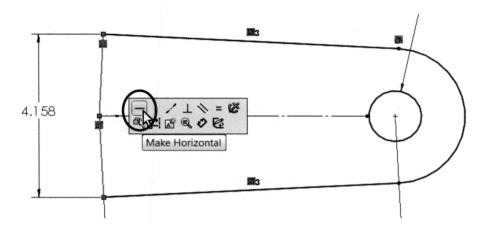

**95. –** Make one of the long lines **"Vertical;"** the other two lines will also become vertical as they have a **"Symmetric"** relation.

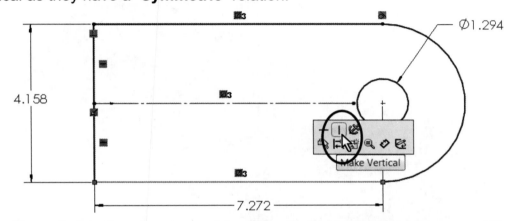

**96. –** To complete the changes, add a **"Tangent"** relation between one of the long lines and the arc. Note that one of them is already tangent.

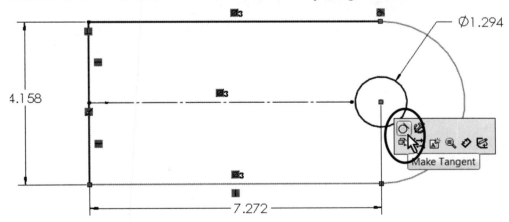

We can read in the status bar that our sketch is now "Fully Defined."

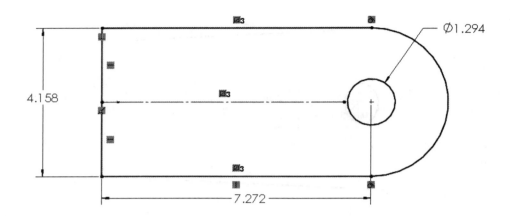

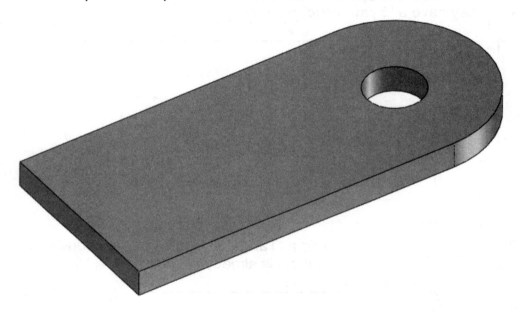

**97. –** Now the part is complete. Exit the sketch to finish, save and close the file.

## *Equations*

One way to help us maintain design intent is by adding equations to our models. Equations are commonly used to evenly space features, add or remove instances to a pattern, change a feature's dimensions when other features are modified, etc. All equations in SolidWorks have the following format:

> variable=expression
> where:

**Variable** is the dimension/value to change (dependant value).
**Expression** is the algebraic combination of other dimensions and values that will define the value of *variable*.

For example, if we have a part of length "**L**" where we want to evenly space a pattern of "**N**" number of holes spaced by dimension "**S**", the *variable* dimension will be "**S**", because that's the value we want to change when the number "**N**" and length "**L**" values change. Our equation would look like:

> S=L/N

A good practice when working with equations in SolidWorks is to rename dimensions and features, so instead of an equation looking like this:

> "D1@LinearPattern1" = "D3@Sketch1" / "D2@LinearPattern1"

it would look like this:

> "Spacing@Holes" = "Length@Base" / "Number@Holes"

which is more descriptive and easier to understand. If we have one, maybe two, equations in our part it may not be a problem, but with more it becomes difficult to manage and modify them if needed.

**98.** – To show how equations work, we'll make a simple part, rename features and dimensions and add an equation. Draw the following sketch (any plane will do) and extrude it 0.5″.

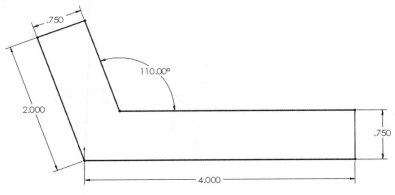

**99. –** Add a through hole in the corner...

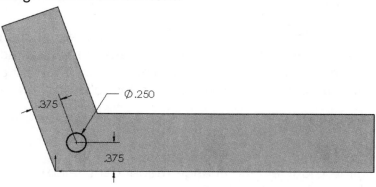

**100. –** Add a linear pattern. In this case the pattern will be made in two directions. Select a diagonal edge for direction 1, three copies spaced 0.5″, and a horizontal edge for direction 2, seven copies spaced 0.5″ (don't finish it yet).

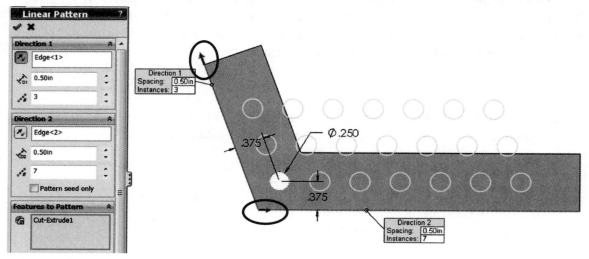

**101. –** Since we only want a single row of copies in each direction, we'll check the option "**Pattern seed only**" under the "Direction 2" options box. By checking this option, we'll get a single row of copies in each direction. Click **OK** to finish.

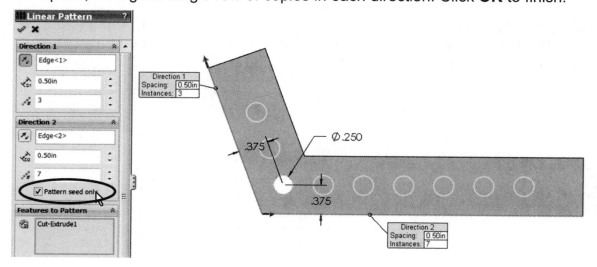

**102.** – We'll now rename the dimensions. To show feature dimensions, right mouse click in the "**Annotations**" folder and select "**Show feature dimensions**;" to show dimension names, activate the menu "**View, Dimension Names**."

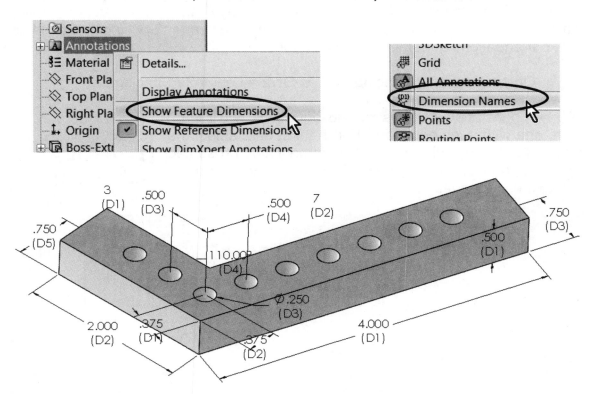

**103.** – Rename the dimensions for the side's length and linear pattern as shown; this way when we add the equations, it will be easier to identify them. Select each dimension and type the name in each dimension's PropertyManager.

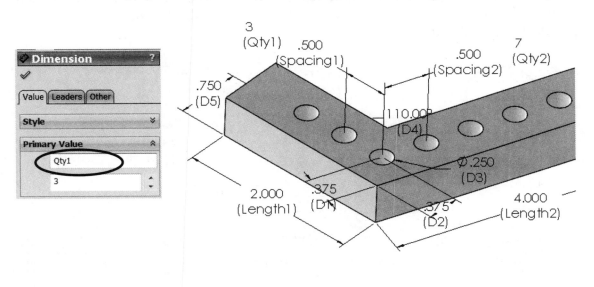

**104.** – Our design intent is to have a pattern of holes equally spaced to fill each side and update accordingly if the length or spacing changes. To accomplish this, we'll need two equations to calculate the quantity of holes (one for each direction). Our "dependant" dimensions will be "*Qty1*" and "*Qty2*", and the driving dimensions will be "*Length1*", "*Length2*", "*Spacing1*" and "*Spacing2*". Based on this, our equations general format has to be:

Qty1 = Lenght1 / Spacing1          Qty2 = Length2 / Spacing2

**105.** – There are two ways to add equations; we'll learn both, one with each equation. For the first one, select the menu "**Tools, Equations**." We are immediately presented with the Equations dialog box. Click the "**Add**" button to create the first equation.

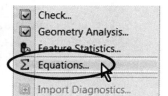

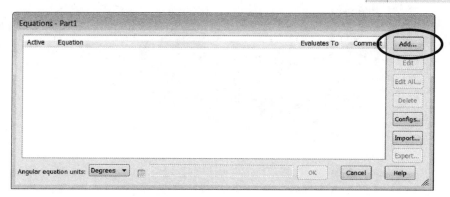

**106.** – In the "**Add Equation**" dialog box we can either type dimensions' names, or select dimensions on the screen. Since the second option is faster and easier, we'll do it this way. Select the dimension "*Qty1*" on the screen to automatically add its full name "*Qty1@LPattern1*" to the "Add Equation" dialog box; type (or click on) the equal sign.

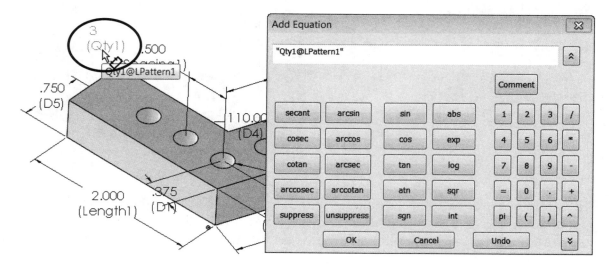

**107.** – In order for our equation to calculate the correct number or holes, we have to subtract a small distance from the length in order to have a minimum space at the end. Otherwise we may get an extra hole at the end. After the equal sign, open a parenthesis, select the *"Length1"* dimension (its full name will be copied), type '**- 0.375**', close the parenthesis, add '*/*' to divide and finally select the *Spacing1* dimension. Click **OK** to finish. Our complete equation looks like:

"Qty1@LPattern1" = ( "Length1@Sketch1" - 0.375 ) / "Spacing1@LPattern1"

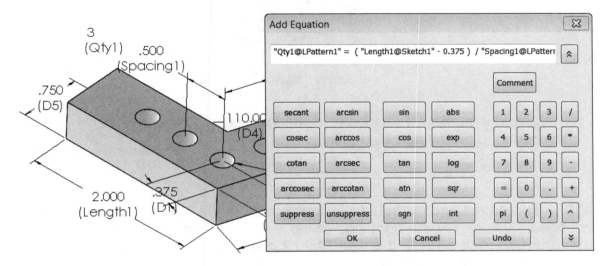

**108.** – In the **"Equations"** dialog we see the first equation is added, and the value for the *Qty1"* dimension evaluates to 3. The green checkmark indicates the equation is valid. Click **OK** to finish.

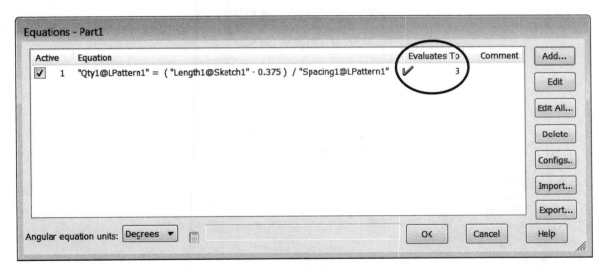

**109.** – After adding the equation, we can see a red ∑ symbol next to the dimension; this is telling us that it is driven by an equation and its value cannot be changed directly. It will only change when the dimensions driving it change.

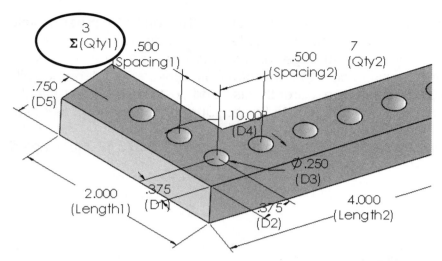

 A folder named "Equations" is automatically added to the FeatureManager.

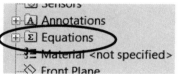

**110. –** To add the second equation, double click in the "*Qty2*" dimension as if to change its value. On the right side of the value input box, we see a drop-down menu arrow; click on it and select "**Add Equation...**" By doing this, the "**Add Equation**" dialog automatically adds *"Qty2@LPattern1"* = to the equation.

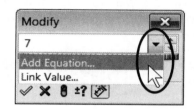

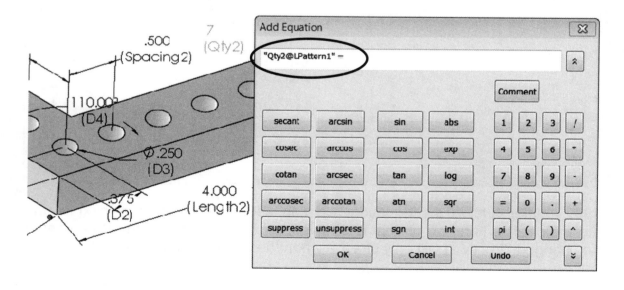

**111.** – Just as we did with the first equation, we'll open a parenthesis, click in the "*Length2*" dimension, type ' **- 0.375** ', close the parenthesis, add ' **/** ' and click in the "*Spacing2*" dimension. The completed second equation looks like:

"Qty2@LPattern1" = ( "Length2@Sketch1" - 0.375 ) / "Spacing2@LPattern1"

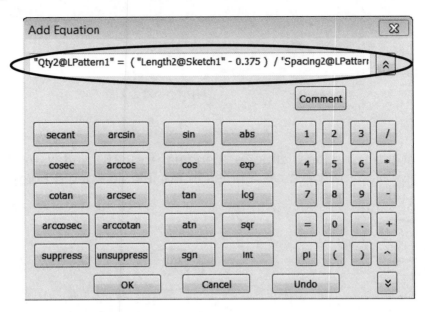

Click **OK** to finish. Now "*Qty2*" evaluates to 7. Click **OK** to close the "Equations" dialog. Both "*Qty1*" and "*Qty2*" have the red ∑ symbol added to alert us that these dimensions are equation driven.

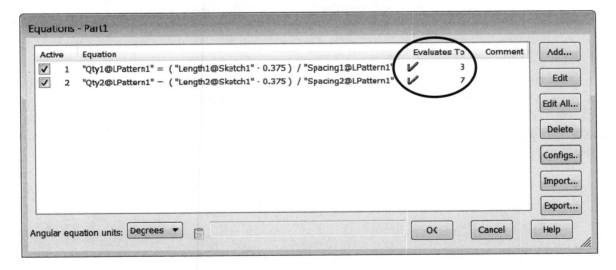

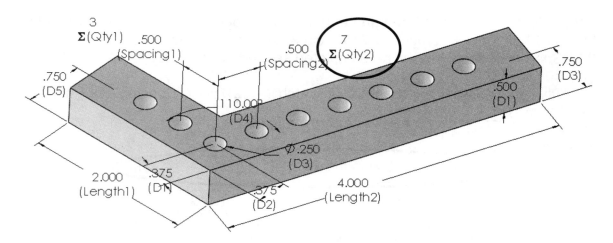

**112.** – To test the equations, change "*Length1*" to 2.75″ and "*Length2*" to 4.5″. Rebuild the model. Now we have 5 holes in the left side and 8 holes in the right side.

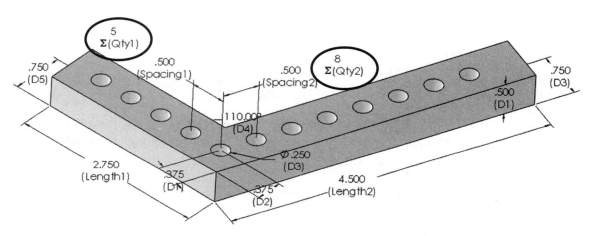

**113.** – Another way to maintain design intent is to "**Link Values**." This is basically a way to make multiple dimensions equal to each other. Right mouse click in one of the 0.75″ dimensions and select "**Link Values**." In the "**Shared Values**" dialog, type the name "*Width*" for this value; it will become a constant value that we can reference throughout the part. Click **OK** to link this dimension.

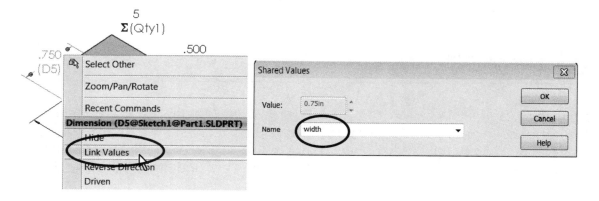

**114.** – After linking the dimension we see an icon of two chain links (*linked*, get it?) next to the dimension and the dimension's name is changed to "*Width.*" Linking only one dimension doesn't make much sense, so we'll link another dimension to the "*Width*" value. Another way to link dimensions is similar to adding an equation. Double click in the other 0.75″ dimension, and from the drop-down menu next to the value box select "**Link Value.**"

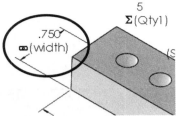

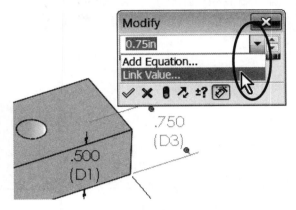

**115.** – We are now presented again with the "**Shared Values**" dialog, but in this case instead of typing a name for the value, we'll select one from the drop-down list. Click on the arrow and select the value "*Width.*" Click **OK** to finish.

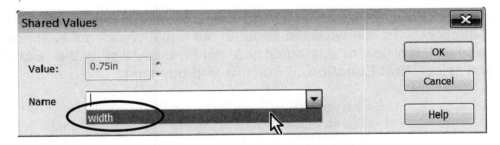

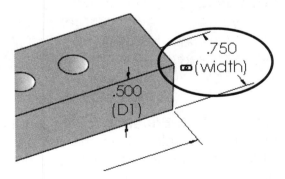

Now this dimension is also linked to the "*Width*" value; it's listed under the "**Equations**" folder in the FeatureManager and as a constant in the "**Equations**" dialog box. To change a linked value, double click one of the linked dimensions and type a new value. All other linked dimensions will update at the same time.

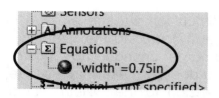

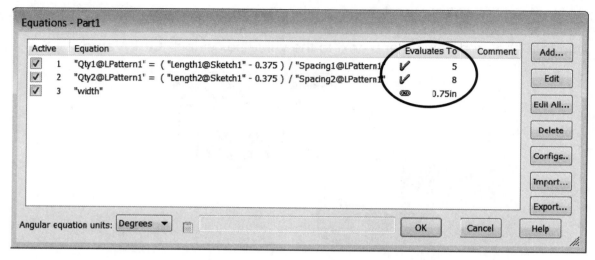

 In an equation we can't change the dependent dimensions ("*Qty1*" and "*Qty2*"), only the referenced dimensions ("*Length1*", "*Lenght2*", "*Spacing1*" and "*Spacing2*"). With "Link Values" we can change *any* linked dimension.

**116.** – In the "**Equations**" folder in the FeatureManager we can Add, Edit or Delete equations. To see what the effect to our equations of not subtracting the 0.375″ and to learn how to edit equations, right mouse click in the "**Equations**" folder and select "**Edit Equation…**" from the pop-up menu.

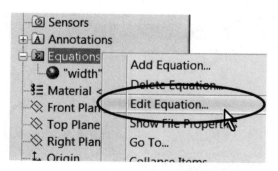

**117.** – "**Delete Equation**" and "**Edit Equation**" only open the "**Equations**" dialog. To edit (or delete) an equation, select it in the list and press the "**Edit**" (or "**Delete**") button. Select the first equation in the list and press "**Edit**". Immediately the equation is opened.

**118.** – Edit both equations to remove the ' **– 0.375** ' portion (it doesn't matter if we leave the parenthesis or not):

"Qty1@LPattern1" = ( "Length1@Sketch1" ) / "Spacing1@LPattern1"
"Qty2@LPattern1" = ( "Length2@Sketch1" ) / "Spacing2@LPattern1"

 If we select the "**Edit All…**" button, all equations are listed in a text editor where we can change any of them as needed.

Now the equations evaluate to 5 and 9 respectively. Click **OK** to finish and rebuild the model to see the changes.

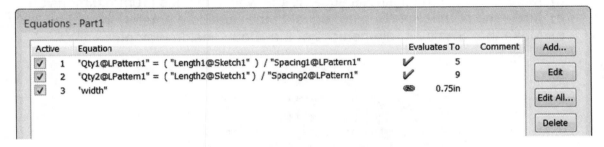

**119.** – What just happened with this change is that a sixth instance is added that breaks the edge of the part. That is the reason why we are subtracting 0.375″ from the length in the equations.

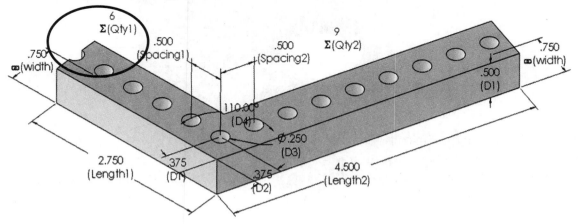

Edit the equations to subtract the 0.375″ again as originally done. Save and close the part to finish.

## Equations Review

**120.** – Add new equations to center the holes about the "*Width*" dimension. Change the "*Width*" value to 0.875″. The holes should remain centered.

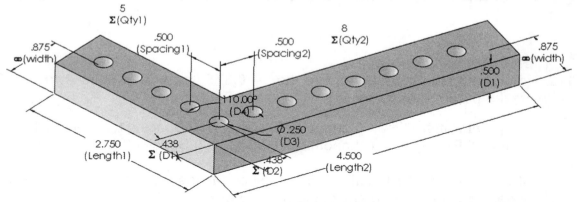

**121.** – Download the part *Equations-Review.sldprt* and give all dimensions used in an equation a meaningful name. Add equations and/or linked values to:

a) Make the bottom thickness equal to the wall thickness (10mm dimension).
b) Make the number of "Copies" equal to the outside diameter divided by 8.
c) Make the "ShaftCut" diameter ¼ of the "Body" inside diameter.

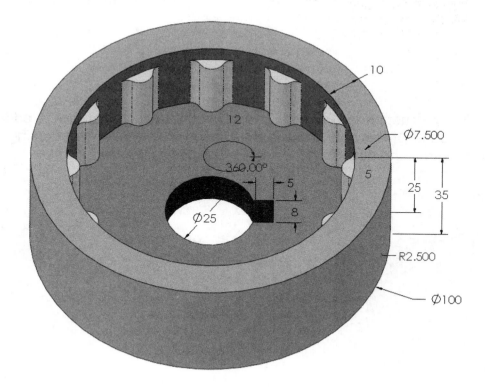

 When making equations we can use almost any algebraic expression to evaluate values. As a general guide, you can write equations with the same algebraic format as you would with Excel formulas.

# *Sheet Metal and Top Down Design*

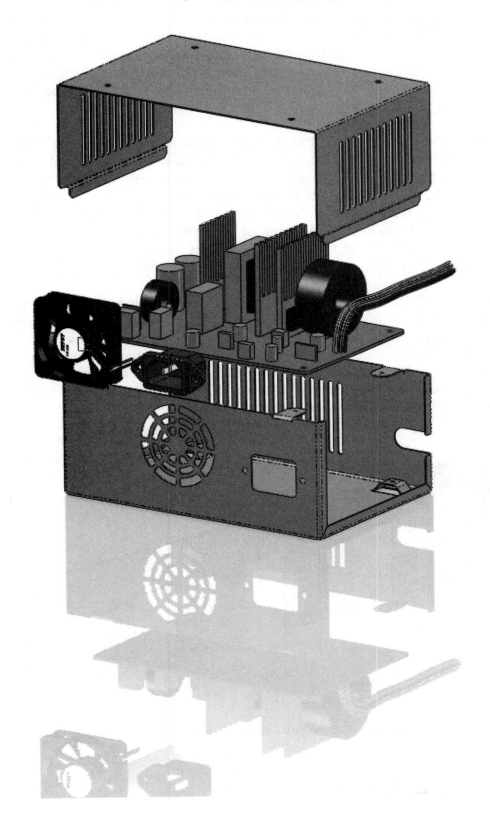

When we talk about a sheet metal process, we are talking about trimming and bending sheets of metal beyond their yield strength causing a permanent deformation. Sheet metal components are made from steel, aluminum, bronze or pretty much any malleable metal and, while the sheet metal process can produce components with tight tolerances, this process is more frequently used when high precision is not required and the components manufactured need to have flexibility in an assembly process, like the power supply we'll be making in this lesson or a school's locker.

Due to the inherent nature of the process of cutting and bending metal, this manufacturing technique is used mostly for internal components that are "out of sight" or don't have a high aesthetical requirement, since the resulting components are not always as pretty or good-looking as a plastic injection molded part and have a more "industrial" look. A very good example is a computer's case. If you look at the back of a your PC's case, you'll see that most likely it is made from sheet metal, and the front (more visible parts) are likely made of plastic to give it a more attractive look as a consumer product.

Sheet metal tends to be a relatively cheap manufacturing process, and lends itself very well for mass produced components using multiple stations or progressive dies, where a long sheet metal strip is fed in one end, and is progressively trimmed, cut, punched and bent until a finished part is completed at the other end. Other manufacturing techniques include cutting the metal with computer controlled torch, plasma, laser or water jet machines and bending the part afterwards using presses and bending tools.

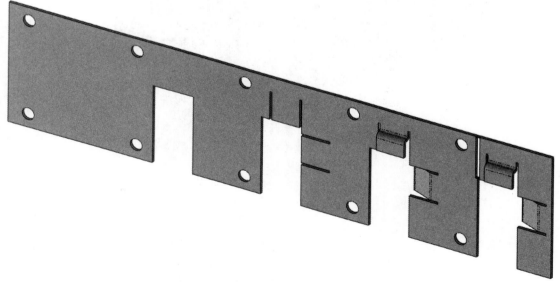

*Example of a progressive die sheet metal part*

## Understanding Top Down Design

In designing the power supply, we'll use different sheet metal and advanced assembly techniques including Top Down Design.

**Top Down Design** is generally referred to as the process where we create and/or add features referencing other components in the assembly; in our example, we'll design a sheet metal enclosure for the power supply *around* the actual electronics of the power supply. In other words, we'll make an enclosure where the internal components fit, instead of building an enclosure and *then* trying to fit the components inside. That's the difference.

One of the biggest advantages of Top Down Design is that when the component referenced is modified, the components designed around it (driven), also change. Looking at this example, the base component is the DRIVING component, the circular hole's edge is the driving feature, and the DRIVEN part will update when the BASE part updates. Here the hole's diameter changed from 1″ diameter to 1.625″ and the pin changed accordingly.

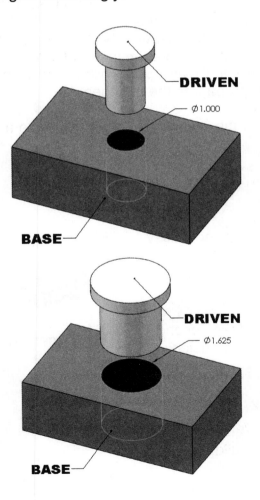

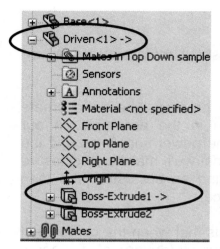

When designing components in the context of an assembly (**Top Down Design**), you can reference other parts or assemblies, including geometry, sketches, planes, axes, etc.

The relations created this way are called **External Relations** and are indicated in the Feature Manager with "**->**" both in the part's file name and each feature that references external geometry. External relations are created every time dimensions, geometric relations or feature end conditions reference other components (parts or assemblies) while editing them in an assembly.

As a primer to **Top Down Design** before we jump into **sheet metal**, we'll make the components illustrated on the previous page as a simple example of working in the context of an assembly, or Top Down Design.

In a **Bottom Up Design** approach, we would make both parts and then assemble them together; the problem is that if a part is changed, the other has to be manually changed. In a **Top Down Design** approach, only one change is needed. For our simple Top Down example we'll make the "Base" part, add it to a new assembly, create the "Driven" part while in the assembly and finally modify the hole's dimension to propagate the changes.

The steps we'll follow for the Top Down Design example are the following:

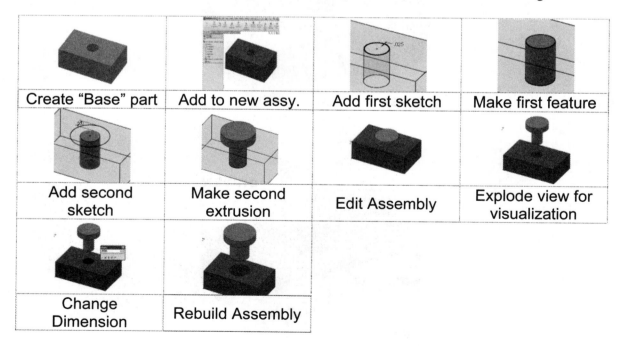

| Create "Base" part | Add to new assy. | Add first sketch | Make first feature |
| Add second sketch | Make second extrusion | Edit Assembly | Explode view for visualization |
| Change Dimension | Rebuild Assembly | | |

**122.** – Make the following part using the dimensions given and save it when done. Name this part *Top Down Base*. The hole is centered in the part.

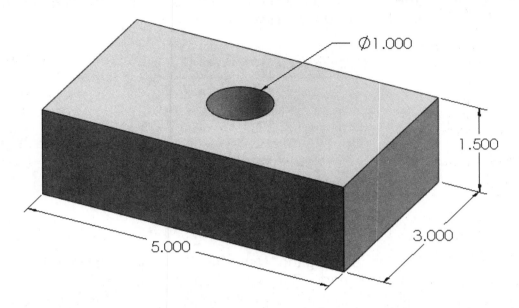

**123.** – Add the *Top Down Base* part to a new assembly. The location of this part in the assembly is not important for this example. Save the assembly with the name *Top Down Assy*.

 It is important to know that one requisite of Top Down Design is that the assembly must be saved before any external references can be added. The reason for this is because SolidWorks needs to know in which assembly the external reference was created.

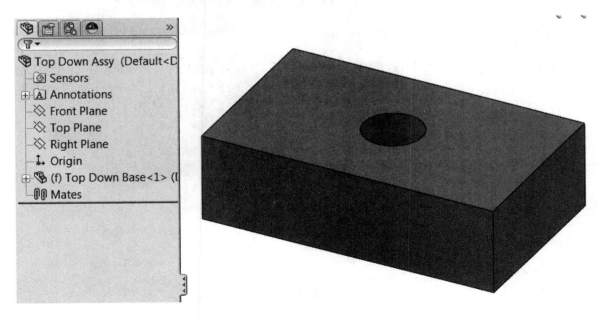

**124. –** The next step is to add a new component. The new component will be created *inside the assembly* or *in context*. Click on the drop-down arrow from the "**Insert Components**" icon in the Assembly toolbar, and select "**New Part**" or from the menu "**Insert, Component, New Part**."

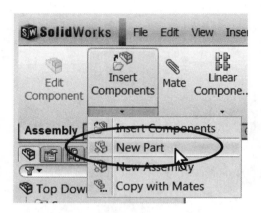

**125. –** Immediately after selecting the "**New Part**" icon, SolidWorks will ask us for a plane to locate the new part. Select the Top face of the "Base" part in the assembly. By selecting the Top face, we are creating the first external reference in the new part; the Front plane of this new part will be coincident with the face selected. This is an "**InPlace**" relation and will fix the new part to the selected face.

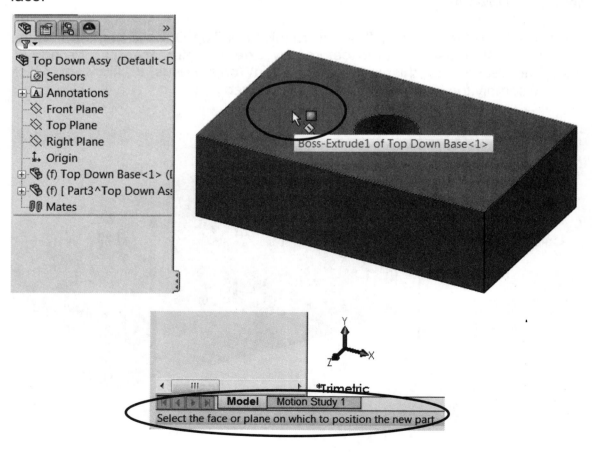

**126.** – After selecting the Top face several things will happen:

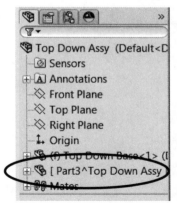

A new part will be added to the FeatureManager tree and its name will be shown in blue. The name in blue indicates that we are *editing* this component in the assembly.

A new Sketch will be created in the Front plane of the new part as indicated by the usual editing sketch indicators, plus an additional one: an

"**Edit Component**" icon will be added to the CommandManager and will be activated. This indicates a component (part or subassembly) is being edited *in* the assembly. This icon will be visible in every CommandManager toolbar.

The most obvious indicator to know that we are editing a new part in the assembly is that the existing component(s) will become transparent. This is a System option in the "**Display/Selection**" section, and it has three options:

**Opaque Assembly** will force every component in the assembly to be opaque regardless of the component's transparency setting in the assembly.

**Maintain Assembly Transparency** will leave components as they were; no changes to transparency will be made. Using this setting it will be less obvious that we are editing components in the assembly.

**Force Assembly Transparency** (default setting) will make every component transparent except the one being edited. The level of transparency can be set with the slider.

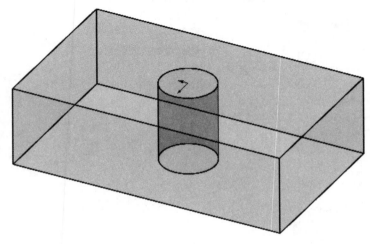

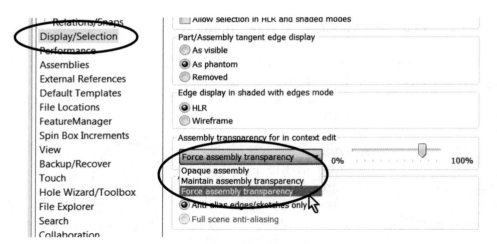

 If, after selecting the face to insert a new part, you are asked to name the new part, the System Option "**Assemblies, Save new components to external files**" is set. The default setting is *off*.

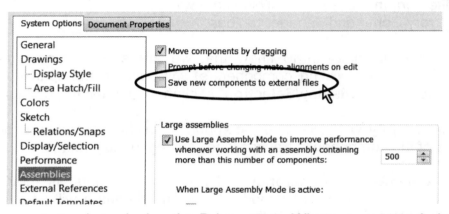

**127. –** The next step is to design the Driven part. What we want to do is to make the pin 0.025″ smaller than the hole. We'll use the **Offset Entities** command to offset the hole. The only new thing here is that when we make the offset we are selecting the edge of a *different* component. Select "Reverse" if needed to offset the edge to the inside of the hole; click **OK** to finish.

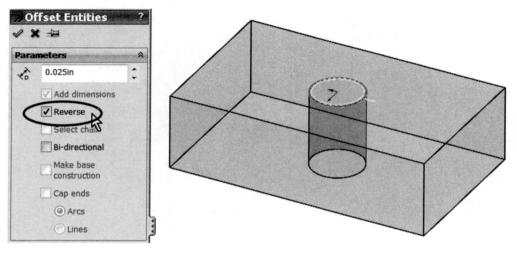

Your sketch will now look like this:

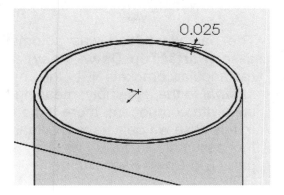

**128.** – Extrude the sketch to the bottom of the *Top Down Base* part using the end condition "Up to Surface" and select the bottom face of the *Top Down Base* part.

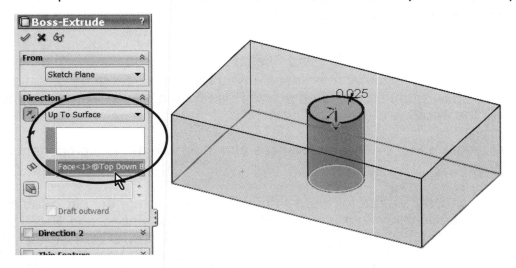

Your assembly should now look like this:

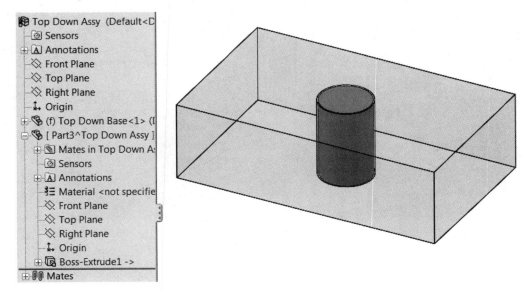

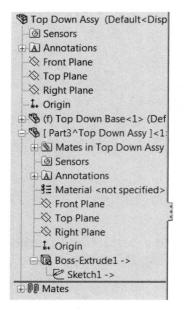

Take a look at the FeatureManager for a second; there are a few things we have to pay attention to:

The part we added was automatically named, in this case **[Part3^Top Down Assy]**. Notice the name is in rectangular brackets [ ]; this means that the part is *internal* to the assembly, meaning that while the part is a separate component, there is no external file for it (yet). In this case we only have 2 actual files on the hard drive: the assembly (*Top Down Assy.sldasm*) and the Base part (*Top Down Base.sldprt*).

The name and all of its features are shown in blue; this means that the part (or subassembly if that was the case) is being edited.

At the end of the Boss-Extrude1 and Sketch1 names we can see **->**; this means that the feature has external references. If you remember, Sketch1 was made by making an offset from the hole's edge and Boss-Extrude1 was extruded up to the bottom of the *Top Down Base* part.

We'll talk more about external references and internal/external components later in the lesson.

**129.** – The second feature for the new part will be the top of the pin. Remember that we are editing the new part in context of the assembly, and EVERY part modeling command is available here as well. Add a new sketch on top of the part we just made. Using the **Offset** command, make a sketch 0.5″ bigger than the hole in the Base part, just as we did for the first sketch.

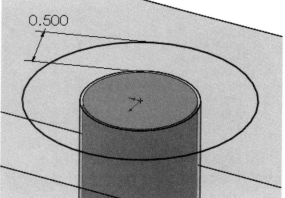

Extrude the sketch 0.5″ up to finish the part.

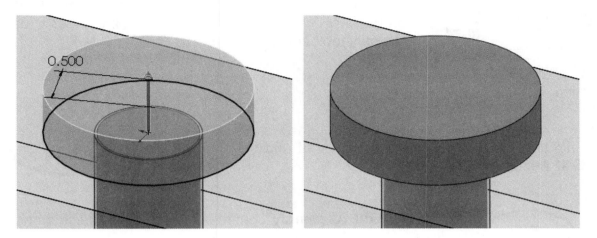

**130. –** We have finished the new part in the context of the assembly. What we need to do now is return to editing the assembly. As a reference, the different editing levels within SolidWorks are:

| Icon | Editing Level |
|---|---|
| | Part Sketch |
| | Part Feature |
| | Part |
| (Yellow & Blue) | Part in Assembly |
| (Yellow & Blue) | Subassembly |
| * As many Subassembly levels as needed. | |
| (Yellow & Blue) | Subassembly |
| (Yellow & Green) | Main Assembly |

 Additionally, SolidWorks has assembly sketch and assembly features in assemblies and subassemblies which will be covered later.

 When we are at the part (or subassembly) editing level inside an assembly, we can right mouse click in the graphics area, and change the assembly transparency from the pop-up menu "**Assembly Transparency**" or select the "**Assembly Transparency**" icon in the CommandManager.

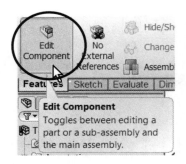

Currently we are editing the part *inside* the assembly. To return to editing the main assembly, select the "**Edit Component**" icon in the CommandManager (or Assembly toolbar if visible) or,

**Edit Component**
Toggles between editing a part or a sub-assembly and the main assembly.

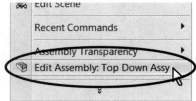

…right mouse click in the graphics area and select "**Edit Assembly: xxxx**" or,

…select the **Edit Assembly** confirmation corner (just like when we close a Sketch).

Now that we are editing the assembly, everything should look as we are used to, and the status bar at the bottom will read "**Editing Assembly**." Notice that when editing a part in the assembly, the assembly tools are disabled.

Editing part        Editing Assembly

**131. –** At the assembly editing level, add an exploded view and pull the Driven part out for visibility.

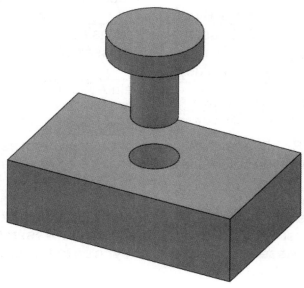

**132.** – Double click in the hole to display its diameter dimension and change it from 1″ to 1.625″. Rebuild the assembly to see the changes propagate to the driven component.

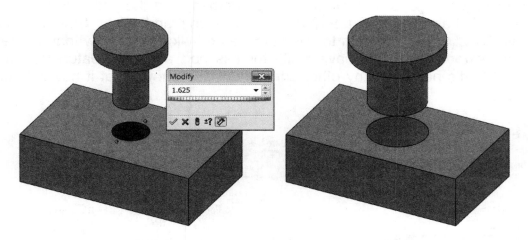

**133.** – Save the assembly and when asked, select "**Save All**," and "**Save internally**" for now.

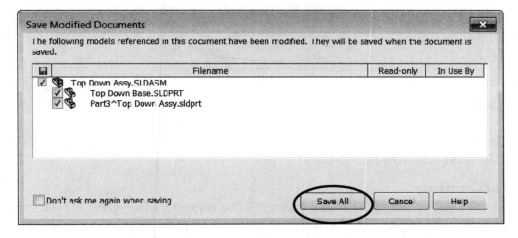

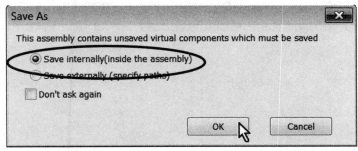

 It may seem a little confusing at first, but it's very simple. Edit assembly or Edit part. Just like that. The rest is what you do while you are editing the part or the assembly. The important thing is to be *aware* if we are editing an assembly or a part.

**134.** – Saving the part "internally" means that there is no file that we can reference, and therefore we cannot make a drawing of an internal part. To externalize the part and make a file for it, we have to rename it like a regular feature (with a slow double click or in its properties) and then save it. Rename the internal part as *Driven Part*. Right mouse click on it and select "**Save Part (in External File).**" Select the path to save the file and click **OK**. Now that the part has been *"externalized"*, we have a file for this part and the FeatureManager shows the part's name as any other component and shows that it has external references (->).

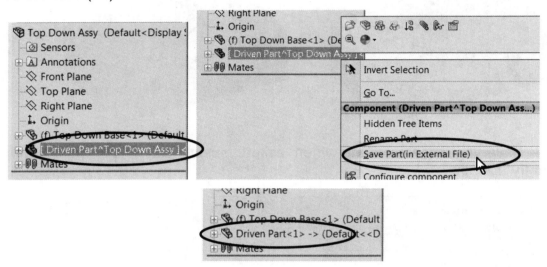

## More about external references

 External references can have four different states: In Context, Out of Context, Locked and Broken.

**In Context:**

When a part with external references and the assembly where those references were created <u>are open</u> in SolidWorks (loaded in memory), if a referenced part (driving) is modified, the driven part updates automatically, as in the previous example. External references are displayed as "**->**" in the FeatureManager.

Assembly view

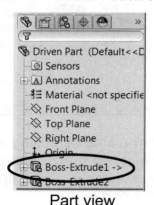
Part view

## Out of Context:

Out of Context is when a part with external references is open, but the assembly in which those references were created is not (not loaded in memory). If a part referenced (driving) is modified, the driven part **WILL NOT** update until the assembly where the references were made is opened.

Open the *Driven Part* and *Top Down Base* parts but **not** the assembly. Change the *Top Down Base* part's hole size and then go back to the *Driven Part*; the changes will not propagate. Open the assembly and see the changes propagate.

**Out of Context** references are listed with "**- >?**"

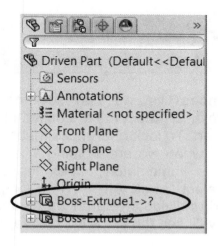

## Locked:

When external references are locked changes will not propagate, even if the assembly is open (loaded in memory or In context). To lock a part's external references right mouse click at the top of the part's FeatureManager and select **"List External Refs…"**

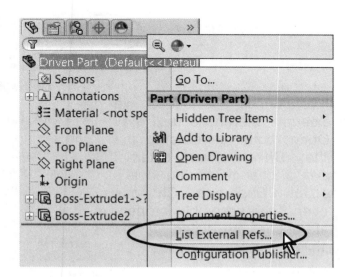

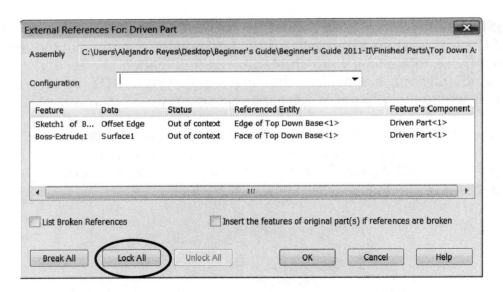

In the "**External References**" list we can see the features with external references, status (In context, Out of context, Locked or Broken) and which part and entity is being referenced. To lock references means that we can temporarily *freeze* them. This is useful when we are working in an assembly and we don't want to propagate changes immediately. Open the *Driven Part* file, list the external references and select "**Lock All**." When locking external references, ALL references are locked; individual references cannot be selectively locked. When locking references, we'll see the following message; click **OK** to continue.

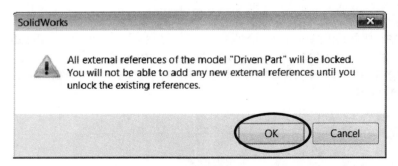

When the external references are locked, we cannot add more external references until they are unlocked. Open both parts and the assembly, lock the *Driven Part* external references and make a change to the hole's diameter in the *Top Down Base* part. Changes will not propagate, even if the assembly is open. Locked external references are listed in the Feature Manager with "**- > \***."

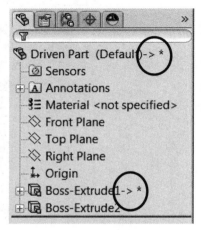

To unlock external references, repeat the same process and select the "**Unlock All**" button. After unlocking, changes will propagate following the same rules when parts are "**In Context**" or "**Out of Context**."

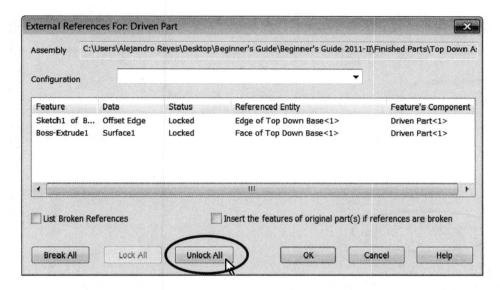

### Broken:

Broken external references work exactly the same way as "**Locked**;" the difference is that Broken references **CANNOT** be re-established. Once a part's external references have been Broken, there is no way to recover them. Broken external references are listed with "**- > x**."

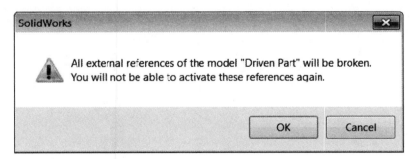

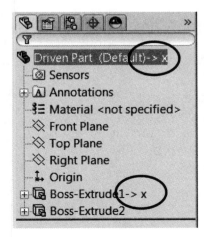

When listing External References for a part with Broken references, the list will be empty unless we use the "**List Broken References**" checkbox.

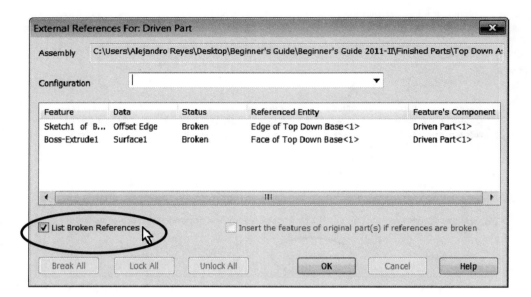

## *Sheet Metal and Top Down Design*

**135.** – Now that we have a basic understanding of what **Top Down Design** is and how it works, let's design a computer's power supply enclosure. For our example we'll start with the assumption that the electronic components are already designed and they will drive the size of the enclosure. Download the *Power Supply.sldprt* part file from www.mechanicad.com/download.html.
Our electronics board looks like this:

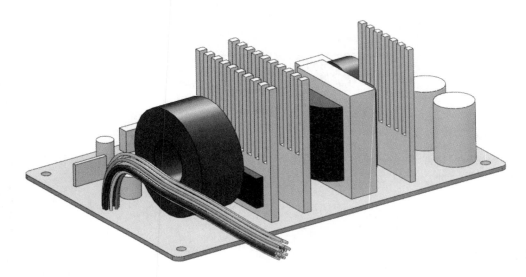

**136.** – The first thing we need to do is to make a new assembly, locate the board at the assembly's origin and save the assembly as "**Power Supply Assy**."

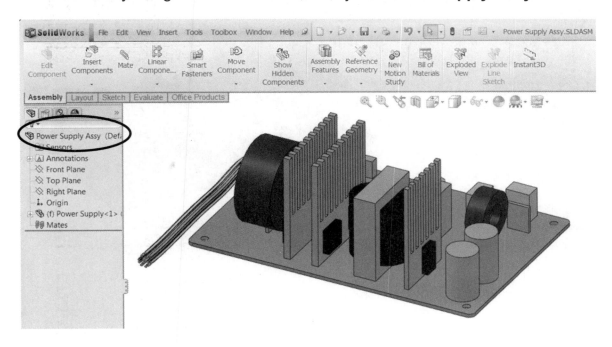

**137. –** The first component we are going to design in the context of the assembly is the bottom of the enclosure. Select "**New Part**" from the drop down list in the "**Insert Components**" icon in the Assembly toolbar, or from the menu "**Insert, Component, New Part**."

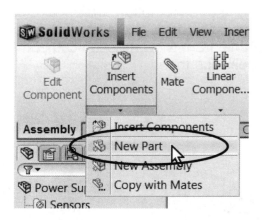

**138. –** Select the assembly's Right plane in the FeatureManager to locate the new part's Front plane, adding the "InPlace" mate.

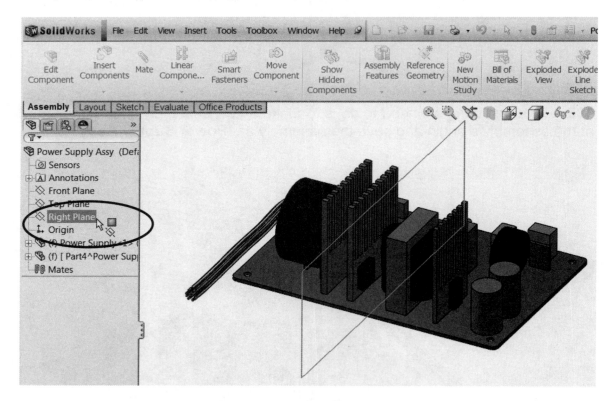

Immediately after selecting the Right plane in the FeatureManager, this is what will happen:

- Our existing electronics board will become transparent (if the option is set in **"Tools, Options, System Options: Display/Selection, Force assembly Transparency"**).
- The **"Edit Component"** icon in the CommandManager will be enabled.
- A new name will be assigned to the new part in the FeatureManager tree if the option **"Tools, System Options: Assemblies, Save New Components to external files"** is NOT checked; OR you will be asked for a new part name if the option is checked.
- The new part's FeatureManager will be blue (default setting).
- A new sketch will be created in the new part's Front plane.
- The status bar will read "Editing Sketch."
- The title bar will read:
  Sketch1 of Part#^Power Supply Assy -in- Power Supply Assy.SLDASM
  Which means:
  *Sketch1*: We are editing the new part's first sketch (Sketch1)/
  of Part#^Power Supply Assy: of **internal** Part# in the Power Supply Assy.
  -in- Power Supply Assy.SLDASM: in the "Power Supply Assy.sldasm" file.
- An **"InPlace"** mate will be added automatically to the new part.

As we can see, there are plenty of visual clues to alert us when we are working on editing a part in the context of an assembly.

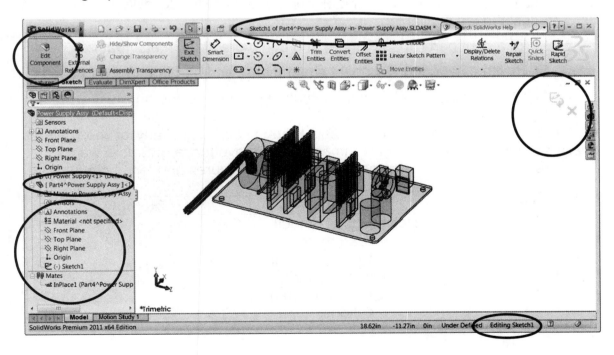

**139. –** If not already visible, activate and select the Sheet Metal toolbar in the CommandManager and/or individual toolbar by either a right mouse click in the CommandManager's tabs and selecting "**Sheet Metal**" from the pop-up menu, or in the menu "**View, Toolbars, Sheet Metal**."

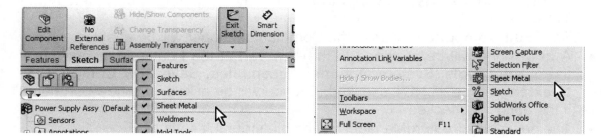

The Sheet Metal toolbar has most of the commands needed, and looks like this:

**140. –** When designing sheet metal components with SolidWorks there are different techniques available:

> Make a bent part (Base Flange) and add more sheet metal features.

> Start with a flat pattern (unbent sheet metal) and add features and bends.

> Convert a solid model to sheet metal adding bends and rips.

In this example we'll start with a **Base Flange**, and use many of the features available in the Sheet Metal environment as we move forward. Before we do that, let's take a look at the most common sheet metal features and terminology.

| Icon | Description | Example |
|---|---|---|
| Sheet-Metal | Definitions of default bend parameters including sheet metal thickness, bend radius, relief type and related options. | N/A |

| | | |
|---|---|---|
| Base Flange/Tab | Base Flange/Tab will be the first sheet metal feature (or additional tabs) in the part. If it's the first feature, it will create the required Sheet Metal features automatically (Sheet-Metal, Base-Flange and Flat-Pattern). | |
| Base Flange/Tab | Tab: Tabs are used to add more material to an existing sheet metal part using a sketch. Tabs can be bent later. | |
| Flat-Pattern | Represents the sheet metal part in its unbent state. If this feature is suppressed, the part is bent; if it's unsuppressed, the part is unbent (flat). | |
| Convert to Sheet Metal | Used to convert a solid, surface or imported model to Sheet Metal by adding bends and rips to allow the part to be flattened. | |
| Edge Flange | Used to add flanges. Flange shapes can be modified and do not need to be the full length of the edge. Circular edge flanges are allowed. | |
| Miter Flange | Used to add flanges on a series of adjacent edges automatically, including non-planar flanges. | |

| | | |
|---|---|---|
| Hem | Used to add a hem to a linear edge. Mostly used to remove sharp edges. | |
| Jog | A jog will add two bends on a model using a single sketch line. | |
| Sketched Bend | A sketched bend will add a bend using a sketch line. | |
| Corners | Used to close corners after relief cuts are made. | |
| Forming Tool | Used to create indentation tools like louvers, lances, flanges, etc. | |

| | | |
|---|---|---|
| 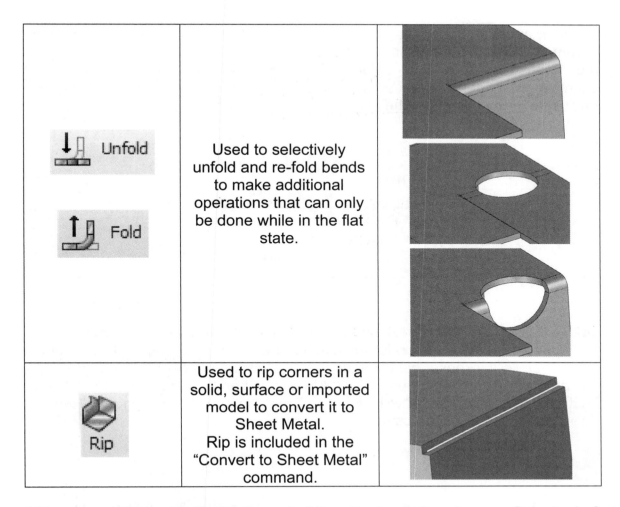**Unfold** **Fold** | Used to selectively unfold and re-fold bends to make additional operations that can only be done while in the flat state. | |
| **Rip** | Used to rip corners in a solid, surface or imported model to convert it to Sheet Metal. Rip is included in the "Convert to Sheet Metal" command. | |

**141. –** Now let's design the lower part of the sheet metal enclosure. Select a Left view orientation (Assembly view orientation), and draw the following sketch. Remember, we are already working in a new sketch in the new part in the assembly. Note that this is an open sketch and is dimensioned referencing the lower and outer edges of the electronic board (both vertical lines are Equal).

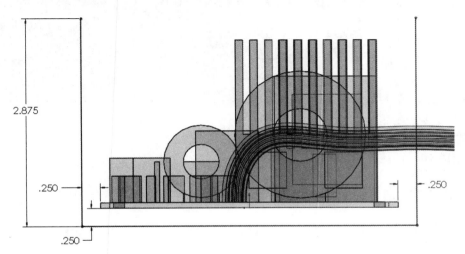

A sheet metal component is essentially a thin extrusion with a few more parameters that we'll explain in the next step. With our sketch complete, create the Base Flange feature selecting the "**Base-Flange/Tab**" icon from the CommandManager's Sheet Metal toolbar. Remember, we are designing the enclosure <u>in the context of the assembly using a Top Down design approach</u>.

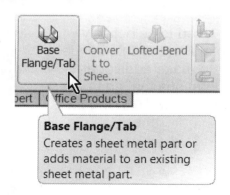

**142.** – Extrude the Base Flange 7″ using the "**Mid plane**" end condition. In addition to the end condition for the extrusion we see more options to control the sheet metal's thickness, bend radius, bend allowance and auto relief type. For our example, use a thickness of 0.030″ with a bend radius of 0.05″ and a K-Factor of 0.5. Auto Relief will be set to Tear. Be sure to turn on the "Reverse Direction" checkbox. Confused?

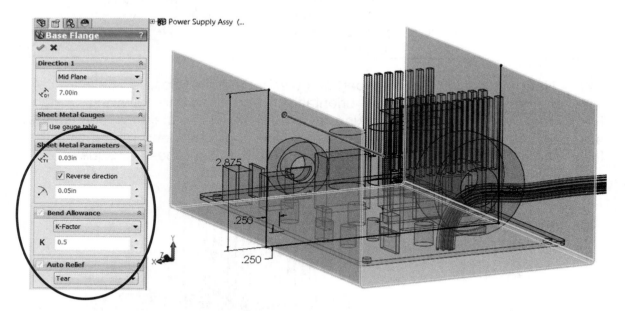

**What it all means:**

In the "Sheet Metal Parameters" options we'll enter:

> **Thickness of the material:** This is the uniform thickness of the material that will be used to make the part.

"**Reverse direction**" **checkbox:** Since a sheet metal part is essentially a Thin Feature (with constant thickness) we need to define which side of the sketch we want the material to be added, in other words, if the dimensions added are *inside* or *outside* dimensions. In our example we want them to be *inside* dimensions and the material will be added *outside*. It may not seem to be very important, but if you ignore the material's thickness in your designs, the result will be a part that is one material-thickness bigger or smaller, and that may ruin your design. We need to pay attention to this important detail when designing sheet metal components and not ignore it.

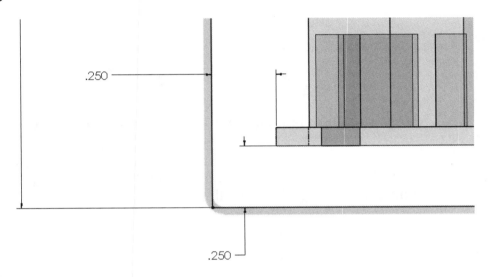

**Default bend radius:** The radius as measured on the inside of the bend.

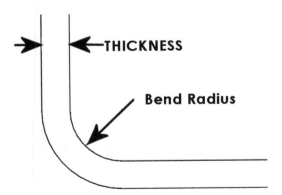

The "**Bend Allowance**" section refers to the way SolidWorks calculates how much material will be consumed by a bend. When we bend a sheet metal component, the material on the inside face of the bend is compressed and the material outside is stretched. For example, if we take a 4″ long strip of metal, and bend it 90 degrees at the center, the length of the flat portions plus the bent region will not necessarily add to 4″. SolidWorks has three methods to calculate the flat pattern length: **Bend Allowance**, **Bend Deduction** and **K-Factor**.

**Bend Allowance:** When we use the Bend Allowance method we specify a length of metal that will become the bent region and is calculated by <u>adding</u> a specified length to the flat regions.

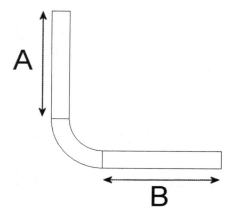

Flat Pattern Length = A + B + Bend Allowance (BA)

**Bend Deduction:** If we use a Bend Deduction we <u>subtract</u> a specified length to obtain the flat pattern length.

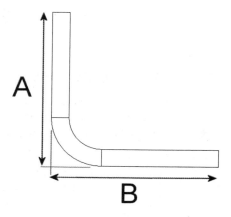

Flat Pattern Length = A + B – Bend Deduction (BD)

**K-Factor:** As we explained before, the material inside the bend is compressed and the material outside is stretched. The line between them is known as the neutral axis, which in essence does not change length. The relation between the distance of the neutral axis to the inside face and the sheet metal's thickness is known as the K-Factor.

K-Factor = t / T

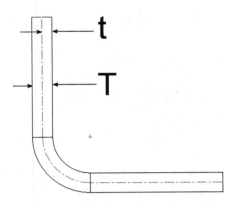

The bend allowance (BA) is then calculated by:

$$BA = \pi (R + KT) A/180$$

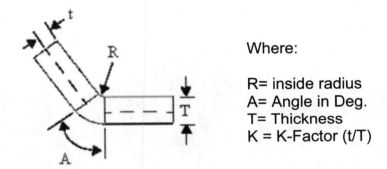

Where:

R= inside radius
A= Angle in Deg.
T= Thickness
K = K-Factor (t/T)

The method to calculate a sheet metal's bend allowance varies by preference, experience, availability of data, etc. There are numerous tables, books, references and guides to calculate it, and since these parameters vary by material, thickness, bend angle, grain direction, process and even temperature, we will not go into those details as it's well beyond the scope of this book and instead we'll use a generic K-Factor value for our examples.

The "**Auto Relief**" section refers to the relief cuts generated by SolidWorks for sheet metal fabrication processes. These cuts are added as needed for bending purposes. During the bending process, it's common to make small cuts (reliefs) at the sides of bends to allow the metal to bend properly and not deform the material unexpectedly.

## The types of reliefs available are:

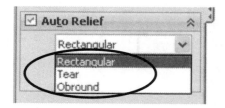

**Rectangular:** In a rectangular relief, a cut is made using a ratio or by specifying dimensions. The ratio is the cut's size (Dim) calculated based on the sheet metal's thickness as follows:

$$Dim = (Material\ Thickness) \times (Relief\ Ratio)$$

**Obround:** Is just like the Rectangular relief, but the relief's cut is rounded.

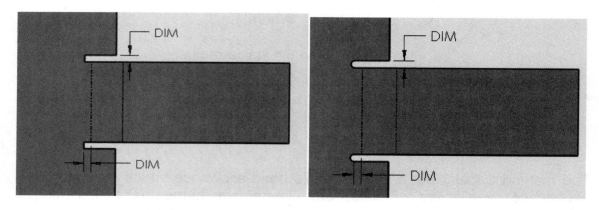

Rectangular Relief                    Obround Relief

**Tear:** In a tear the smallest possible relief cut is made, just enough to allow the metal to bend as intended. This is similar to ripping it at the time of bending.

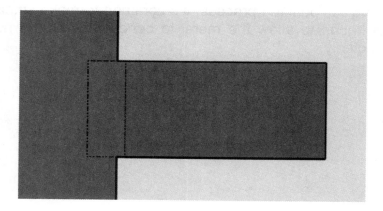

**143.** – After extruding the "Base-Flange," our part looks like this. Keep in mind that we are still editing it in the context of the assembly, and that's the reason why the electronics board is transparent.

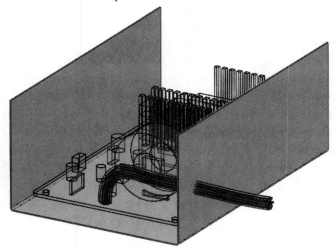

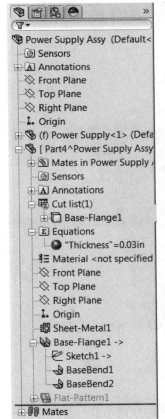

**144.** – The FeatureManager now shows the new part and the Sheet Metal features.

In *"Part4^Power Supply Assy"* (in blue because we are editing it in context of the assembly) we see the new sheet metal features added with the Base Flange operation.

**"Cut list"**: Shows the number of bodies in the part. If multiple sheet metal bodies are added to a part, they will be listed under this folder.

**"Equations"**: Lists the equations and constants in a part. For sheet metal components, a constant is automatically added called "Thickness" which is used to make dimensions equal to the material's thickness.

**"Sheet-Metal1"**: The feature that defines settings for a sheet metal part including material thickness, default bend radius, bend allowance and relief type.

**"Base-Flange1"**: The first feature of the sheet metal part. Just like other sketch-based features, it includes the sketch used to make it and the bends in the feature.

**"Flat-Pattern1"**: This feature is suppressed when the part is bent (default). To show the part's flat pattern (*un-bent part*) we can unsuppress it. It includes a sketch (Bend-Lines1) automatically generated with the part's bend lines and a list all the bends in the part.

**145.** – The next step is to add features to screw the board to the enclosure. The way we are going to create these supports is by using a feature called "**Forming Tool**." A Forming Tool works as a die that forms the sheet metal by bending, cutting and stretching as if it was pressed into the part, hence the "*Forming*" part of the name. SolidWorks has a number pre-loaded tools to make flanges, louvers, lances ribs, etc. In this step we'll learn how to use an existing forming tool and in a later step we'll see how to create one.

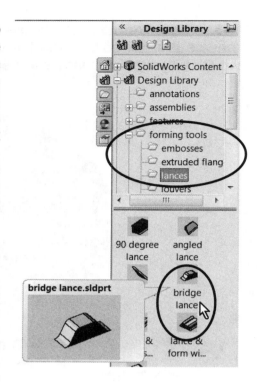

Expand the Design Library, and from the folder "**forming tools**" select the "lances" subfolder. We'll use the "bridge lance" forming tool. To apply it to our model, drag it onto the bottom part of the model, and before dropping it make sure the tool is going 'into' the part (pressing the metal from the outside in), as in the following image. To reverse the direction of the forming tool press the "Tab" key before 'dropping' the forming tool with the mouse.

If SolidWorks asks "*Are you trying to make a derived part?*" when dropping the forming tool, the "forming tools" folder is not defined as such. To fix it, right mouse click in the "**forming tools**" folder in the Design Library and turn on the "**Forming Tools Folder**" option.

**146. –** After dropping the forming tool, we see the **"Position form feature"** dialog. Each form tool has a locating sketch that we can use to accurately locate the form tool; we cannot change its size but we can change its orientation and position.

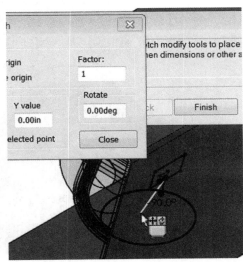

**147. –** To rotate the sketch 90 degrees, we'll use the **Modify** tool from the menu **"Tools, Sketch Tools, Modify."** With this tool we can move the sketch by clicking and dragging the left mouse button and rotate it with the right button.

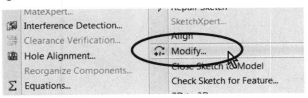

**148. –** With the **"Modify Sketch"** tool we can scale, translate or rotate the sketch by entering values, or clicking-and-dragging. Click and drag with the right mouse button and notice the screen feedback as we move the mouse. When you see *90.0* degrees, stop and release the mouse button. Click on the "Close" button of the "Modify Sketch" dialog.

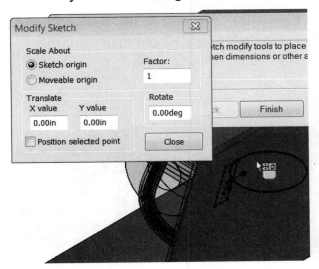

**149.** – To locate the form tool feature, switch to a Top view. (Do not close the "**Position form feature**" dialog yet; just move it out of the way if needed.) Click and drag the center of the sketch onto one of the holes in the electronics board, and capture a concentric relation.

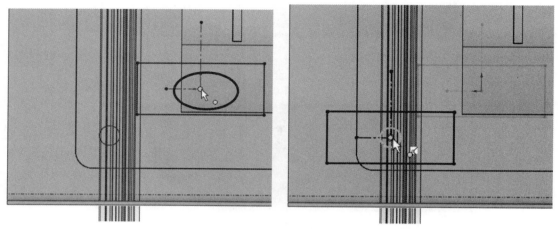

**150.** – Select one sketch line and add a vertical or horizontal relation (depending on which line was selected) to fully define the sketch. Click in the "Finish" button to complete the form feature.

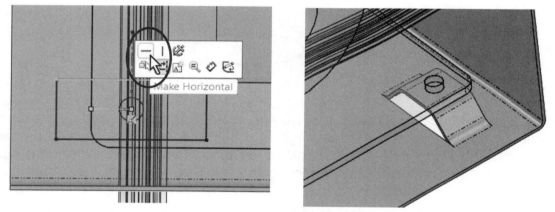

**151.** – Add the other three form tool features to the rest of the mounting holes using the same approach, making one coincident to each hole in the board.

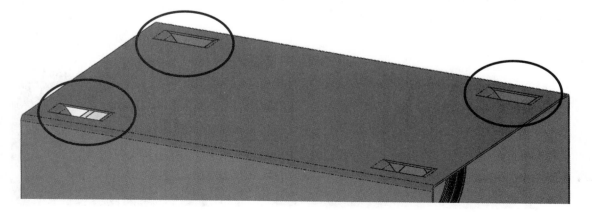

**152. –** After adding the lances to the bottom, we need to make holes for the screws. Switch to a Top view, select the top of any of the form features just added and make a new sketch. Add four equal circles concentric to the electronic board mounting holes. Dimension them 0.1″ in diameter.

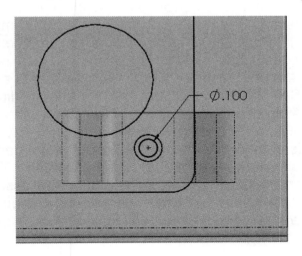

**153. –** Select the "**Extruded Cut**" icon to make a cut using all four circles at the same time. Notice the extra options under "Direction 1." Using the "**Link to Thickness**" option will make the cut exactly as deep as the sheet metal thickness.

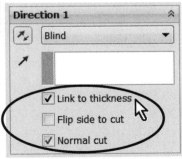

The second new option is "**Normal Cut**." Normal cut means the cut will be made perpendicular to the sheet metal, even if the cut is being made at an angle. The reason to do this is because manufacturing processes cannot easily make cuts at an angle in thin metal. This option is driven by the nature of the manufacturing process.

Normal cut unchecked
(Difficult to make)

Normal cut checked.
(Easier to make)

**154.** – After adding the mounting holes we need to add a fan to help us cool the power supply. In many cases we'll need to include purchased components in our designs, like electrical components, hardware, etc. Many suppliers provide 3D models of their products, saving designers the trouble of modeling purchased parts, reducing the risk of design errors and at the same time improving the chances of having their products selected for our designs, making it a win-win situation. There are multiple sources of 3D models, from manufacturer's web sites to portals that consolidate multiple suppliers and user submitted models, like SolidWorks' 3D Content Central. 3D Content Central is a free portal that is also integrated in SolidWorks, and can be accessed directly from within SolidWorks or on the web at www.3dcontentcentral.com.

Remember that at this point we are editing the sheet metal part *in* the assembly, and now we need to add a new component to the assembly. To do this we need to stop editing the part for now, and return to editing the assembly. Select the **"Edit Component"** toggle button in the toolbar or CommandManager, *or* the confirmation corner *or* right mouse click and select **"Edit Assembly: xxxx"** to stop editing the sheet metal part and return to the assembly.

When we stop editing the part and return to editing the assembly...

- The sheet metal part's FeatureManager is no longer blue.
- The Power Supply electronics will become opaque again.
- The status bar will read "Editing Assembly."
- The "Edit Component" button will be disabled (since no component is selected).
- The confirmation corner will be off.
- The title bar will read "*Power Supply Assy.sldasm*."

Basically, the assembly looks like any other assembly and now we can add more components to it.

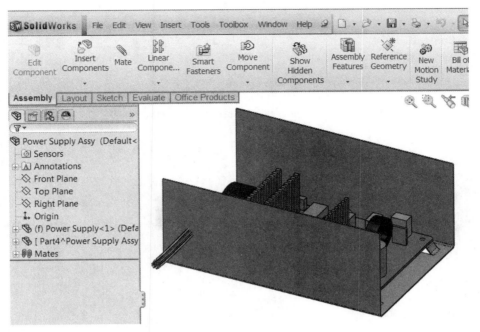

**155.** – In SolidWorks, select the Design Library, go to "**3D ContentCentral**, **User Library, Home Page**" and click on the icon at the bottom to display the **User Library**.

A web browser will be launched where we can search the online catalog for components. As of the writing of this book, you have to register (free) in order to download files. In our example we'll use a user supplied model instead of a supplier certified component. For our power supply we need a new fan.

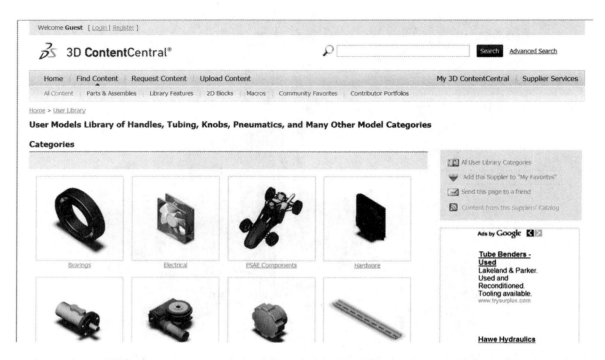

In the search box type *PABST 512F*. This is the exact model we'll use; however, users would typically search by model or part number, make a general search for "Fan", and select a suitable model from the available options. The search now shows the part we are interested in.

Select the model; in the next screen make sure the format selected is SolidWorks 2011 (or earlier) and download the 3D model. After we are presented with the download window, drag the model's name into the assembly to add it to our Power Supply. When asked for a part name, select the folder to save the downloaded part and save as "**Fan-PABST 512F**". The model will be automatically added to your model. Save it and return to the assembly.

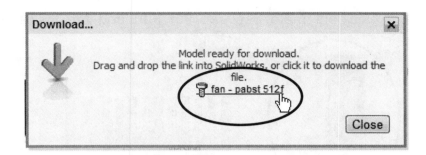

After adding the Fan to our assembly, locate it approximately as indicated.

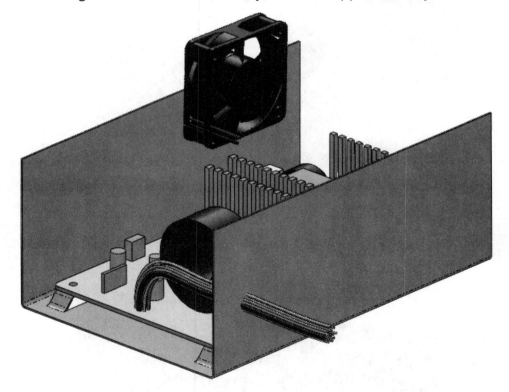

**156. –** Add a Coincident mate between the Fan and the inside wall of the enclosure.

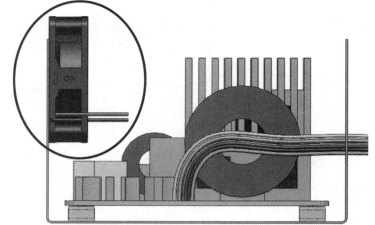

…then a second Coincident mate between the Right plane of the Fan and the face indicated in the electronics board.

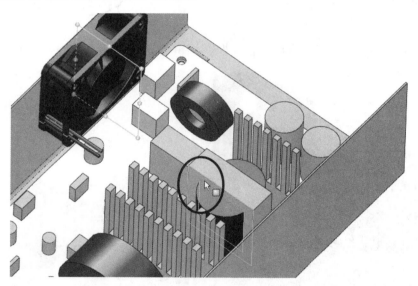

**157. –** To finish locating the Fan, add a 0.2″ Distance mate from the Top face of the Fan to the top of the enclosure. Our Fan is now fully defined in the assembly.

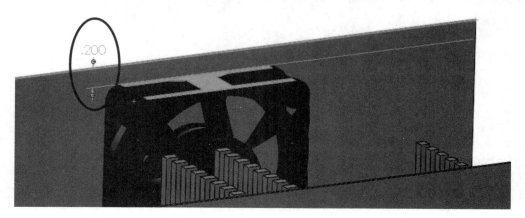

**158. –** Now with the Fan in place, we need to edit the sheet metal part to make a cut for ventilation. Select the sheet metal part in the FeatureManager or in the graphics area and from the pop-up menu select "**Edit Part**".

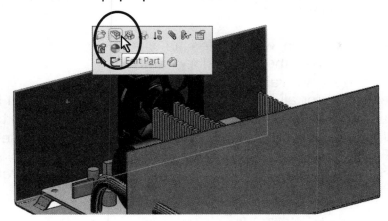

**159. –** We are now editing the sheet metal part again; the electronics board and the fan are transparent and the box is opaque. Switch to a Back view and hide the electronics board component for visibility. Change the display mode to "Hidden Lines Visible".

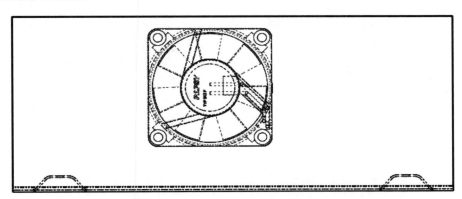

**160. –** Select the face in the back and make the following sketch. We'll use the Fan as a reference to make the ventilation cut using the "**Vent**" feature. By matching the vent's location to the fan, if the fan's position is changed the vent will update; that is the idea behind designing in the context of an assembly. Notice the sketch used for the vent has intersecting lines, and the only reference to the fan is a Concentric relation to the fan's center.

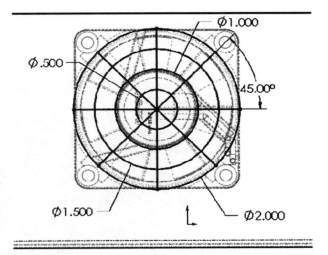

**161.** – From the Sheet Metal toolbar select the "**Vent**" feature. This icon is also located in the "**Fastening Features**" toolbar, or in the menu "**Insert, Fastening Feature, Vent**".

Vent
Uses sketch elements to create a vent for airflow in both a plastic or sheet metal design.

**162.** – In this step the fan was hidden for clarity. Select the outer circle as the "**Boundary**" and set the "**Radius for the fillets**" value equal to 0.05″ (this will be the fillet radius for all inside edges). In the "**Ribs**" selection box select all straight lines and make their width 0.1″. For the "**Spars**" selection box select the 1″ and 1.5″ diameter circles and make them 0.1″ wide. Finally, select the inner circle in the "**Fill-In Boundary**". The Fill-In Boundary will be completely covered. Note the "**Flow Area**" section lists the total area and the open area percentage for reference. Click **OK** to complete the Vent feature.

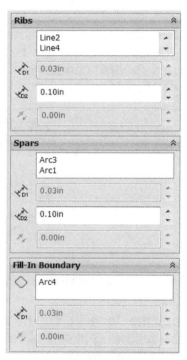

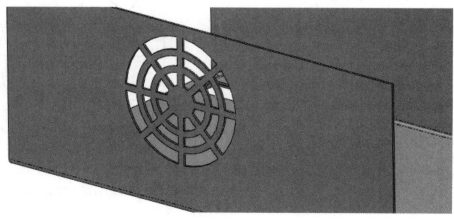

**163. –** So far the sheet metal component has been an '*internal*' component in the assembly. This means that it only exists inside the assembly; there is no file on the hard disk that we can make a reference to.  Since we need to have a *part file* to make a drawing of, we need to *externalize* the part. It's not possible to make a drawing of a part internal to an assembly.  If you remember, we never gave the part a (file) name; it was automatically assigned by SolidWorks.  This step will make the part external; we'll give it a name and SolidWorks will create a file at the same time. To externalize the part, select the part in the FeatureManager with a right mouse click and select "**Rename Part**" from the pop-up menu. Rename the part "**Box Bottom**" in the FeatureManager.

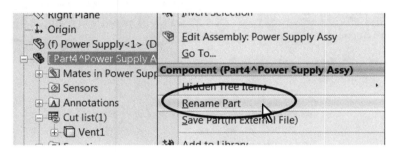

**164. –** After renaming the part, select it again with a right mouse click and select "**Save Part (in External File)**" from the pop-up menu.

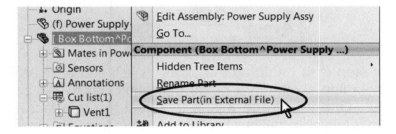

Make sure the path is correct and click **OK**.  The *Box Bottom* has been saved as a part file and looks the same as any other part in the assembly.

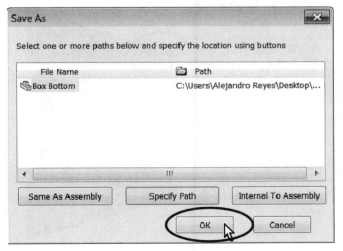

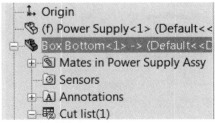

**165. –** At this point we can stop editing the part in the assembly and open it in its own window, or continue working in the context of the assembly. We'll edit the part in its own window as much as possible to make it easier to visualize the process, and revert to editing in the assembly as needed to take into consideration other components. To stop editing the part in the assembly, turn off the "**Edit Component**" icon and open the *Box Bottom* part.

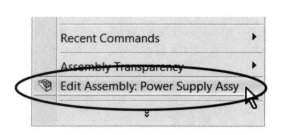

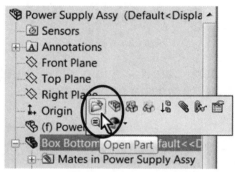

**166. –** The next step is to reinforce the sides. We'll add a Miter Flange to each end using a single line sketch in a plane perpendicular to the edge we want to add the miter to. One way to do this is to select the thin face at the end and insert a sketch in it (which is difficult unless we zoom in really close), or select the **Miter Flange** icon and click near the end of the edge. SolidWorks will automatically create a plane perpendicular to the selected edge and start the Miter Flange command.

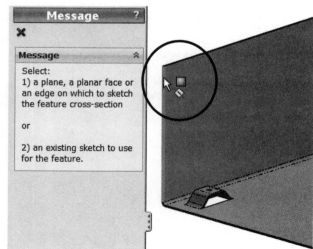

**167. –** Draw a single line perpendicular to the edge and dimension it 0.25″. This will be the profile of the miter flange.

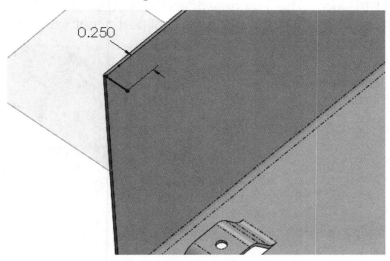

**168. –** Click on the **Miter Flange** command icon (or Exit Sketch) to continue. Notice the preview in the first edge. To continue the flange along the bottom and other side, either click on the "**Propagate**" icon to automatically select these edges, or manually select them. Leave the "**Use default radius**" checkbox selected to make the flange's bends the default radius. "**Gap Distance**" is the gap at the corners of the miter. "**Trim side bends**" removes material when a bend of the miter touches an existing bend (no difference in this case). Select the "**Material inside**" flange position.

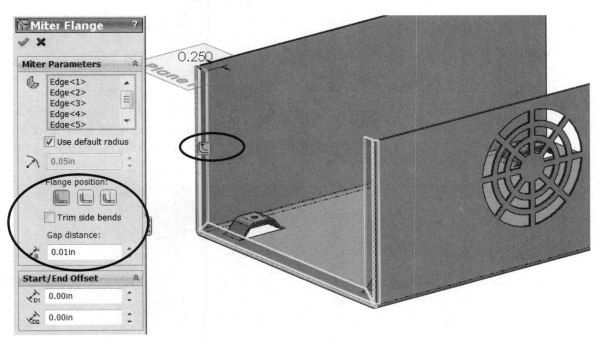

The "**Flange Position**:" section means:

**Material Inside**: The Flange added will not extend beyond the existing edge of the part, maintaining the original part dimensions.

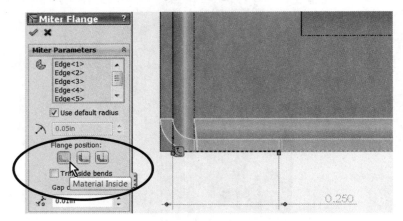

**Material Outside**: The flange added will be *one thickness* outside the existing edge.

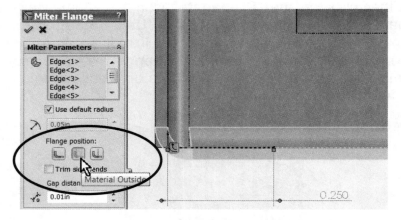

**Bend Outside**: The flange will leave the existing edge intact and add all the material and the bends outside. The part will increase in size by one thickness and one bend radius.

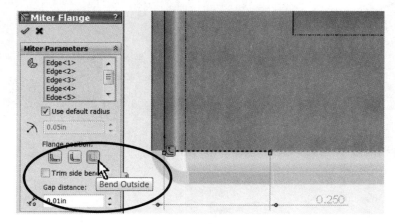

**169.** – Add a second Miter Flange to the other side of the enclosure using the same parameters as the first one.

**170.** – Now we need to add a cut on one side to allow the power supply wires to exit the enclosure. Go back to the Power Supply assembly and make the electronics board visible. Edit the *Box Bottom* part in the assembly.

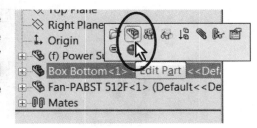

**171. –** To make the cut, first we need to unfold the miter's edge closer to the wires. We'll use the "**Unfold**" command from the Sheet Metal toolbar, or from the menu "**Insert, Sheet Metal, Unfold**".

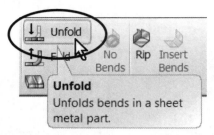

In the "**Fixed face**" selection box select the model's face that will remain fixed; in other words, when we unfold the miter flange, the flange will move out instead of the other way around. In the "**Bends to unfold**" select the bend region of the flange. Click **OK** when done.

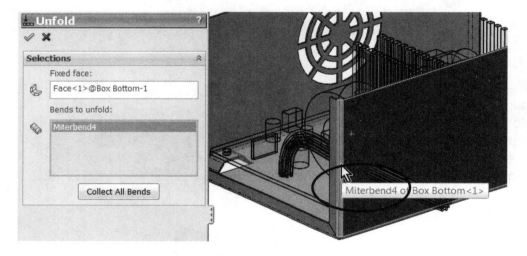

The miter flange will unfold.

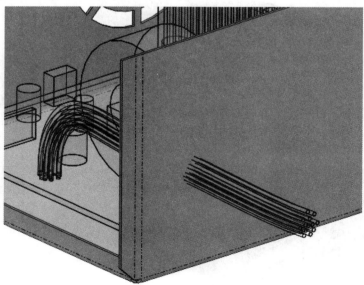

**172. –** While unfolded we can add the cut for the wires and then re-fold the flange. Switch to a Front view and make the next sketch around the wires. Make a cut using the "**Link to thickness**" option.

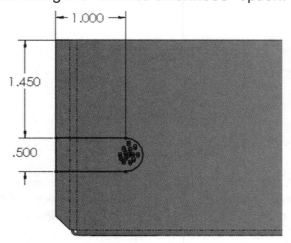

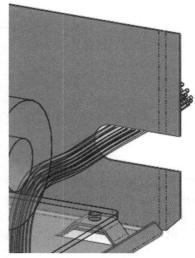

**173. –** To re-fold the flange, select the **Fold** icon from the Sheet Metal toolbar or from the menu "**Insert, Sheet Metal, Fold**".

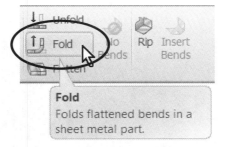

The "**Fixed face**" is automatically selected; all we have to do is select the bend region (SolidWorks will only let us select bends). Clicking in the "**Collect All Bends**" button will add all unfolded bends.

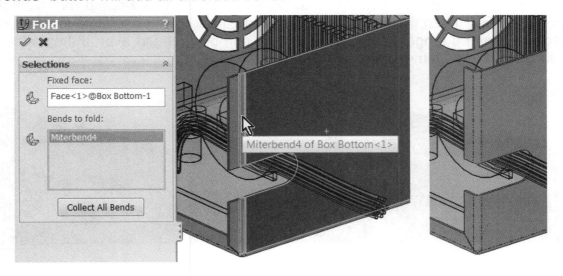

**174. –** The next step is to add flanges at the top of the box to screw the cover in place. Select the "**Edge Flange**" command from the Sheet Metal toolbar, or the menu "**Insert, Sheet Metal, Edge Flange**".

In the "**Flange Parameters**" selection box, select the top edge of the side with the vent. As soon as the mouse pointer is moved, you can see a preview of the edge flange. Click inside the box to make the flange inside. Then click on the "**Edit Flange Profile**" button to modify the shape of the flange. (If we want the flange to be the full length of the edge, there is no need to edit the profile.)

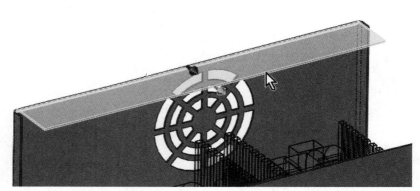

We can modify the sketch as much as we want, as long as we end with a single closed profile. Drag the end lines to the inside, remove the short line in front and replace it with a tangent arc. The end lines can be dragged even if they appear fully defined. Add dimensions as needed.

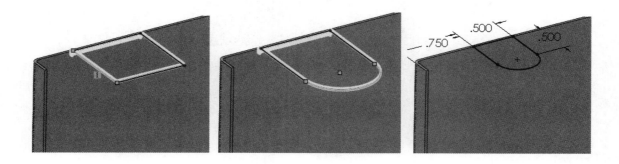

**175. –** Click the Back button to return to the **Edge Flange** command when the sketch is complete.

 If you click Finish, the flange will be completed with the parameters entered before editing the sketch.

In the "**Flange Parameters**," set the angle to 90 degrees. In the "**Flange Position**" selection box, select the "Material Inside" option, and turn on the "**Custom Relief Type**" checkbox. We'll use an Obround relief for the flange with a 0.5 ratio. Click **OK** to finish.

 For rectangular or obround types we can optionally define the relief by width and depth.

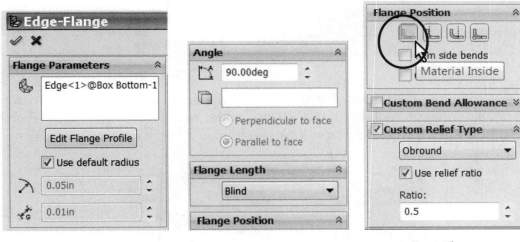

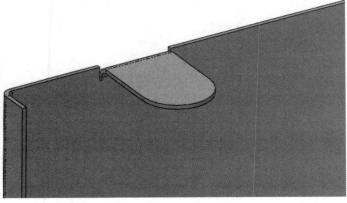

**176. –** Now we need to add a hole for a screw to the tab we just made. In this case we'll use one of the built in Form Tools to do it. Open the "**Design Library**" in the task pane, and scroll down to "**forming tools, embosses**". From the list of tools select "**extruded hole**". Drag-and-drop it in the Top face of the tab just made. Make sure it is going *into* the part, and not out of it. Remember that we can reverse the direction of the tool by pressing the TAB key before releasing the mouse.

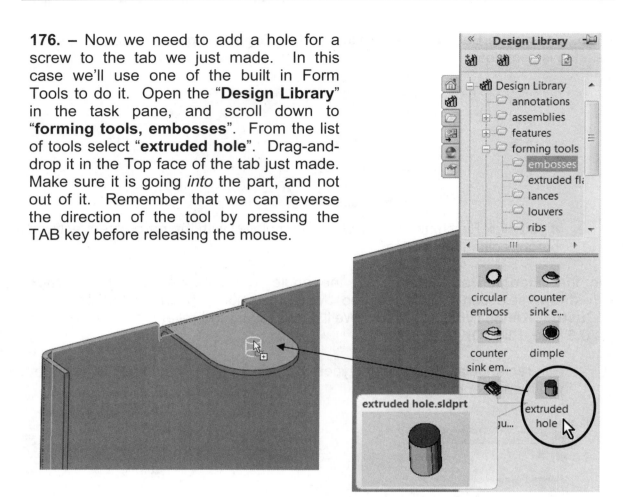

**177. –** When the "**Position form feature**" dialog box is displayed, make the locating sketch concentric to the round edge of the tab and click Finish to complete it. Your part should now look like this:

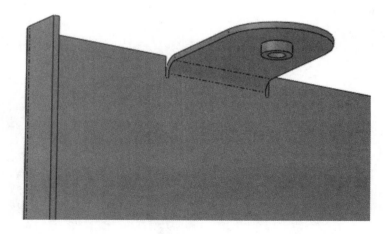

**178.** – The enclosure requires four flanges (and holes); add the other three using the Mirror feature about the Front plane, and then about the Right plane. We are still working in the context of the assembly.

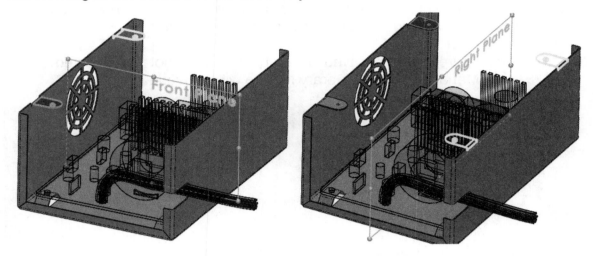

**179.** – Form tools can only be used in sheet metal parts, but a **library feature** can be used in any part, not just sheet metal. To make a library feature we have to make a new part, add the feature(s) we want and save it as a library.

We still need to add a cutout for the power supply cable connector next to the vent. We'll make a library feature with the cutout for the power connector and then apply it to the *Box Bottom* part. To build a library feature, make a new part, add a new sketch with a 3″ x 2″ square and extrude it 0.125″ thick. After extruding it, make the following sketch and make a cut using the "Up to next" end condition. The size and thickness of the first feature are not really important; it just has to be big enough to hold the feature we want to make a library from.

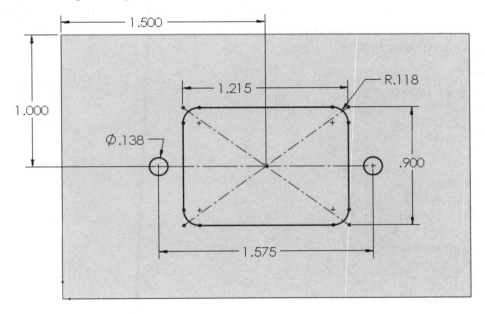

**180. –** Once the cut is made, select the Cut-Extrude1 feature in the Feature-Manager, select the menu "**File, Save as...**" and from the "Save as type" drop down selection box select "Lib Feat Part (*.sldlfp)".  Name it *Power Connector Cutout*.  Notice as soon as the library feature type is selected, we are switched to the "Design Library" folder.  Save the library in this folder.

 If the feature(s) to be saved as a library is(are) not pre-selected in the FeatureManager, saving a library feature will not work.

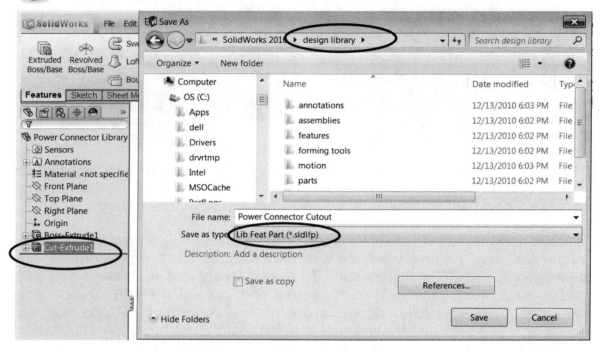

The FeatureManager changes to reflect it is now a library feature. A green letter "L" is superposed in the feature(s) that are the library, and the icon at the top is changed to a library feature.

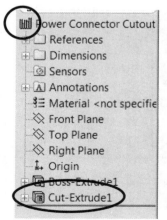

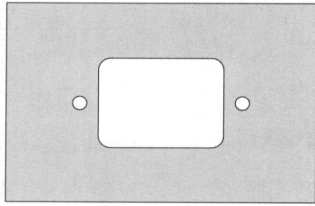

When the library is saved, the folder "**Dimensions**" is added to the Feature-Manager tree. Right mouse click in the "Annotations" folder, turn on "**Show Feature Dimensions**," and display dimension names from the menu "**View, Dimension Names**." Rename the indicated dimensions as shown.

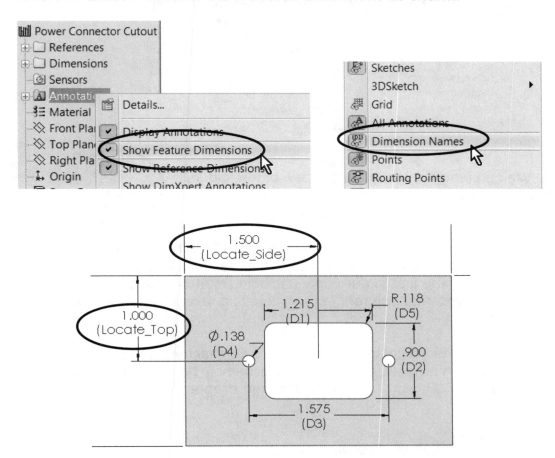

**181. –** The reason for renaming the dimensions is that in the library file we can define which dimensions will be used to locate the feature when inserted into a part, which dimensions can be changed by the user, and which cannot. Expanding the "**Dimensions**" folder we can see all the dimensions listed. What we need to do is drag-and-drop the "*Locate_Top*" and "*Locate_Side*" dimensions to the "Locating Dimensions" folder, and the rest in the "Internal Dimensions" folder.

**Locating Dimensions** will be used to position the feature when we add the library to a part. **Internal Dimensions** cannot be changed by the user and the dimensions not added to either folder can be changed when adding the library. After adding the dimensions to the folders, turn off the dimension display, save the changes and close the library file. The library we just made is now listed under the "Design Library" folder in the task pane.

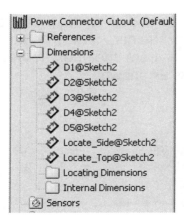
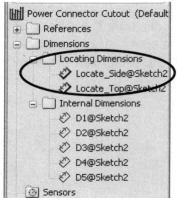
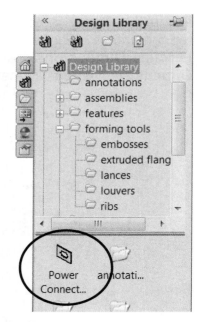

 We can drag the library files to one of the folders in the top to keep libraries organized. More folders can be added as needed.

 Library features can have more than one feature. The best way to make multi feature libraries is to make the second and subsequent features referencing the first feature only (including sketch locations if possible). This way the external references and locating dimensions can be kept to a minimum.

**182. –** We are now ready to add the "Power Connector Cutout" library to the *Box Bottom* in its own window, or edit it in the assembly (your choice). Open the task pane, select the "Design Library" folder, and drag-and-drop the library onto the part.

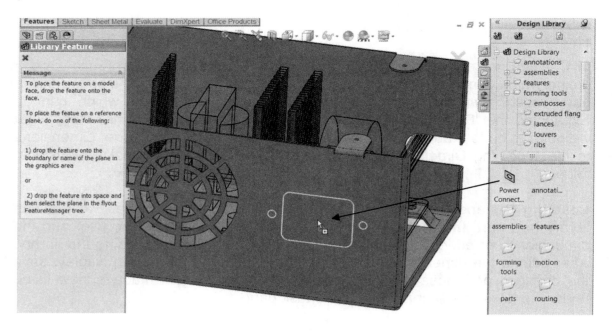

After dropping the library, a preview pop-up window will show us the edge that we need to select in the part for each of the locating dimensions. When an edge is selected, the "References" selection box will show a checkmark next to each edge listed. Select the reference asked for, in this case it is "Locate_Top" (yours may be the Side); select the edge at the top.

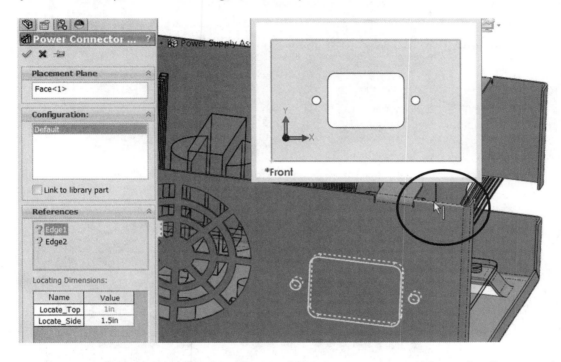

Immediately after selecting the first reference we are shown in the preview window, select the second reference. Select the indicated reference in the part.

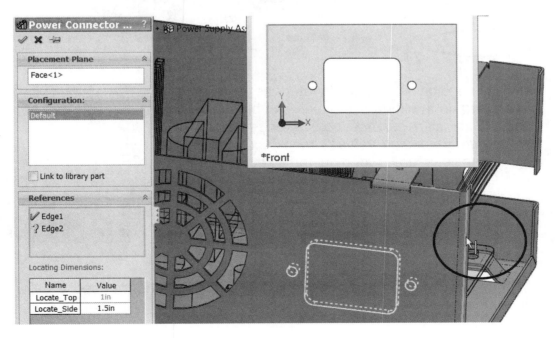

Click inside each dimension in the "Locating Dimensions" box, and change their values. Locate_Side = 1.25″; Locate_Top = 1.5″. Click **OK** to finish.

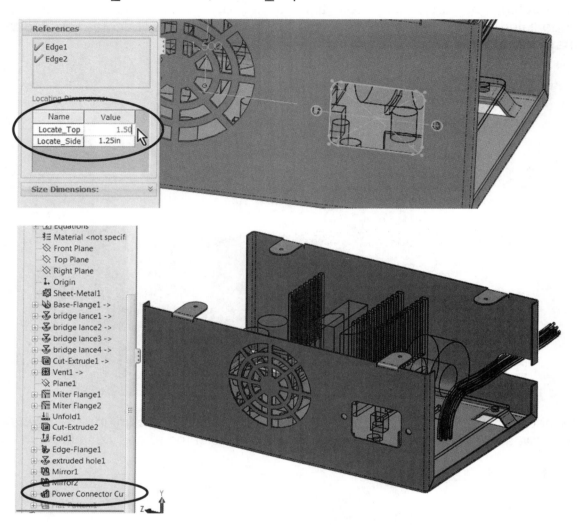

 If a dimension is not designated as "*Internal*" or "*Locating*" in the library, its value can be changed in the "*Size Dimensions*" box after selecting the "*Override dimension values*" checkbox. Also, if no locating dimensions are added to the sketch when the library is added, we'll see an "Edit Sketch" button to define the location of the library, as seen in this example with two external dimensions and no locating dimensions.

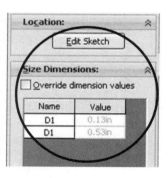

A library feature can have configurations, and each time it's used, a different one can be selected.

**183.** – We can also make libraries of parts and even assemblies, not just features. In the next step we'll create a library part and use it in our assembly. The part we want to make a library of is the Power Connector for which we just made a cut out.

A library part can be any SolidWorks part, and can be used as such simply by putting it in the "**Parts**" folder of the "Design Library." What makes library parts useful is that we can define mate references so that when we drag them into an assembly, the mate references will attempt to find a matching face or entity. Open the part *Power Connector,* or download it from our website (www.mechanicad.com/download.html). As an extra exercise you can download the drawing and build the part.

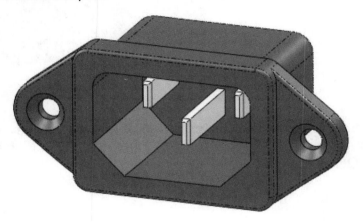

**184.** – Once the connector is open, go to the menu "**Insert, Reference Geometry, Mate Reference**." Mate References will automatically add mates when the library part is inserted into an assembly, and will try to match the references defined.

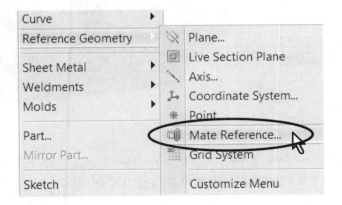

 Up to three mate references can be defined in a part; for our example we'll only use one Concentric and one Coincident mate.

For the "**Primary Reference Entity**" select the circular edge in the left mounting hole of the connector.

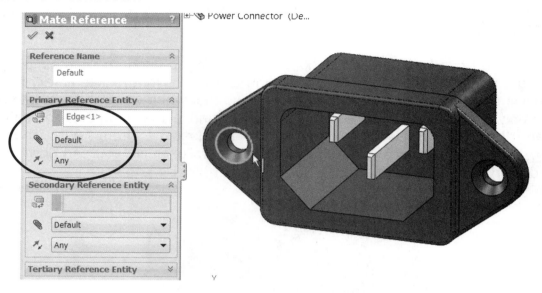

For the "**Secondary Reference Entity**" pick the flat face shown. Select "Coincident" mate and "Anti-Aligned" for the orientation. This is the mate that will be added. Click **OK** to continue.

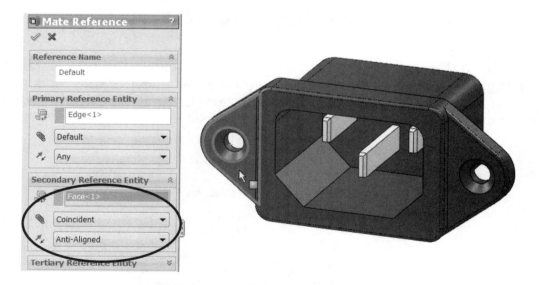

Mate Alignment refers to how the mated faces will be oriented. For flat faces imagine an arrow (Vector) going out of each face. "**Aligned**" means both arrows are pointing in the same direction; "**Anti-Aligned**" means they are pointing at each other. There is no analogy for cylindrical surfaces; just flip them as necessary. A good practice is to position parts as close to the wanted orientation before adding mates; SolidWorks will not rotate a part more than 180 degrees to add a mate.

**185. –** Save the *Power Connector* part with the Mate References. After adding the Mate References, a new folder is added to the FeatureManager listing the references defined.

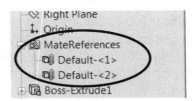

Before adding the part to the library, we need to keep the Design Library visible by clicking on the auto-show pin.

Expand the Design Library and drag-and-drop the part <u>from the top</u> of the FeatureManager to the task pane in the desired folder. We'll select the "**parts**" folder for our example.

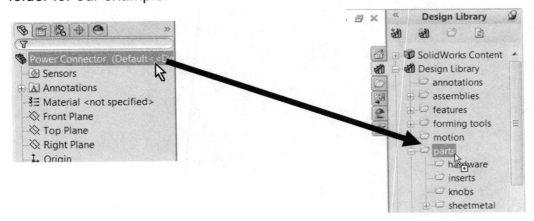

We are asked to select the folder to add the library to, and optionally give it a different name. Click **OK** to continue and close the *Power Connector* part; it's already saved as a library in the "**parts**" folder.

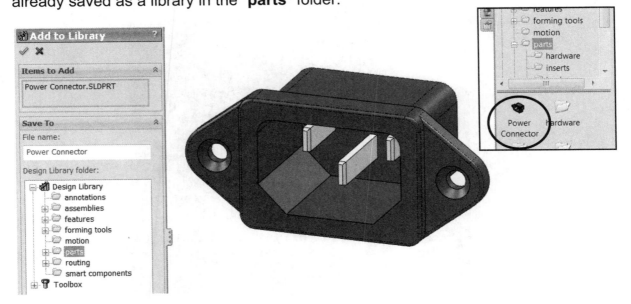

**186. –** Now, back to our assembly. After making the library part, it's time to add it to our assembly. From the "**Design Library**," drag-and-drop the *Power Connector* into the assembly. Notice, as we move it close to a hole or a flat face, the part is automatically mated to it. The mate references we gave it are trying to find a match. Drop the part when we get to the cutout we previously made for it. Just like the Toolbox, it will offer us the opportunity to add more copies. Since this is the only one we need, close the "**Insert Components**" message or hit the "Esc" key.

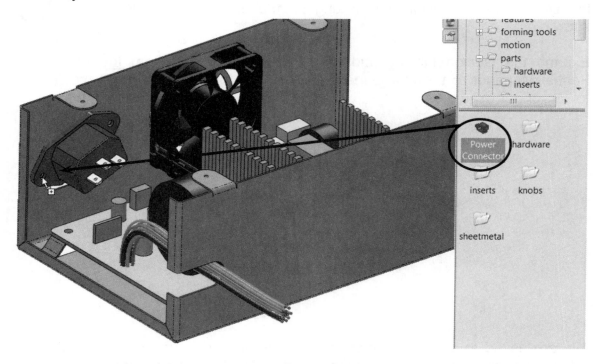

The only thing left for us to do is to add a Parallel mate to align the connector.

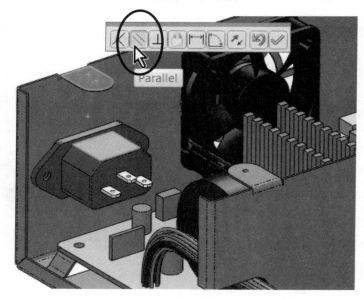

**187. –** In order for the fan to properly cool the power supply, add a series of slots for air to go into the enclosure. Open the *Box Bottom* part; in the face opposite to the vent add the following sketch using the "Slot" tool and make a cut with the "Link to thickness" option.

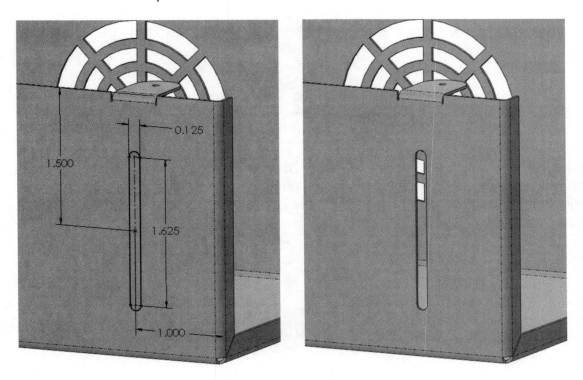

**188. –** Make an array of 15 copies spaced 0.25″.

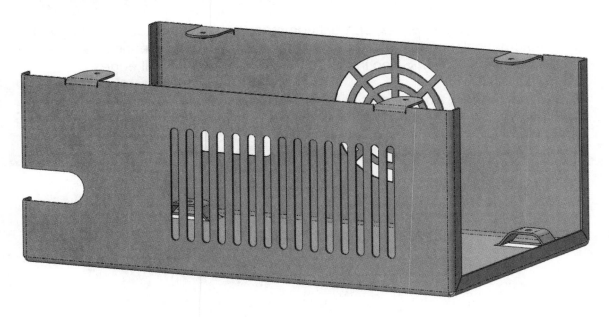

**189. –** The last operation to complete our first sheet metal part is to eliminate all the sharp edges. When fabricating sheet metal components, it's common to see sharp edges due to shearing and punching operations. The "**Break Corners**" command is in the Sheet Metal toolbar, under the drop-down "**Corners**" icon.

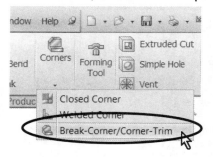

**190. –** There are two options for the "**Break Corners**" command to add a chamfer or a fillet. For this part of the enclosure, we'll use a 0.050″ chamfer. Select all edges that could potentially have a sharp corner.

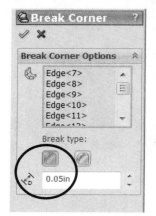
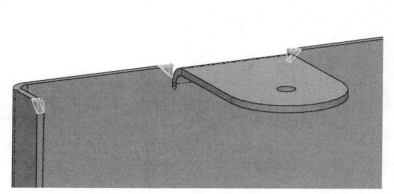

 When using the "Break Corner" command. a filter to select small edges is automatically enabled to make selection easier. Small edges can also be window-selected. Selecting a face will add all of its small edges.

**191. –** Save the *Box Bottom* part. Our finished component now looks like this:

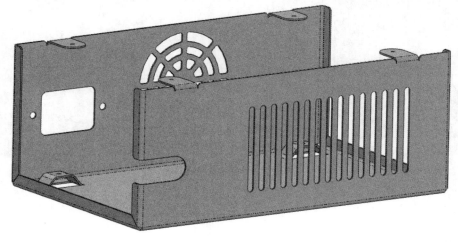

**192.** – Sheet metal components can be flattened at any time. The "**Flat-Pattern**" feature at the end of the FeatureManager is suppressed while the part is in the bent state, and when we select the "**Flatten**" command from the Sheet Metal toolbar, it is unsuppressed and the part unfolds.

A flat pattern is required for manufacturing to know what size the metal needs to be cut and how to bend it. Using the correct bend allowance is extremely important, because otherwise when the calculated flat pattern is bent, the resulting part would not have the expected design dimensions. To see the flat pattern for the *Box Bottom* select the "**Flatten**" command.

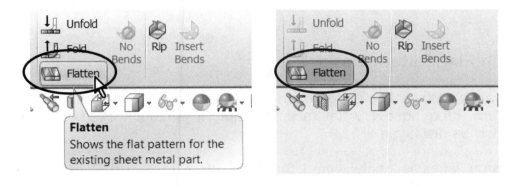

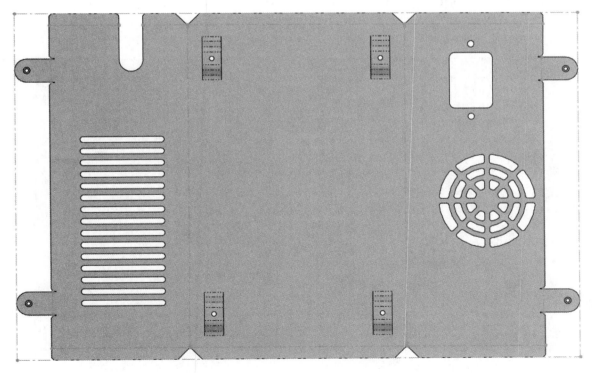

The "Flat-Pattern1" feature is now unsuppressed, and we can see the flattened sheet metal part and a sketch that represent the minimum material size needed to make this part.

**193.** – Editing the "**Flat-Pattern**" feature will show the following options:

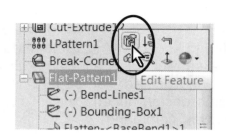

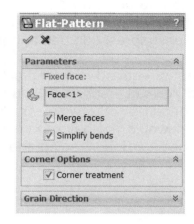

## More on Flat Pattern Options

**Merge faces**: When this option is checked, no bend regions are shown in the flat pattern, merging every flat face together. If left unchecked, all the bend regions will be displayed.

 Merge faces is useful when the flat pattern is exported to a computer numerical control (CNC) software to avoid multiple broken lines and faces.

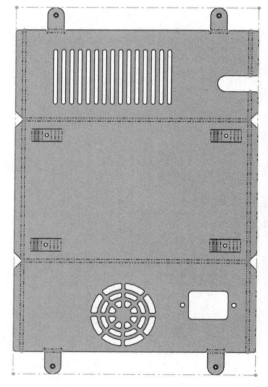

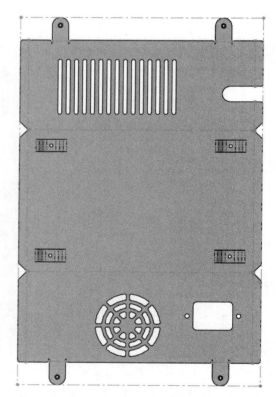

Merge faces unchecked                    Merge faces checked

**Simplify bends:** When flattening complex bends (like bends across a curved area), this option will make a straight edge in the bend region, making the manufacturing process easier.

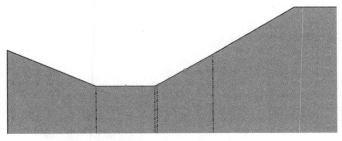

Simplify bends checked

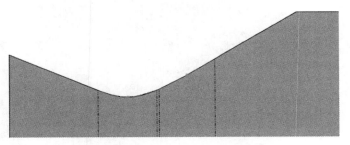

Simplify bends unchecked

**Corner Treatment**: Will make a flat pattern correct for manufacturing by eliminating complex cuts in the corners.

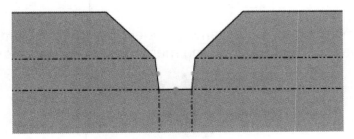

No corner treatment

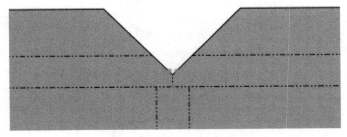

With corner treatment

**194. –** The second component to be designed is the cover of the power supply. Just like the bottom part, we'll design the cover in the context of the assembly. Change to the assembly window, if not already there, and make sure we are editing the assembly and not a part.

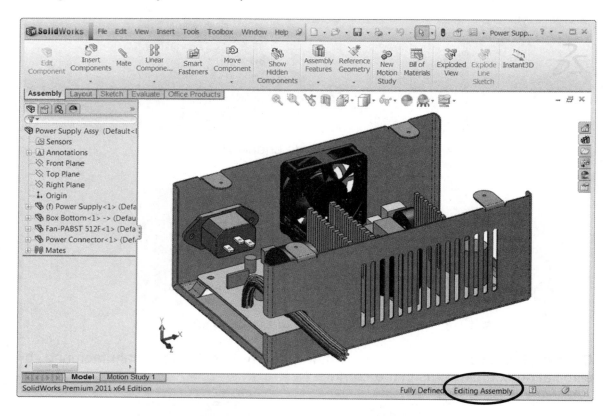

Insert a new component in the assembly. Select the "**Insert Components**" drop-down icon and select "**New Part**," or the menu "**Insert, Component, New Part**."

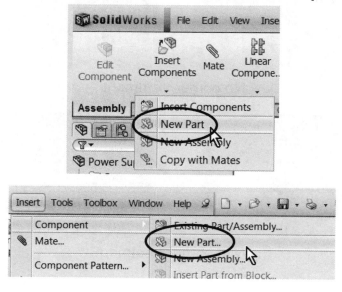

**195. –** In the FeatureManager, select the Front plane to insert the new part. Remember, the Front plane of the new part will be aligned and constrained to the selected plane with an "**InPlace**" mate.

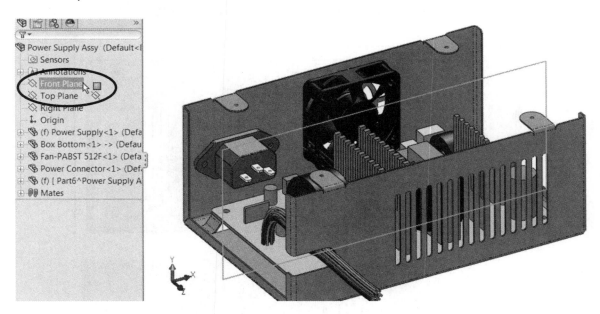

As soon as we select the assembly's Right plane, a new part is added to the FeatureManager; it's displayed in blue. The other assembly components turn transparent (if the option is set), and a sketch is ready for us to start working.

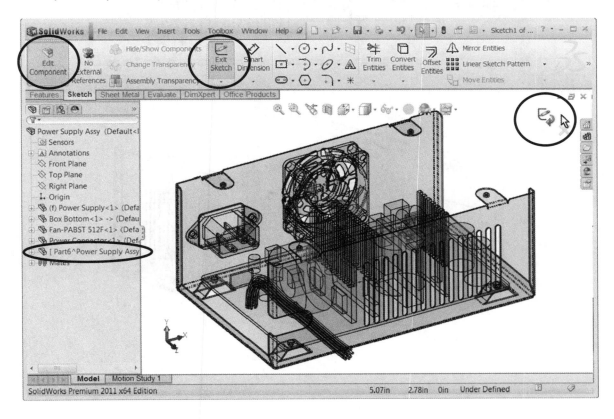

**196. –** Switch to a Front view. Hide the electronics board, the fan and the connector; they will not be needed to design the cover and keeping them visible makes the screen unnecessarily busy. Draw the sketch as three lines; add the necessary Coincident relations to make the lines coincident to the top and sides.

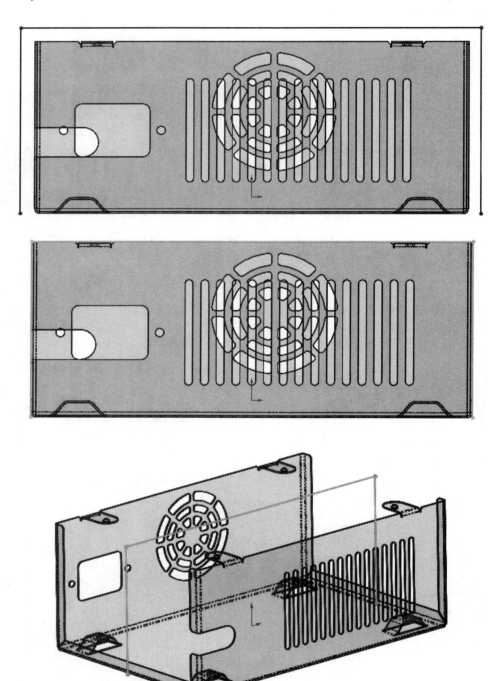

**197. –** After completing the sketch, select the "**Base-Flange**" icon from the Sheet Metal toolbar.

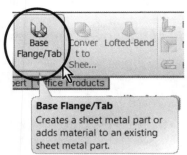

**Base Flange/Tab**
Creates a sheet metal part or adds material to an existing sheet metal part.

**198. –** This sketch represents the inside dimensions of the sheet metal cover; therefore, we'll change the settings to add material *outside* the sketch. Extrude the base flange in Direction 1 "**Up To Surface**" and select the Front face of the *Box Bottom*; in Direction 2 "**Up To Surface**" and select the Back face. Select the same parameters as we did for the bottom part, except make the default Bend Radius 0.015″. "K-Factor" is 0.5 and "Rectangular" relief ratio is 0.5.

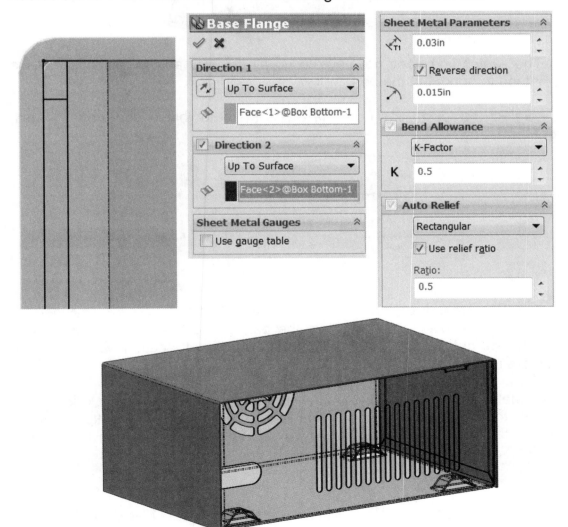

**199.** – The next step is to add two jogs, one in each side. To add a jog we need to draw a line before opening the Jog command, or draw it after selecting it.

**Before option**: Select the side of the cover, and draw a single line sketch.

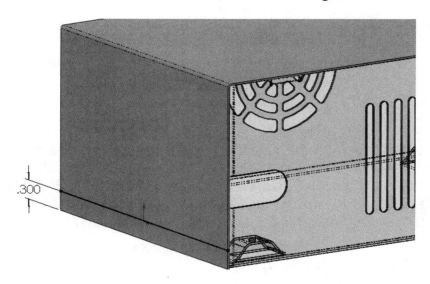

 The sketch line does not have to go all the way across the face that we intend to bend, but the bend will.

**200.** – Select the "**Jog**" icon from the Sheet Metal toolbar or the menu "**Insert, Sheet Metal, Jog**."

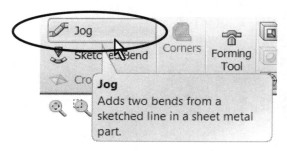

In the "**Jog**" command, under the "**Fixed Face**" selection box, click anywhere in the sketch face above the line; this is the part of the face that will not move. Leave "**Use default radius**" checked. In the "**Jog Offset**" section we'll define the parameters for the bend.

We can make the jog a fixed distance, up to a surface, vertex or offset. The purpose of the jog in our part is to bend the material inside the miter flange of the bottom part. There are three different ways to define how the Jog distance is measured:

 Outside Offset      Inside Offset      Overall Dimension

If the option "**Fix projected length**" is checked, enough material will be added to the flat pattern for the bends and jog. If it's unchecked, the flat pattern will remain the same size.

Fixed projected length option:

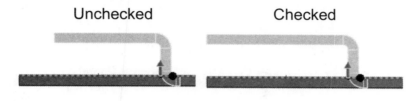

Flat pattern (The Jog area size changes):

The "**Jog Position**" is essentially the same definition as when making flanges. Change to a Front view and zoom in the jog area for visibility. Select "Blind", 0.1″ going into the enclosure; use "**Overall Dimension**" and "**Material Inside**." For "**Jog Angle**" use 90 degrees for the bend's angle.

Notice "Fix projected length" is not checked; if it was checked, the jog would go through the bottom part. Click **OK** to finish.

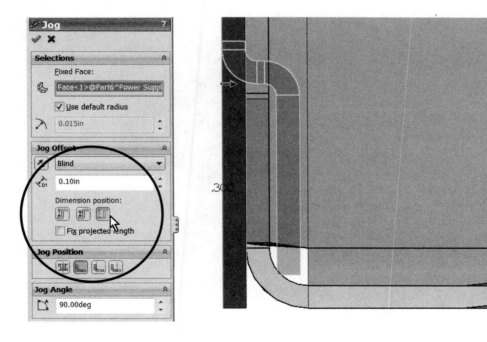

**201.** – For the other side, select the "**Jog**" command first. When asked to select a face on which to draw the sketch (or select an existing sketch), select the other side's face. Draw the same sketch and add the second jog with the same settings as the first one. Your model should now look like this on both ends.

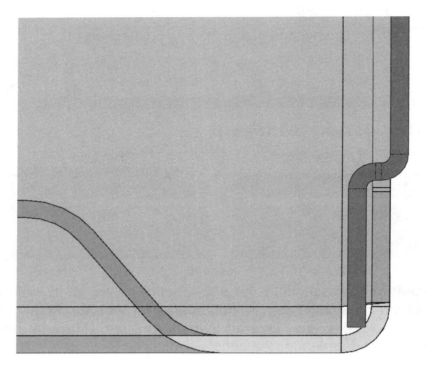

**202.** – With the jog we bent the entire length of the cover to fit behind the miter flange of the *Box Bottom* part, but now we have interferences at the corners (Assembly Transparency set to "Opaque" for visibility).

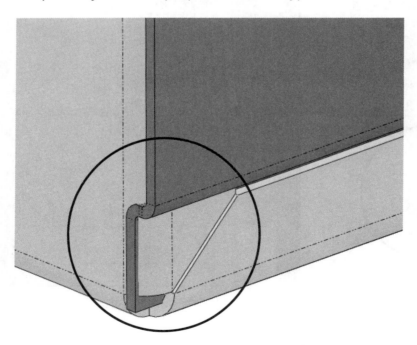

**203.** – To correct this situation we'll make a cut at the corners. Add a sketch on one side of the cover (either side will work). Dimension the inside of the rectangle 0.050″ past the miter flange corner. Add a Coincident relation at the beginning of the bend region and the lower outside corner to fully define the sketch. Mirror the sketch about the part's center and make a cut using the "**Through All**" end condition to cut all four corners at the same time.

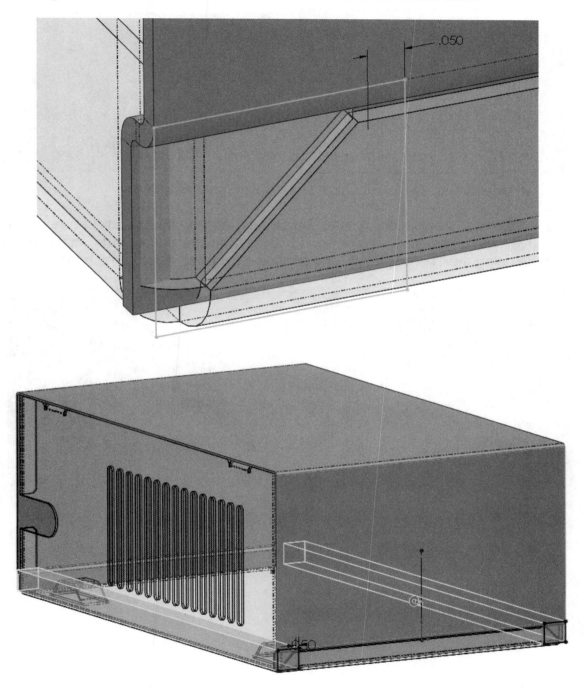

**204. –** The next step is to add holes to screw the cover to the *Box Bottom* part. Switch to a Top view and add a sketch on the Top face. Change to "Hidden lines visible" and add four circles concentric to the holes in the tabs. Dimension one circle 0.150″ diameter and make all circles equal. Cut using "**Link to thickness.**" (The "Shaded" view was added for clarity, as a HLV is difficult to distinguish.)

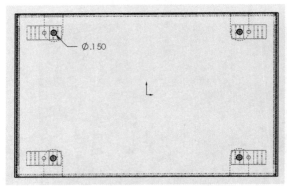
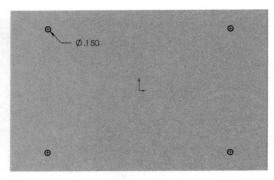

Hidden lines visible (HLV)                    Shaded

**205. –** Now add ventilation slots to the cover. Add a new sketch in one side of the cover and dimension as shown. Just as with the corner cuts, make a Cut Extrude using the "**Through All**" end condition. Use the "**Slot**" sketch tool.

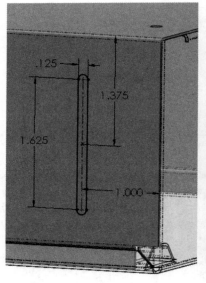
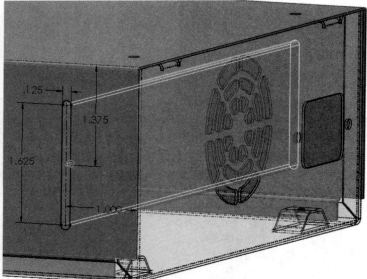

146

**206. –** Make a linear slot pattern with 12 instances spaced 0.250".

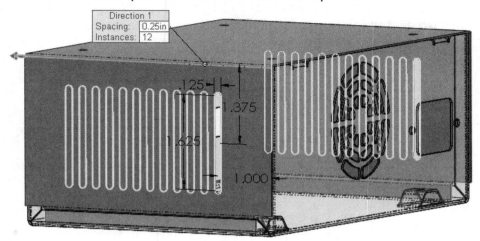

**207. –** As a final step, break all sharp corners using the "**Corners, Break-Corners**" command from the Sheet Metal toolbar. Add a 0.1" chamfer break. Select the side and the jog faces to automatically select all corners.

**208. –** Now that the part is finished we'll *externalize* it from the assembly. All this time the part has been internal, meaning it only exists in the assembly and there is no "file" we can reference. Stop editing the cover in context of the assembly and return to editing the assembly. Press the "**Edit Component**" button in the CommandManager *or* right mouse click in the graphics area and select "**Edit assembly: Power Supply Assy**."

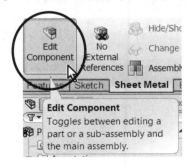

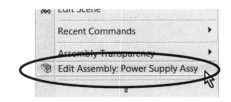

**209. –** Rename the part *Box Cover* with a slow double-click, or from the right mouse click menu select "**Rename Part**". Right mouse click in it again and select "**Save Part (in External File)**" from the pop-up menu. Make sure the path is correct and click **OK** to save the file.

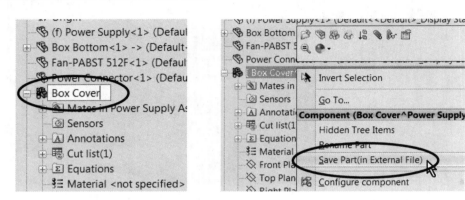

**210. –** Open the *Box Cover* part in its own window and view the flat pattern by selecting the "**Flatten**" command in the Sheet Metal toolbar. Turn off the "Flatten" command and return to the assembly.

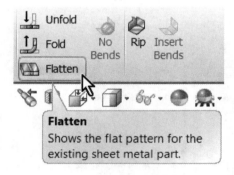

**211.** – Show the Power Supply, Fan and Power Connector parts in the assembly and if needed, make an exploded view to finish. We'll work on the sheet metal drawings next.

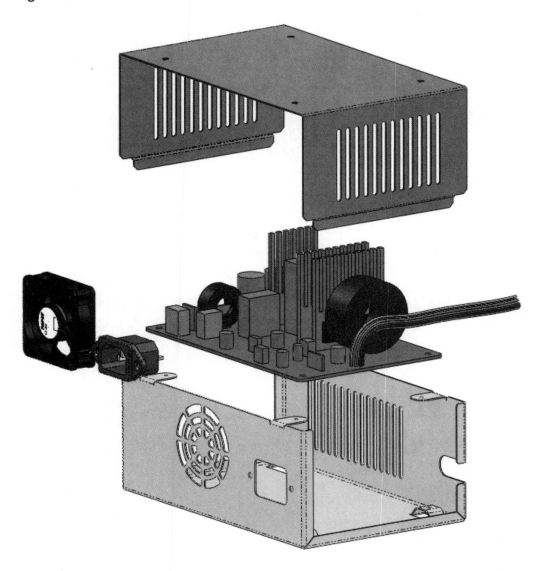

**Notes:**

## Sheet Metal Drawings

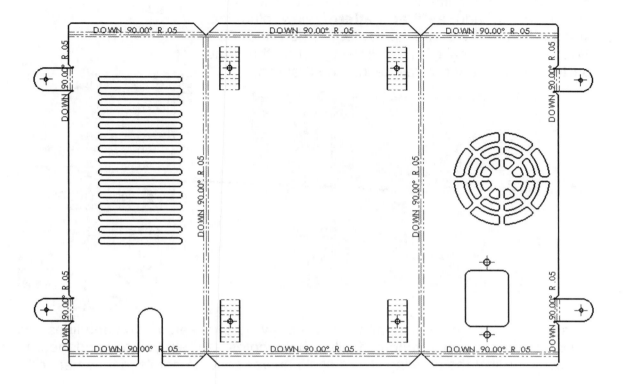

**212.** – There are a few differences when we talk about a Sheet metal part's drawing. When we make a new drawing, the first thing to notice is that we have the option to add a "**Flat Pattern**" view plus the standard views we are used to. Open the *Box Bottom* part and make a new drawing. Drag the "**Flat pattern**" from the View Palette into the drawing.

As soon as we drop the flat pattern in the drawing, the sketch with bend lines and bending notes is added automatically. These notes will help you to bend the part correctly. Adjust the drawing view's scale and/or bending note's font as needed.

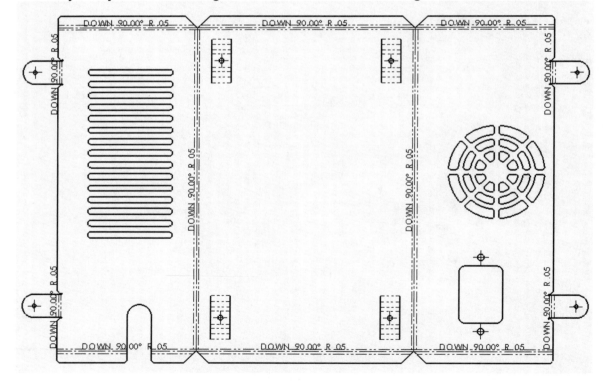

**213. –** Open the *Box Bottom* part; edit the "**Flat-Pattern**" feature and check the "**Merge faces**" option.

All of the flat faces are merged and the only thing visible is the sketch with the bend lines. Go back to the flat pattern drawing to see the effect.

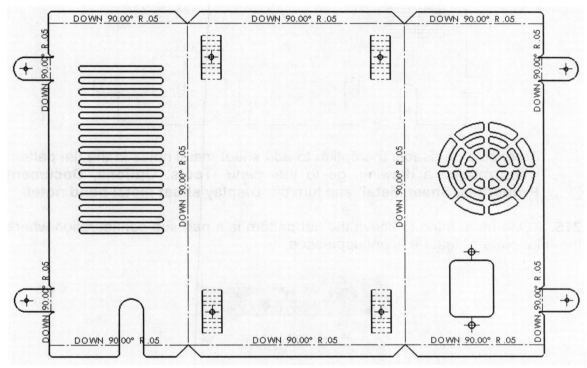

**214. –** It is common to export a 1:1 scale drawing in DWG or DXF with "Merge faces" on for manufacturing (CNC), and you may or not want the bend lines and notes. To turn off all notes and bend lines, you can right mouse click in the "**Annotations**" folder of the drawing and turn off "**Display Annotations**," or hide the sketch with bend lines in the "**Flat pattern**" feature and delete the notes.

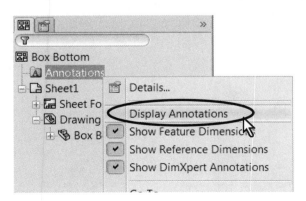

Flat patterns usually have to be manually dimensioned.

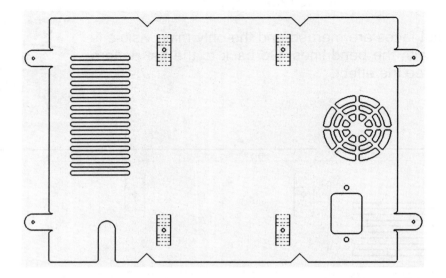

 To enable or disable the option to add sheet metal notes in the flat pattern when making a drawing, go to the menu "**Tools, Options, Document Properties, Sheet Metal**" and turn off "**Display sheet metal bend notes.**"

**215.** – One more thing to know: the flat pattern is a part sub-configuration where the "Flat pattern" feature is unsuppressed.

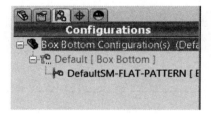

**CHALLENGE:**

Make manufacturing drawings from the power supply sheet metal parts including a flat pattern.

## Sheet Metal Locker Top Down Design

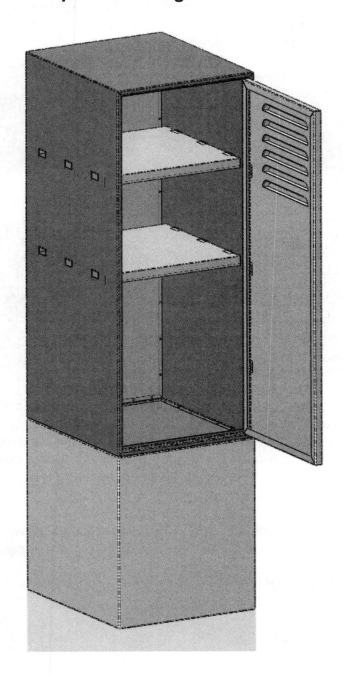

**216. –** For our next sheet metal project we'll build a locker also using a top down design approach. Our locker will have a base to raise it from the floor. In this example, we'll learn how to convert solid parts into sheet metal. A solid or shelled part can be converted directly as shown here:

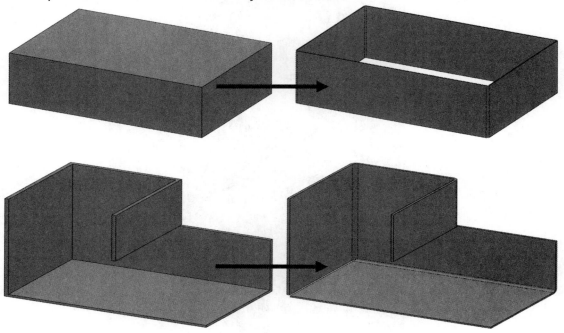

What happens after converting the solid part into sheet metal is that the face selected as "fixed" will remain static, the faces connected to it by edges defined as "Bends" will be part of the sheet metal and the rest of the faces will be deleted. If the part is made of surfaces or a shelled part before converting it to sheet metal, some of the faces not connected by "Bend" edges will also be removed.

**217. –** First, make the locker's base. Make a new part; draw the following sketch in the Top plane and extrude it 10″ up. Note the square is centered in the origin.

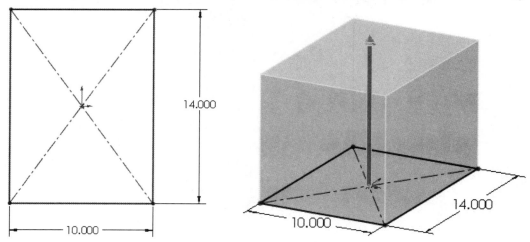

**218. –** From the Sheet Metal toolbar select "Convert to Sheet Metal."

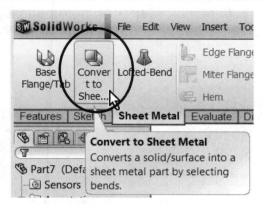

**219. –** We have to select a face that will be the fixed face in the sheet metal, the edge(s) of the part that will become bend(s), and the edge(s) that will be ripped (open). Select the left face of the part to be the fixed face (here we used "Select other"). For our locker's thickness, we'll use a 22 gauge sheet metal. From standard gauge tables for steel* we see that the thickness is 0.03″. Enter the thickness and a default bend radius of 0.05″. Make sure the thickness of the sheet metal is added *'inside'* as we want to maintain the dimensions given as external dimensions. You can zoom into a corner to see if the material is added inside or out and check (or uncheck) the "Reverse Thickness" option.

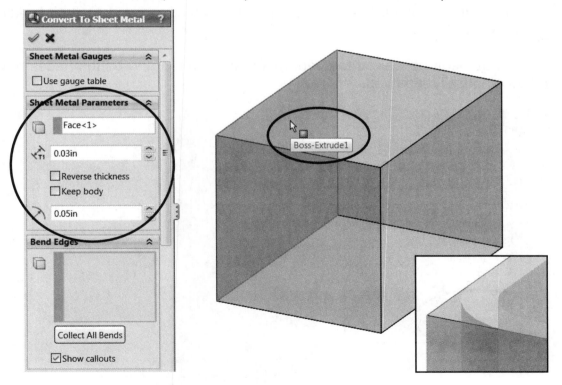

* "Standard" sheet metal gauge tables vary by country, material, etc.

**220.** – Select the 3 vertical edges (labeled "Radius") that will become bends. The remaining vertical edge (labeled "Gap") is automatically selected as a "**Rip Edge**." Set the default gap for rips to 0.01″ and "**Auto Relief**" type to Obround with a 0.5 ratio.

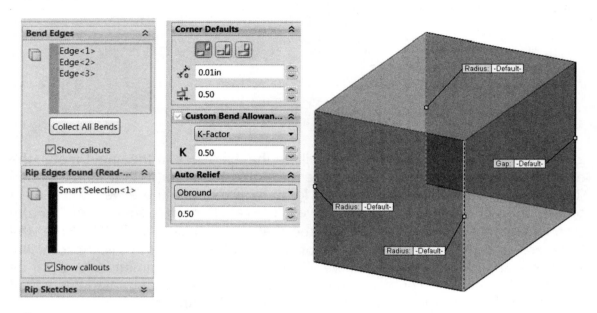

 In the fly-out labels we can override the default settings for bend radius and gap distance.

The part has been converted to sheet metal and the top and bottom faces have been automatically removed.

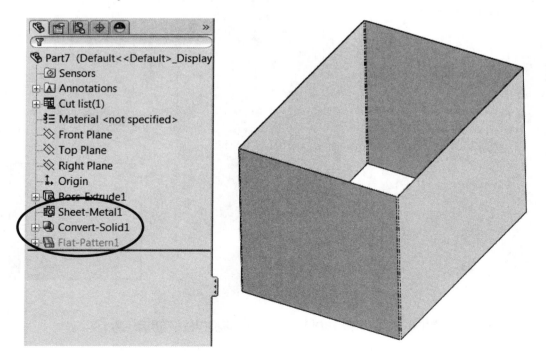

**221. –** Now we need to add miter flanges in top and bottom, but instead of using the "**Miter Flange**" command, we'll use "**Edge Flange**." Select all the indicated edges; the miter cuts will be added automatically in the corners. Make the flange 0.5″ long, with the option "Material Inside." The arrows in each flange can be used to reverse the direction individually if needed.

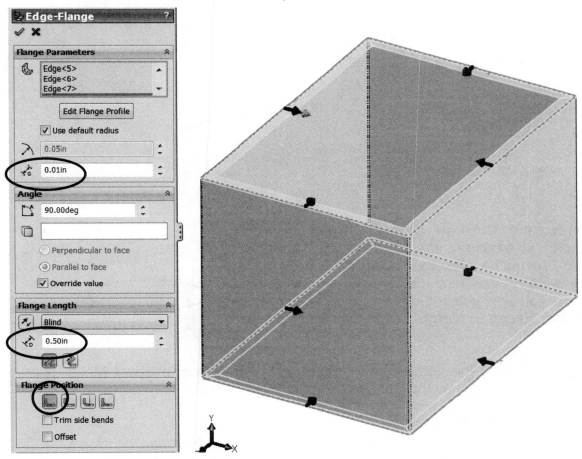

 In this case there is no difference between "Miter Flange" and "Edge Flange," but remember, the "Miter Flange" runs the full length of the edge and can change the profile, and "Edge Flange" can change the length and shape of the flange but not the profile.

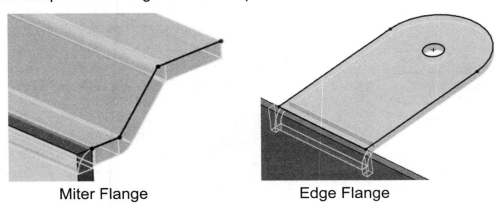

Miter Flange                 Edge Flange

**222.** – After adding the flanges, we need to close the gap in the corner that was ripped when we converted the solid to sheet metal.

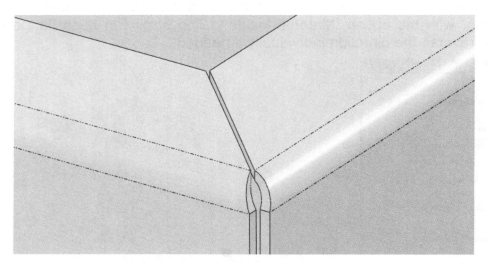

Select the "**Corners, Closed Corner**" drop down icon. This command will extend one sheet metal side to match the other using a butt, overlap or underlap extension. In the "**Faces to Extend**" selection box, select the flat face on one side, and in the "**Faces to Match**" select the other flat face.

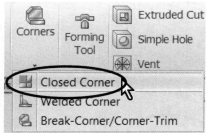

 Closing the corner is an option when converting to Sheet Metal, but we chose to show how to use this command instead.

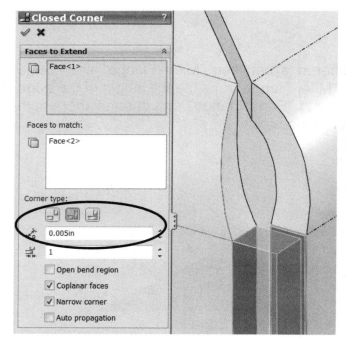

Select "Overlap" to make the first face extend over the second face. *Open bend region* will close the bend region.

*Coplanar faces* will automatically select faces that are coplanar to the one selected.

*Narrow Corner* will attempt to close the gap when using large bend radii.

In the "Gap Distance" we can make the gap in the corner as small as needed. Enter 0.005″.

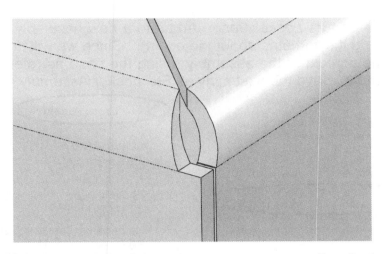

**223.** – Upon closer inspection of the other corners, we realize that an extra piece of metal is in the bend area. To eliminate it, select the "Edge-Flange1" made before, edit it and check the "**Trim side bends**" option under "Flange Position." Click **OK** to finish. Now all of the corners made with this Edge Flange command are trimmed.

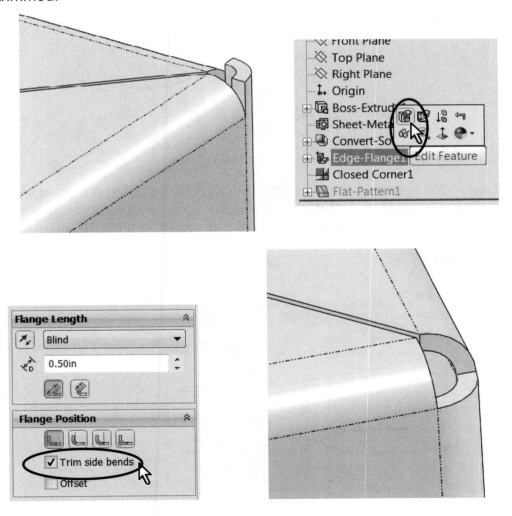

**224. –** Save the part as *Locker Base*.  Add it to a new assembly and locate it at the origin (making it symmetric about the origin).   Since we will design the rest of the locker in the context of the assembly (using the base as reference) we must save the assembly.  Save the assembly as *Full Locker Assembly*.

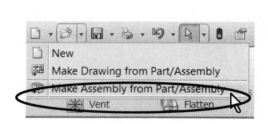

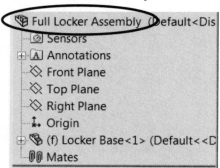

**225. –** The next step is to add a new part to the assembly; it will be the locker's body.  From the Assembly toolbar select the "**Insert Components**" drop-down menu and select "**New Part**."  We are then asked to select a face or plane to add the new part.  Select the Top face of the "Locker Base."

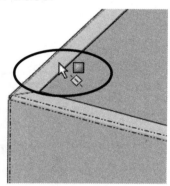

Immediately after selecting the Top face, a new part is added. It's listed with blue in the FeatureManager, the "**Edit Component**" icon is active, the *Locker Base* becomes transparent and a new sketch is automatically added.

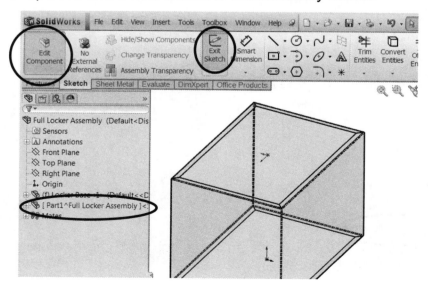

**226.** – Since we want to make the locker's body the same size as the base, we'll make the base's sketch visible and use "**Convert Entities.**" Expand the *Locker Base* "Boss-Extrude1" feature and select "**Show**" from the pop-up menu in "Sketch1." Once the sketch is visible, select "**Convert Entities**" from the Sketch toolbar. Change to "Shaded" view mode to make it easier to distinguish sketch entities and model edges.

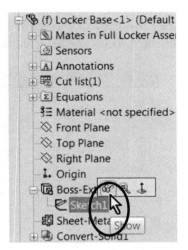

Select the base's sketch lines and click **OK** to project them into the locker's sketch.

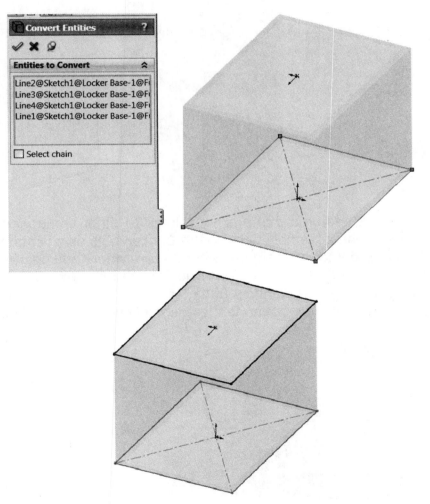

 Optionally we can select the entire sketch from the FeatureManager and then use "**Convert Entities.**"

**227. –** After converting the sketch edges, extrude it upwards 30″. Hide the *Locker Base*'s sketch and switch back to "Shaded with Edges" mode.

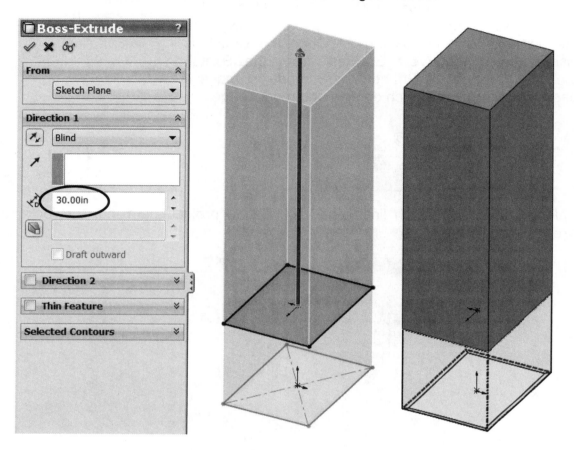

**228. –** When adding features that are not related to other components, we can continue working in the assembly or open the *Locker* in its own window. To some extent it's really a personal preference; however, when adding references to other component's geometry, we have to do it in the context of the assembly. Open the new part in its own window (if it's easier to visualize or convenient) to convert to a sheet metal component. In the assembly we are still editing the part.

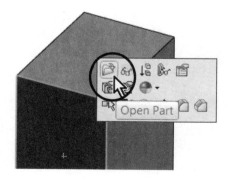

**229.** – Shell the part with a 0.03" thickness removing the top and bottom faces which will become the front and back of the locker's body.

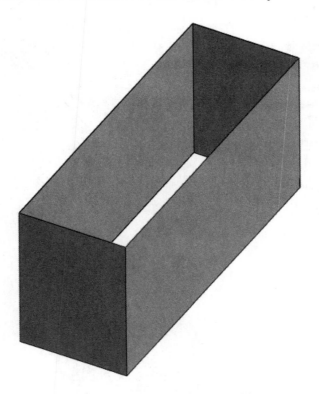

**230.** – We can convert this model to sheet metal without having to use a shell first like we did before, but we are doing it this way to show a different approach.

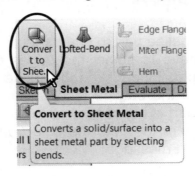

From the Sheet Metal toolbar select "**Convert to Sheet Metal**." Select the face on the left as the fixed face; set the thickness to 0.03" and the default bend radius to 0.05". You *may* have to check the "**Reverse Thickness**" checkbox if the inside or outside face was selected. It doesn't really matter which was picked; what is important is that we make sure the material is added to the side we want. Remember, the dimensions in our part are outside dimensions. Zoom in one corner to verify this. Essentially the sheet metal preview will overlap the existing shell thickness.

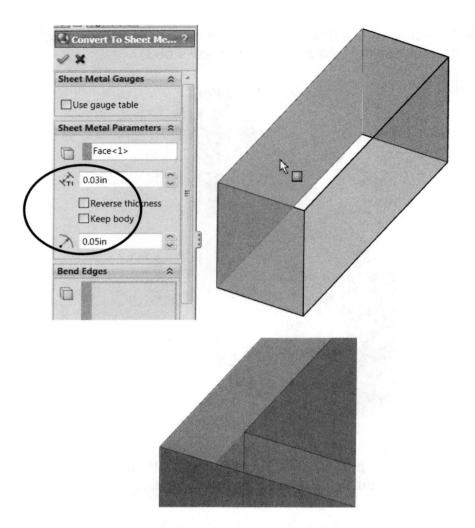

When we convert a shelled part to sheet metal, at the time of selecting the **"Bend Edges"** we have to select the edges connected to the face we selected. For example, if we picked the inside face of the shell, we have to select the inside edges; if the outside face was selected, the outside edges have to be selected. If the part is big compared to the shell's thickness, you may have to zoom in to the corners to make the selections. If the incorrect edge is picked, you'll see the following message:

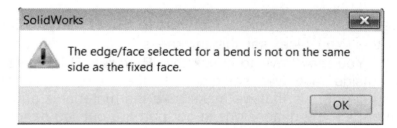

**231.** – Select three edges to convert to bends and the fourth edge will be automatically added to the "**Rip Edges found**" selection box. Set the default gap for rips to 0.01", use a K-Factor ratio of 0.5, and set the default relief type to "Obround" with a 0.5 ratio. Click **OK** to complete.

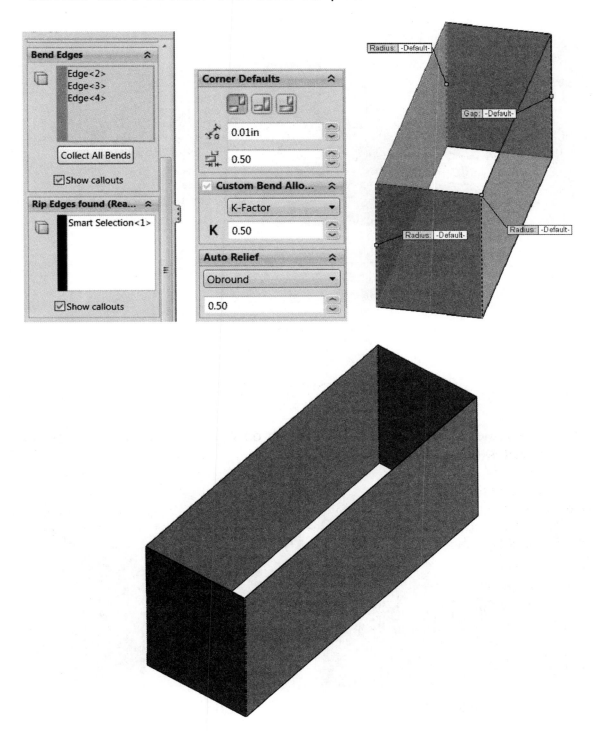

**232. –** The next step is to add a miter flange on both sides of the locker. Zoom in the corner with the rip and select the "**Miter Flange**" icon from the Sheet Metal toolbar. Immediately after selecting it, SolidWorks will ask us for 1) a face or plane to sketch the flange's profile, or 2) an existing sketch with the profile.

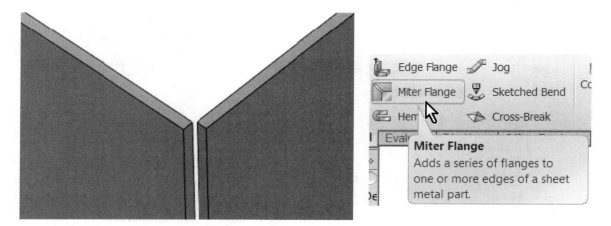

**233. –** Select the flat face to make the sketch on it, or the edge to add a plane perpendicular to the edge at the end of it.

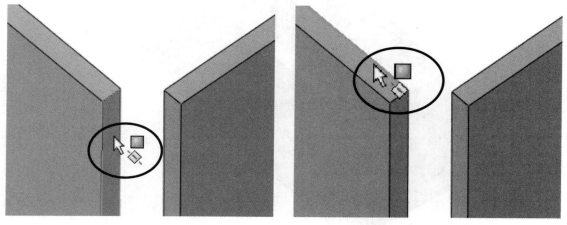

Face selection                    Edge Selection

Selecting faces is easier using a "**Selection Filter**." Selection filters allow us to select only the type of geometry or element desired. In this case press "**X**" on the keyboard (default filter for faces) to turn it on (press "**X**" again to turn it off). We'll know the filter is active with a small funnel added next to the mouse pointer. The Selection Filters toolbar can be enabled selecting the menu "**View, Toolbars, Selection Filter**," right mouse clicking in any toolbar and selecting "**Selection Filter**," or use the default shortcut "**F5**." In this toolbar you can turn on/off any combination of filters as needed.

**234.** – Draw the profile for the miter flange as shown. It's a single 0.375″ long line.

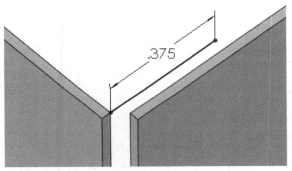

**235.** – Select "**Exit Sketch**" to continue. The "**Miter Flange**" preview is activated. Make the flange with the option "**Material Inside**" and a 0.01″ gap distance. Select the edges in the top individually or click on the "**Propagate**" icon on the first edge to automatically select all the edges connected.

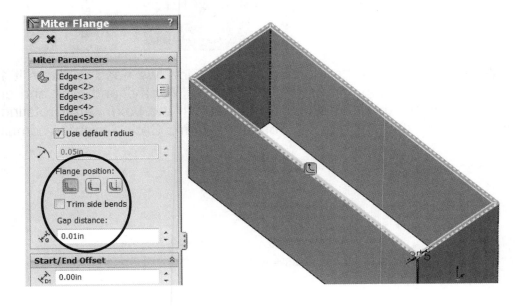

**236.** – Repeat the Miter Flange command on the other side with the same options.

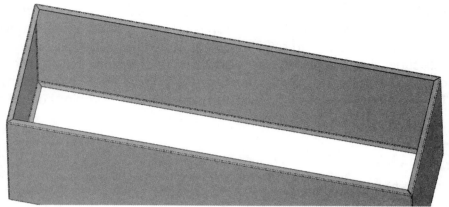

**237.** – Switch back to the assembly (if working in the part's window); notice we are still editing the part. Now we need to add a forming tool feature to support shelves inside the locker. Expand the "**Design Library**" and scroll down to "**forming tools, lances**" and find the "**90 degree lance**" library. Drag-and-drop the lance in the right side of the locker; you may have to press the "Tab" key to flip the lance to go 'into' the locker. After dropping it, we'll need to use the "Modify" tool to rotate the lance.

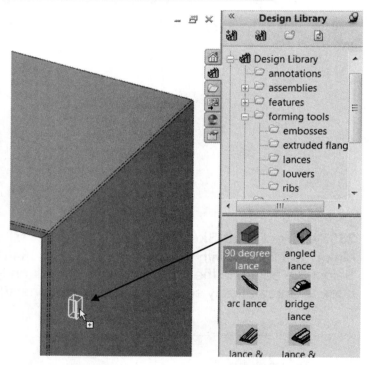

**238.** – We are now editing the locating sketch. First, we need to rotate it 180 degrees. Select the menu "**Tools, Sketch Tools, Modify**" and click and drag with the right mouse button (or type 180 degrees in the box). After rotating it, dimension it 3″ from the front and 18″ from the bottom. Click "Finish" to complete it.

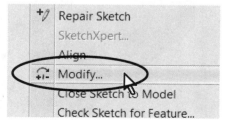

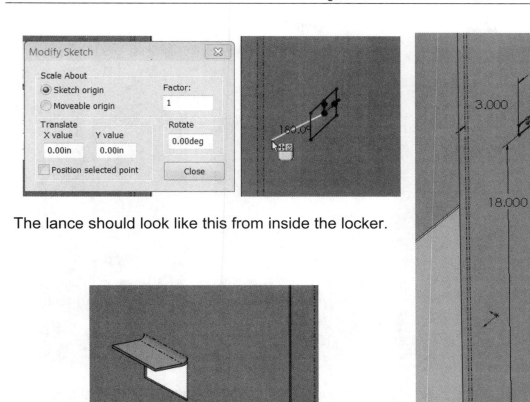

The lance should look like this from inside the locker.

**239.** – Use a linear pattern to make 3 copies horizontally spaced 4″.

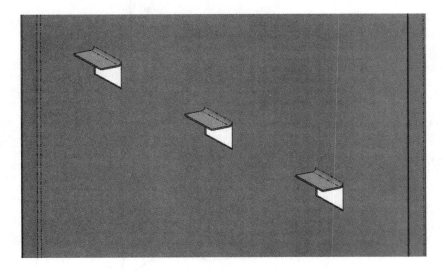

**240.** – Add a linear pattern vertically to copy all 3 instances 8″ up. We'll explain later why we did it this way instead of making the first pattern in two directions. Mirror all lance cuts about the Right plane as shown.

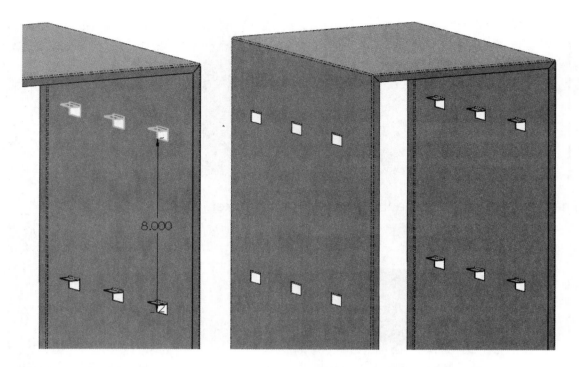

**241.** – Rename the internal part as *Locker Body* and save to an external file.

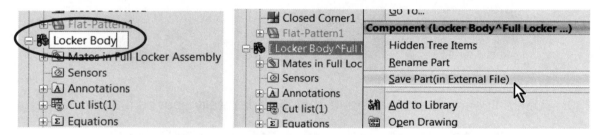

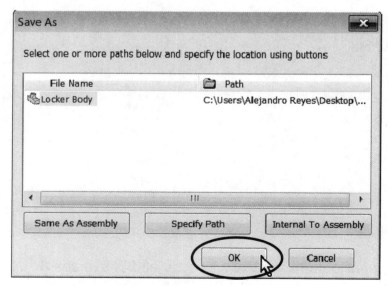

**242.** – Now that we are done with the locker's body we can turn off "**Edit Component**" and go back to editing the assembly. Next, we'll add a cover in the back and a door.

**243.** – The back is a simple sheet metal cover that will be welded or riveted in place. The cover needs to be the same size as the locker's body, and it will also be made in the context of the assembly. Select the "**Insert Components, New Part**" drop down icon and click in the inside face of the back miter flange to locate the new part (the back cover).

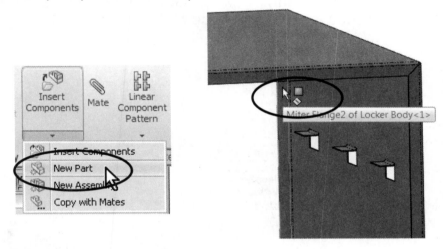

**244.** – The locker's base and body turn transparent, we are editing the new part and a new sketch is ready for us to work on. In this step, it is easier to work in a completely opaque assembly, as it may be difficult and/or confusing to select references. Select the "Assembly Transparency" drop down icon and select "Opaque." If the assembly remains transparent, rotate the model to refresh the image.

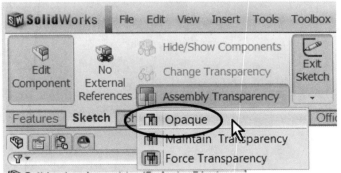

**245. –** Draw a rectangle starting in one of the lower corners (inside the locker) and finishing in the opposite upper corner. Make sure to capture a Coincident relation as indicated. By adding these two relations to the miter flange, we have completely defined the sketch and are now ready to make the base flange.

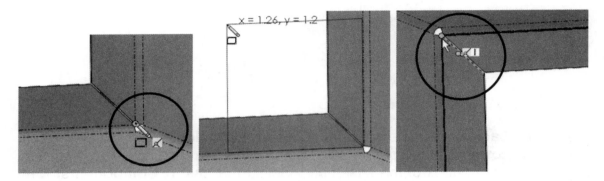

**246. –** Select "**Base Flange/Tab**" from the Sheet Metal toolbar or the menu "**Insert, Sheet Metal, Base Flange.**" Make the base flange 0.03″ thick. Make sure the material is added towards the inside of the locker and does not overlap with the locker's body.

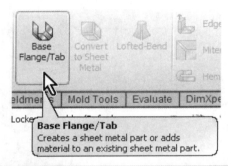

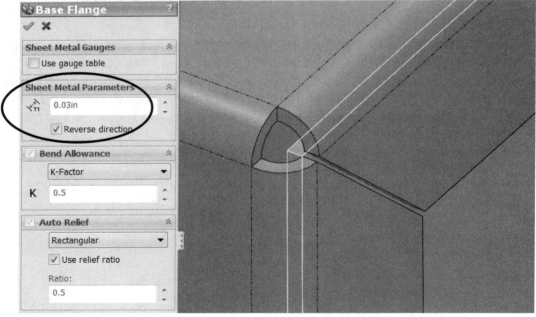

**247. –** Rename the part "**Locker Back**." Save to an external file and turn off "**Edit Component**" to continue editing the assembly.

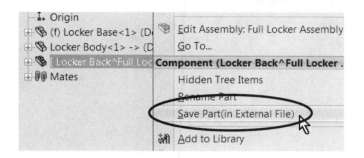

**248. –** The next component to add will be the shelf. Select "**Insert Components, New part**" and select the Top face of one of the lower lances we just made to locate it.

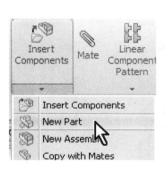

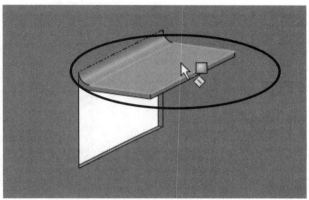

**249. –** Since we changed the transparency setting to "Opaque" in the previous step, the other components will not become transparent; we are now editing the new part's first sketch. Draw a rectangle as indicated, adding collinear relations to the bend lines and dimensions as indicated to the front and back of the locker.

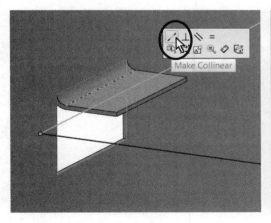

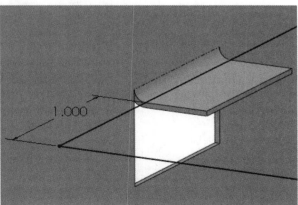

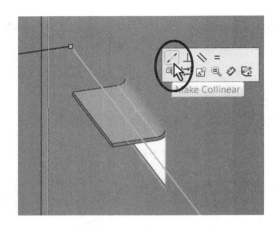

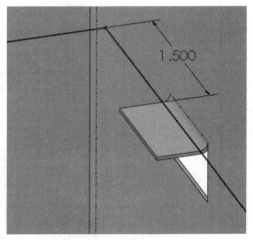

**250.** – Click in the "**Base Flange/Tab**" command from the Sheet Metal toolbar and make the shelf 0.03″ thick going up, K-Factor = 0.5 and Rectangular auto relief with a 0.5 ratio.

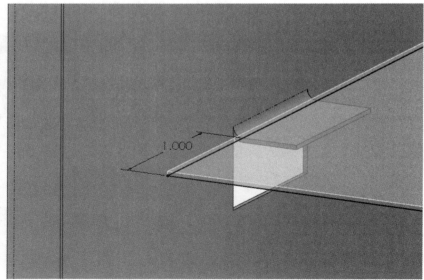

**251. –** Since a flat shelf like this is not strong enough, a flange will be added to all edges for reinforcement. Click in the "**Edge Flange**" icon and select all four edges. Right after selecting the first edge a preview will be displayed, click towards the bottom to define the direction for the flange, then select the other three edges.  Set the flange gap to 0.01″, the length to 0.80″ and the flange position to "Material Outside."

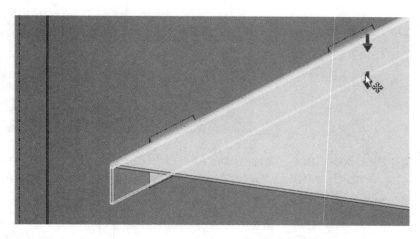

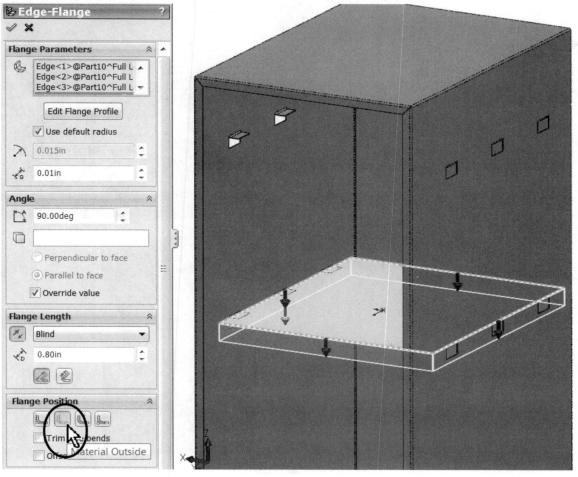

**252. –** The flanges we just made have an interference with the lances. To correct this we'll unfold the side flanges, add cuts to clear the lances and then refold the side flanges. Select the "**Unfold**" command from the Sheet Metal toolbar; click in the Top face of the shelf part to select it as the fixed face.

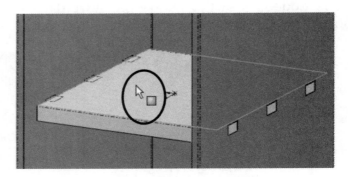

After selecting the fixed face, select the two side bends (the ones interfering with the lances) to unfold them. SolidWorks will filter your selections to bends automatically. Click **OK** when done.

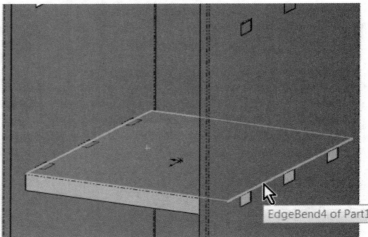

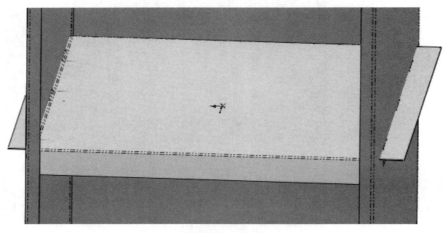

Unfolded bends

**253.** – To better visualize the next operation, we'll turn the locker upside down and make the cuts needed in the bottom face of the shelf; the reason for this is that from this angle, we can see the lances that we need to clear. Rotate your locker assembly until you can see the lances in one side.

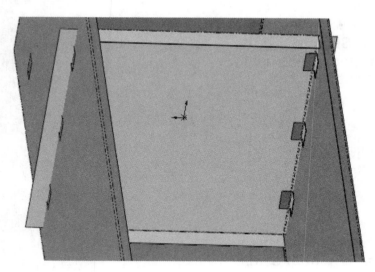

**254.** – Create a new sketch in the bottom face. Add dimensions and relations to clear the lances as shown. Make the rectangle Coincident to the edge of the unfolded flange and the bend line.

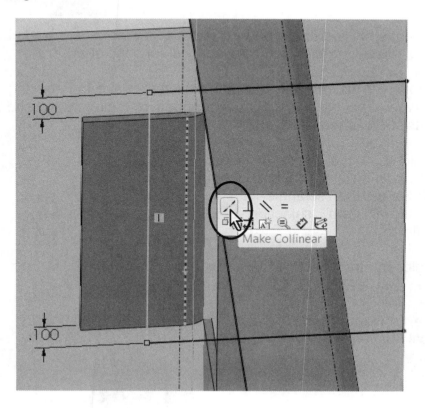

**255.** – With the sketch fully defined, our next step is to add a Sketch Pattern. Not only can we make feature patterns, we can and also make linear and circular patterns *in the sketch*. Select the menu "**Tools, Sketch Tools, Linear Pattern**" (the icon is not in the Sketch toolbar by default).

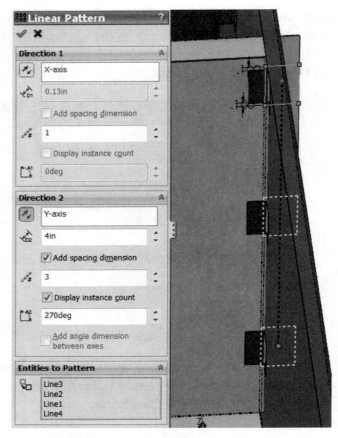

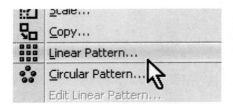

The sketch Linear Pattern behaves similar to the Feature Pattern. By default the "**X-axis**" direction is the sketch's horizontal direction and the "**Y-axis**" direction the vertical.

Pattern directions can be changed by selecting model edges or sketch entities. Our pattern will have 3 copies vertically spaced 4 inches apart.

Check the option "**Add spacing dimension**" *on* to make the spacing dimension visible; otherwise spacing can only be changed by going to the menu "**Tools, Sketch Tools, Edit Linear Pattern**."

Fill in the values for the Y-axis *or* select an edge for direction in the "Direction 1" options box. Select the rectangle lines in the "Entities to Pattern" selection box. Click **OK** to finish.

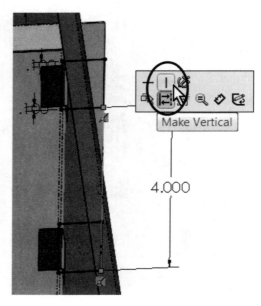

If you look closely, the sketch is not fully defined. To fully define it, select the construction line added between the rectangle we drew and the first copy and add a Vertical relation.

**256.** – With the sketch fully defined, we can make a sketch mirror to make all six cuts at the same time, OR make a cut *and then* make a feature mirror. We'll leave the option to the reader. Just remember to use the "Link to thickness" option when making the cut.

Our part should now look like this (still unfolded):

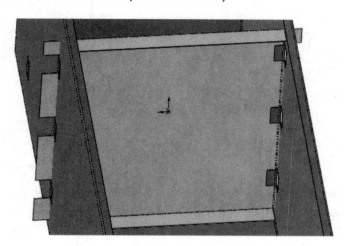

**257.** – To finish the part select the "**Fold**" icon from the sheet metal toolbar. Either select both unfolded bends or click on the "**Collect All Bends**" button. In this case, it is the same since we want to re-fold all bends. Click **OK** when done.

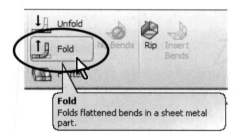

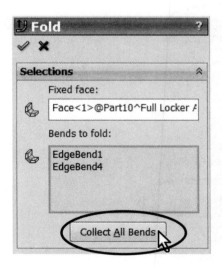

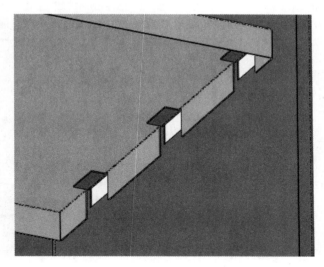

**258.** – The shelf part is complete; finish editing it by clicking on the "**Edit Component**" icon or the confirmation corner. Rename to *Locker Shelf* and save as an external part.

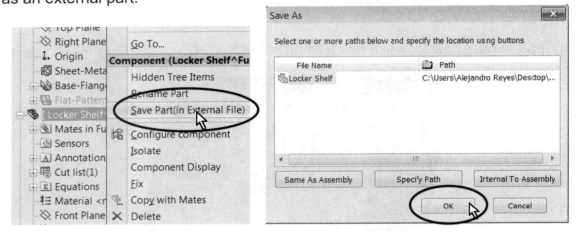

**259.** – The next step is to add another *Shelf* at the top. We can add it using the "**Insert Component**" command, but in our example we'll use a component pattern. Components can be patterned in the assembly in a linear or circular fashion, just like features in a part, but in this case we'll use a "**Feature Driven Pattern**." A copy of the seed part will be added at each position of the feature pattern (this is the reason why we patterned the lance vertically). Select it from the "**Linear Component**" drop down list or the menu "**Insert, Component Patten, Feature Driven**."

**260. –** Pick the *Locker Shelf* part in the "**Components to Pattern**" selection box and one of the lances at the top position as the "**Driving Feature**." Turn *on* the "**Propagate component level visual properties**" checkbox to make the patterned copies look like the seed part. Click **OK** to finish.

 This type of pattern is very handy when adding fasteners to an assembly; we can add one fastener to a hole, and use the pattern of holes to add the rest of the fasteners. An advantage is that, if the feature's pattern is changed, the number of fasteners is also updated.

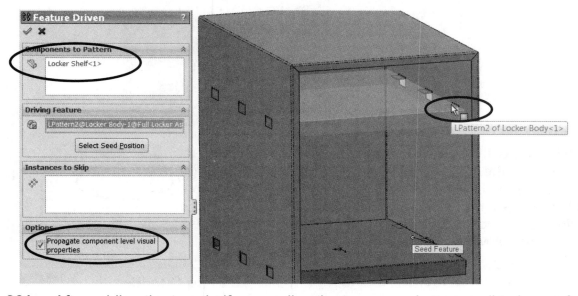

**261. –** After adding the top shelf, we realize the top space is too small to be useful and we need to change it. Expand the *Locker Body* part's FeatureManager and find the "**90 degree lance**." Double click oin it to display its dimensions and change the 18″ height to 14″. Rebuild the model when done to finish.

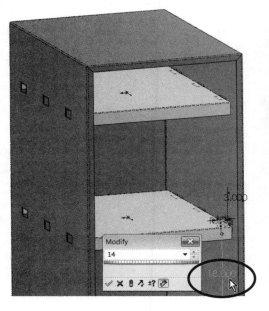
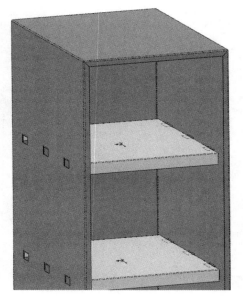

**262.** – The next thing we need to do is to add a "Hem" to the *Shelf's* front flange. Hems are used to eliminate sharp edges and to reinforce a sheet metal part by folding or rolling the edge. The first thing we need to do is to edit the *Shelf* in the assembly. Select it in the graphics area or FeatureManager and click in the "**Edit Part**" icon. Remember the other parts won't become transparent when editing the *Shelf* because we have the Assembly Transparency setting to "Opaque."

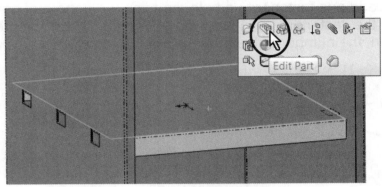

**263.** – Select the "**Hem**" command from the Sheet Metal toolbar. In the "**Edges**" selection box, pick the front edge of the *Shelf*. A preview will show the hem's direction. Make sure the hem is inside; click on "Reverse Direction" if needed. Besides editing the hem's width, we have the following options:

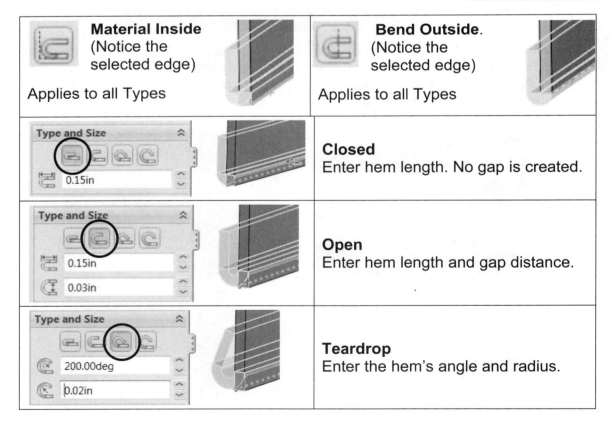

| | | |
|---|---|---|
| **Material Inside** (Notice the selected edge)<br><br>Applies to all Types | **Bend Outside.** (Notice the selected edge)<br><br>Applies to all Types | |
| *Type and Size* — 0.15in | **Closed** Enter hem length. No gap is created. | |
| *Type and Size* — 0.15in / 0.03in | **Open** Enter hem length and gap distance. | |
| *Type and Size* — 200.00deg / 0.02in | **Teardrop** Enter the hem's angle and radius. | |

| | |
|---|---|
| 270.00deg | **Rolled**<br>Enter the hem's angle and radius. |
| 0.02in | |

**264.** – For the *Shelf* use a "**Closed**" hem, 0.20″ long, and the Material inside option.

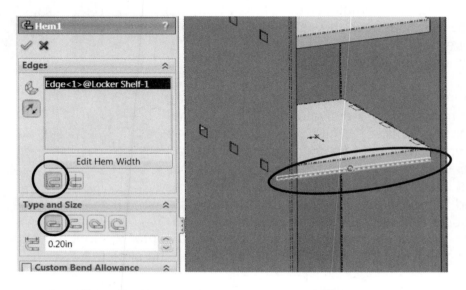

**265.** – Turn off "**Edit Component**" and return to editing the assembly. The last component we are adding is the locker's door. Select the "**Insert Components, New Part**" icon and click in the Front face of the *Locker Body* to locate the new part.

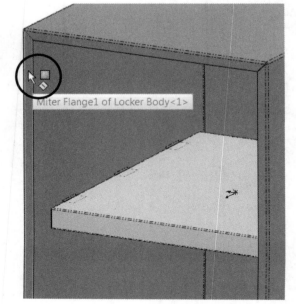

**266.** – The purpose of adding relations in the context of the assembly is to propagate changes; however, in the case of the door, we don't want to because we want to be able to open the door and move it. If we capture relations to make the door the same size of the body, when we open the door later, it will be rebuilt and its size will be smaller, fail to rebuild with an error, or produce unexpected results trying to maintain the in-context relations. Notice how the door is smaller when we open it and have in-context relations to define its size.

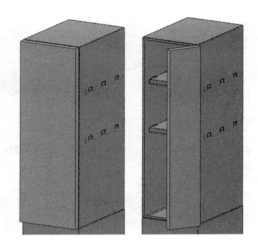

**267.** – One thing we can do to prevent capturing external relations is to activate the "**No External References**" option. While this command is active, we will not capture automatic (or manual) references to other components. Activate "**No External References**" and draw a rectangle as indicated for the door. Dimension it to match the locker's size and add a Midpoint relation between

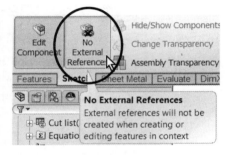

the lower rectangle's line and the part's origin to center it about the origin (almost always a good idea). This relation will fully define the sketch.

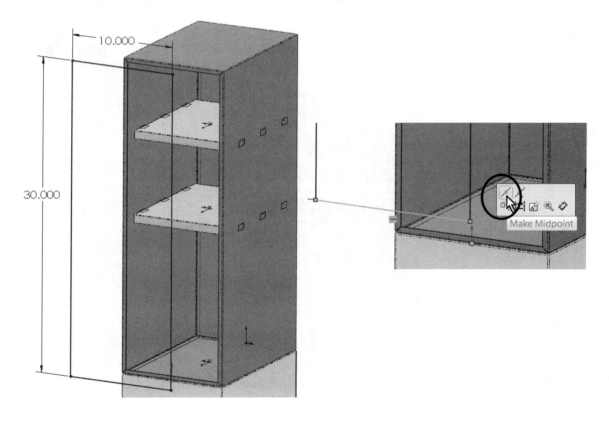

**268.** – Extrude the rectangle 0.625″ outward.  Now we need to convert the part to sheet metal.  Select "**Convert to Sheet Metal**," select the front of the door to be the fixed face, and add its four edges to the "**Bend Edges**" selection box.  Once the bend edges are selected, the corner edges will be automatically added to the "**Rip Edges found**" selection box.

**269.** – Set the sheet metal thickness to 0.03″ as the rest of the locker, a default bend radius of 0.05″ and a default gap for rips of 0.02″. Set "Auto Relief" to "Tear."

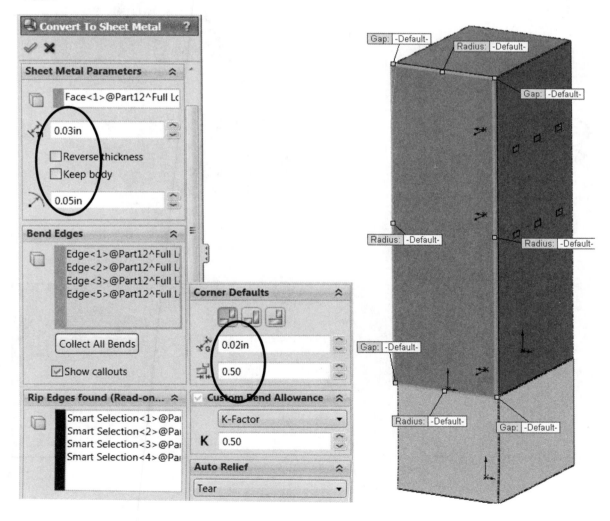

**270.** – After converting to sheet metal, we need to add flanges to the inside of the door. Open the part in its own window and turn it to see the back.

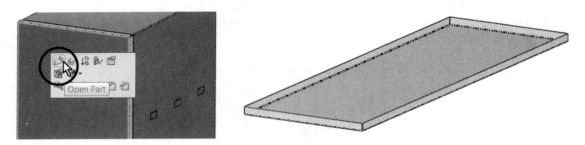

**271.** – Select the "**Edge Flange**" command and add all four edges in the back to the "Edge" selection box. Make the flange 0.625″ with a gap distance of 0.01″ and "Material Inside" option.

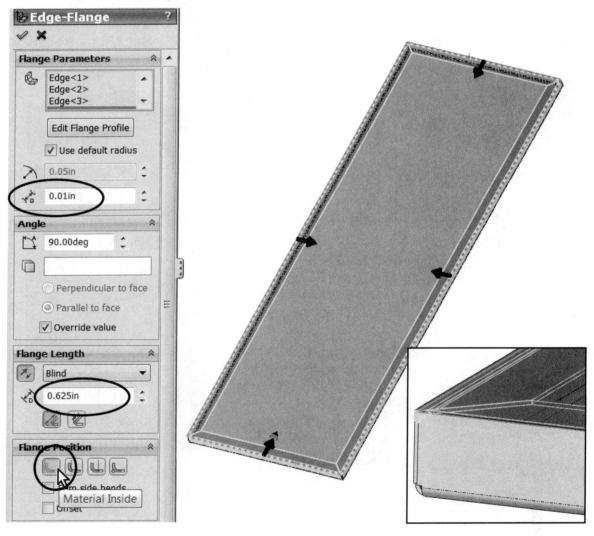

**272. –** Switch back to the assembly. Rename the new part as *Locker Door* and save in an external file.

**273. –** Our next step is to add a set of louvers to the door. The louver in the built-in library is too small. Its dimensions cannot be changed after adding it to a part and therefore we need to make a new one. In order to make a new library, we need a part with the shape that we want to obtain. Our library will be slightly different from the louver in the "Design Library" and bigger. To design a "Forming Tool" library, first we need to make the shape of the tool, and then define a *stopping face*, which is how deep the tool will be, and optionally the face(s) that will be removed (cut) as openings in the part. Make a new part. Add a sketch in the Top plane and draw the following rectangle as shown. Extrude 0.375″.

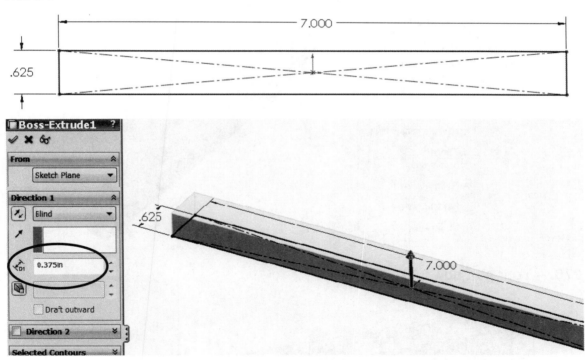

 **IMPORTANT:** At this writing there was a software issue with "Forming Tools" not working correctly. This is a simplified version of the originally intended louver design, since the original did not work, and custom made "Forming Tools" would not cut the sheet metal part or accept certain fillets. A Cut-Extrude *was* added to the finished files on our website to show the cut the "Tool" should make.

**274.** – Add a Fillet to round both of the indicated corners with a radius of 0.625″.

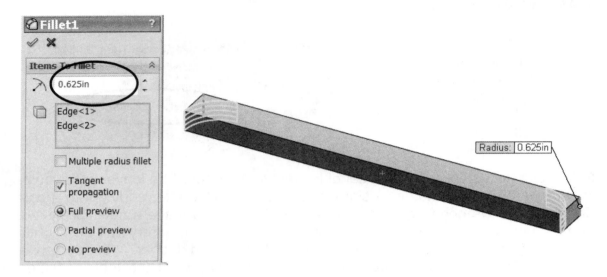

**275.** – Add a second Fillet to the top edge with a 0.25″ radius.

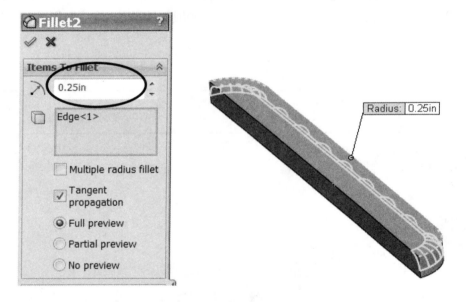

**276.** – Your part now looks like this:

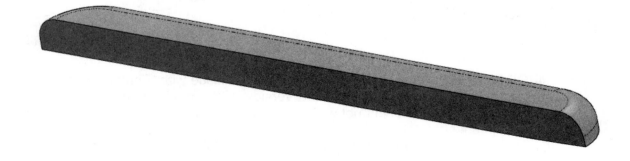

**277. –** After the part is complete, select the "**Forming Tool**" icon from the Sheet Metal toolbar or the menu "**Insert, Sheet Metal, Forming Tool**."

**278. –** Select the bottom face as the "**Stopping Face**." This is the face that will define how deep the tool will go *into* the sheet metal part.

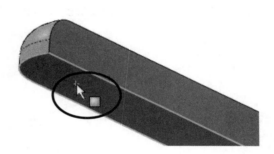

**279. –** Select the front flat face in the "**Faces to Remove**" selection box. This is an optional selection, but in our case we want this face to be open. Click **OK** when done.

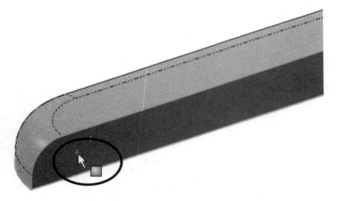

**280.** – SolidWorks automatically changes the face's colors; this is how it knows where to stop and which face(s) to remove.

**281.** – Open the "**Design Library**" and set it to visible (click on the 'push pin'). It will help us when we add the forming tool to the library.

Drag-and-drop the part's name from the top of the FeatureManager to the "**louvers**" folder. When prompted for a name, save it as *7in louver*. It will be automatically placed in the "louvers" library folder. Now we are ready to use it in our locker's door.

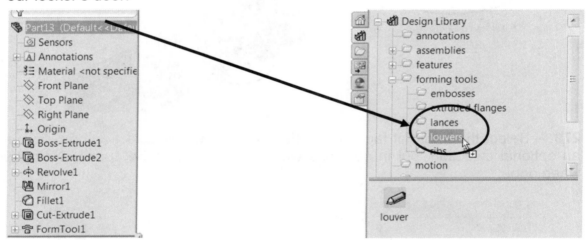

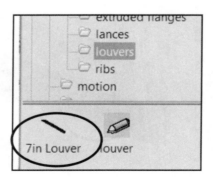

 The forming tool adds a sketch automatically created called "**Orientation Sketch**." This is the sketch that will be used to locate and orient the form tool when it is used in a sheet metal part.

**282.** – Close the *7in louver* library part and switch back to the assembly. Make sure we are still editing the *Locker Door* in context of the assembly to continue. Drag the new louver to the front of the locker door; if the preview is not going out, press the TAB key before releasing it to reverse the direction.

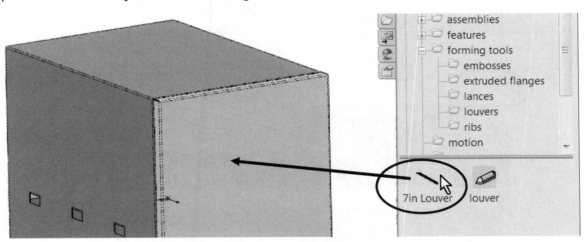

**283.** – **IF** the locating sketch is upside-down, select the menu "**Tools, Sketch Tools, Modify**" to rotate the sketch and orient the louver correctly. Type a rotation of 180 degrees or right mouse click-and-drag until the sketch is completely rotated. Close the "**Modify Sketch**" dialog when done rotating.

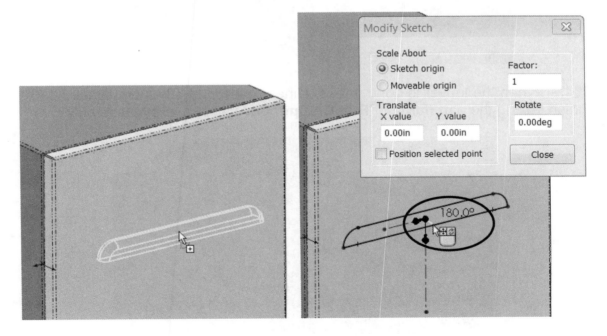

Add a "Coincident" relation between the vertical construction line and the door's origin to center it, then dimension to the top edge as indicated and click **Finish** in the "Position form feature" dialog box to complete the louver.

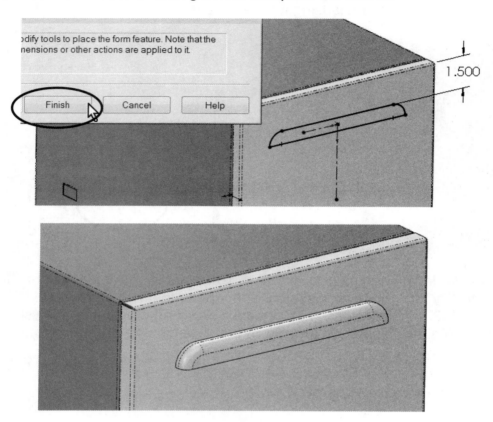

**284. –** When the louver is done, make a linear pattern of 6 louvers spaced 1.25″. Finish editing the part (turn off "**Edit Component**") and save the assembly.

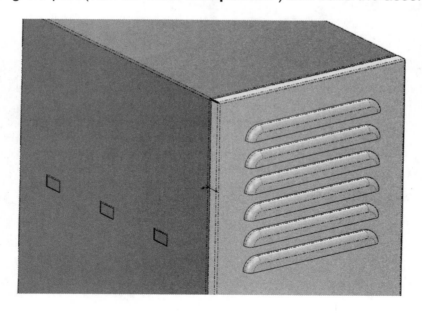

**285.** – After reviewing the assembly in a Right view, we notice that the door and the locker's body are bigger than the base. Measuring the difference we can see the *Locker Body* needs to be 0.625″ smaller to make the door flush with the base. To correct this we'll edit the first sketch of the locker's body. Expand the *Locker Body* FeatureManager and edit the "Boss-Extrude1" sketch. When we edit a part's sketch in an assembly, we automatically activate the "**Edit Component**" mode.

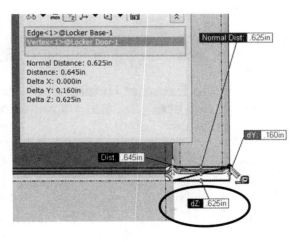

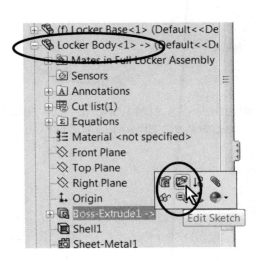

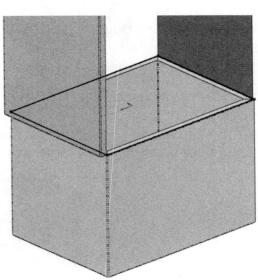

**286.** – Select the front sketch line and delete the "**On Edge**" relation (added by the "**Convert Entities**" command).

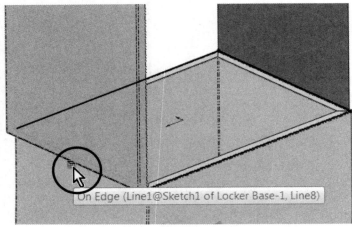

After deleting this external relation (we know it's external because it is followed by the "**->**" symbol), drag the front line a little to the back and dimension it. (Be sure to reference the edge of the base and not the door to locate it.)

 If the "**No External References**" command is activated, you will NOT be able to add dimensions (or relations) to other components. Turn it *off*.

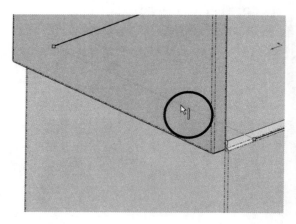 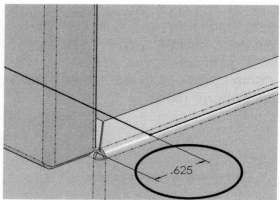

Close the sketch and turn off "**Edit Component**." All components will rebuild correctly. Your assembly now looks like this (colors were changed for visibility):

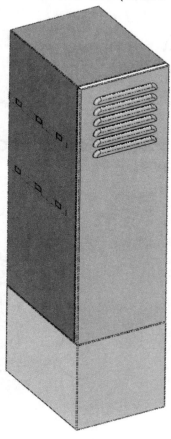

**287. –** The last thing we want to do is to add hinges to the locker so that we can open the door. However, if we try to move the door, we'll get the message:

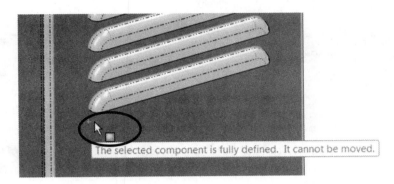

When we create components in the context of the assembly, an **InPlace** mate is automatically created when we select the face where we want to locate the new part. This mate completely immobilizes a component, and in order to be able to move it, we have to delete (or suppress) this mate. Expand the FeatureManager for the *Locker Door* part and scroll down to the folder "**Mates in Full Locker Assembly.**" This folder contains all the mates referencing the door in this assembly. If you remember, we did not make the door the same size as the body with external relations, but with dimensions. The reason was to be able to move the door using dynamic assembly motion. If we had added relations in the sketch, after moving the door, its size would have changed and most likely produced undesired results.

Delete the **InPlace** mate; click-and-drag to move the door and separate it from the locker. We'll add the hinges in the next step.

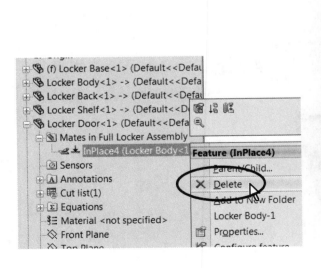

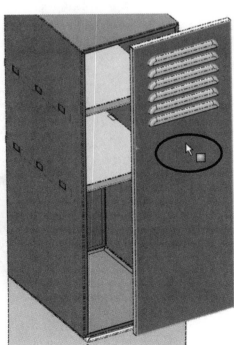

**288.** – Download the hinge assembly from our website and add it to the locker assembly (www.mechanicad.com/download.html). Be sure to set the file type to Assembly when adding it.

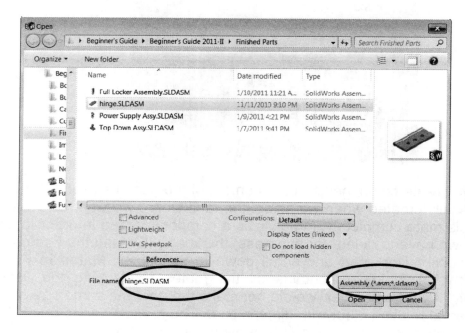

**289.** – Move the door to the left; we'll add the hinges in the right side of the locker. Mate one side of the *Hinge* Coincident to the front flange of the body…

**290.** – … the top of the *Hinge* Coincident to the upper shelf (the faces selection filter can be used to pick the smaller faces of the hinge; default shortcut "X").

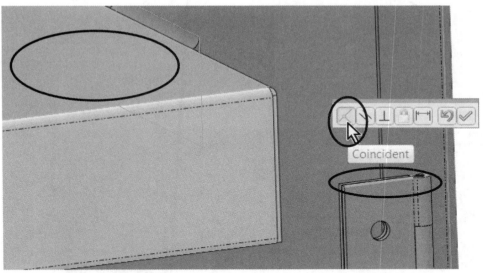

 If you use the Selection Filter, don't forget to turn it *off* when done!

**291.** – And finally make the edge of the *Hinge* Coincident to the outside face of the *Locker Body*.

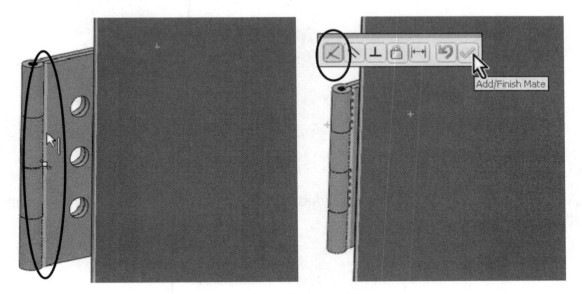

**292.** – With the hinge located in place, make a linear pattern and add two more *Hinges* spaced 8 inches. Select the menu "**Insert, Component Pattern, Linear Pattern**" or the "**Linear Component Pattern**" from the Assembly toolbar. Use the *Hinge* subassembly as the component to pattern and any vertical edge for the direction.

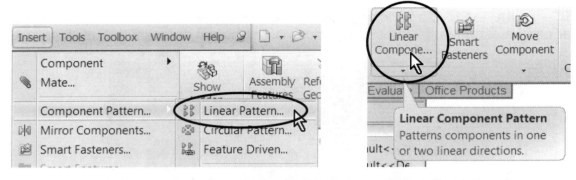

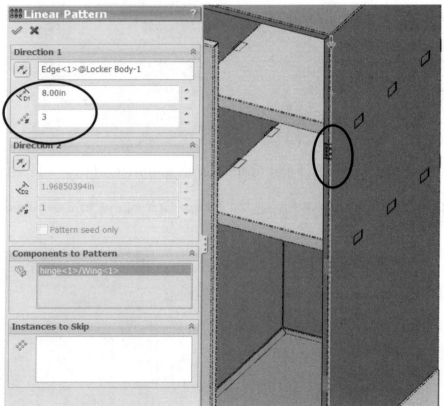

A component pattern feature is added to the assembly's FeatureManager with the additional two *Hinges*.

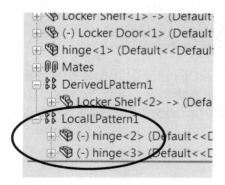

**293.** – Now we have to add mates to locate the door. Add a Coincident mate between the inside face of the door and the hinge.

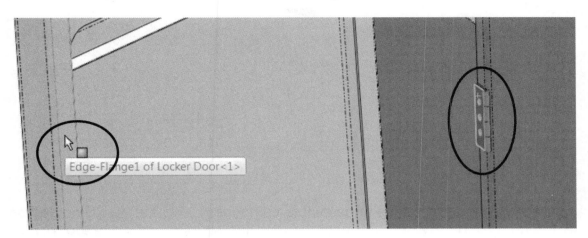

**294.** – Make the side of the door Coincident to the edge of the hinge (similar to how we mated the hinge to the locker's body).

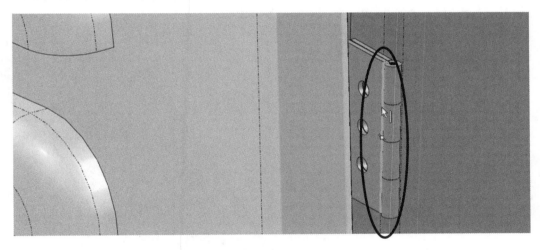

**295.** – Finally, add a Coincident mate between the top face of the door and the top face of the locker's body.

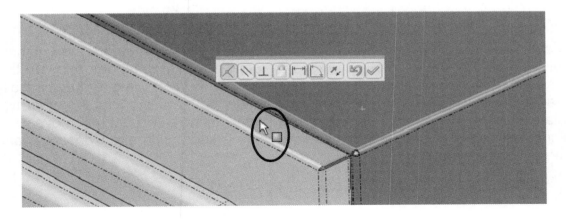

**296. –** When we try to move the door, we get the same "**Fully defined component**" message, and the door cannot be moved.   Open the hinge assembly.

**297. –** When we add mates to assemble components, we are removing degrees of freedom (dof).   By default, a component has six degrees of freedom. Three translations along the X, Y and Z axes, and three rotations about the X, Y and Z axes.   When a component is under defined, it means that *at least* one dof is not constrained, and it can move. If a part is fully defined, it cannot move or rotate. This is the basis for assembly motion in SolidWorks.

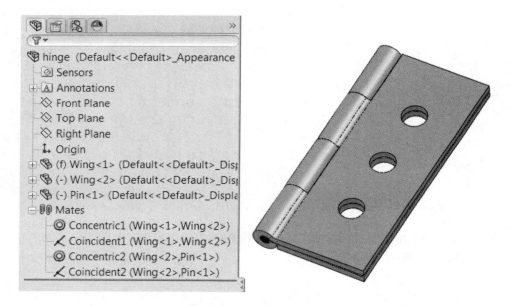

In our hinge assembly one Wing and the Pin have a (-) sign before their names. This means that these parts can move or rotate about *at least* one axis.   In this case, both can rotate about the Pin's axis.   Since the first Wing is automatically fixed in place (because it was the first part added to the assembly) the other two rotate about it.   If we click-and-drag the under defined Wing, it will move as a hinge (as expected) because it was restrained (mated) with one Concentric and one Coincident mate.

**298. –** If we keep moving the Wing, it will go past through the fixed Wing. This is the normal behavior. We can optionally activate the "**Collision Detection**" to make parts stop when they touch each other. Click in the "**Move Component**" icon in the Assembly toolbar; in the "**Options**" select "**Collision Detection**." By default "**All components**" is selected; as we move any part, SolidWorks will calculate collisions between every part in the assembly.

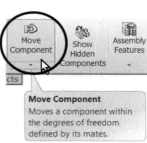

**Move Component**
Moves a component within the degrees of freedom defined by its mates.

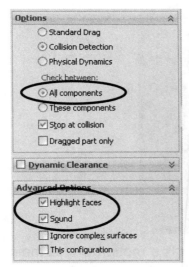

If the assembly has a small number of components, this is fine ("*small*" varies, from a few to tens or even hundreds depending on the computer's capacity); but if we have a large number of components (and "*large*" also varies..) we can limit the scope of detection by selecting the "**These components**" option and select only the ones we are interested in, greatly enhancing the speed and accuracy of the calculation. With only three parts, "**All components**" should be fast enough in just about any computer. Turn on the "**Stop at collision**" option to prevent a part from going through another, "**Highlight faces**" to visually identify the component faces that are colliding, and "**Sound**" to hear when a collision is detected. Drag the Wing in the hinge; it will stop when the faces touch each other.

 If we start "**Collision Detection**" with an interference between the components being analyzed, the "Stop at Collision" option will be ignored. The assembly must be set to a non-colliding position to re-activate this option.

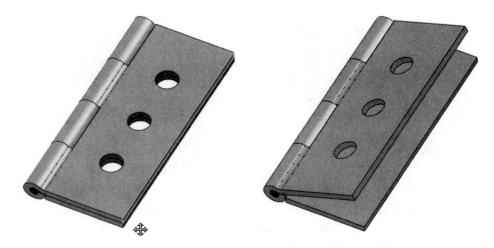

**299. –** Leave the hinge partially open as shown above and switch back to the locker assembly; we'll be asked to rebuild it. After selecting "Yes," the hinge remains in the same position as we left it in its own assembly, but this is not really the behavior we want.

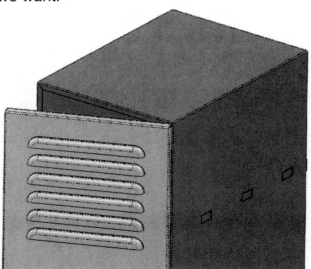

**300. –** What we need to do is to enable the subassembly's motion in the main assembly. By default, subassemblies are calculated as rigid bodies without motion. Select the "**hinge**" subassembly in the FeatureManager (and only in the FeatureManager), click on the "**Component Properties**" icon from the pop-up menu and activate the "**Solve as Flexible**" option. Click **OK** when done.

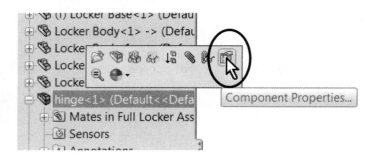

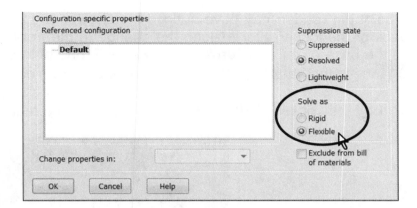

Note the different icon when a subassembly is made flexible.

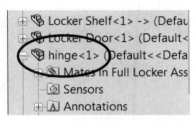

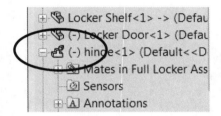

**Rigid sub-assembly**          **Flexible sub-assembly**

**301.** – By making the "hinge" subassembly "Flexible" we can move the door freely. Make the other two hinges flexible and mate them to the door. We only need to add a Coincident mate to the each of the patterned hinges.

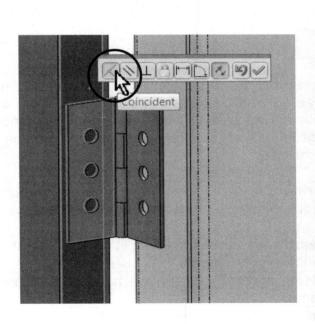

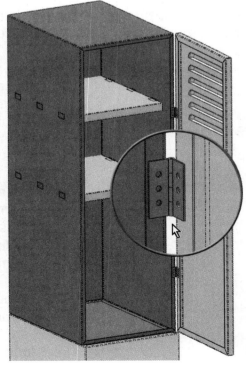

**302. –** At this point the reader may have noticed the shelves are too big and go through the back of the locker after making the change in the front to make the door flush with the base. To fix this error, double click in one of the shelves and change the distance in the back from 1.5″ to 1.25″. Rebuild the model to finish.

**CHALLENGE:** Edit the *Locker Shelf* and make it 0.25″ from the rear.

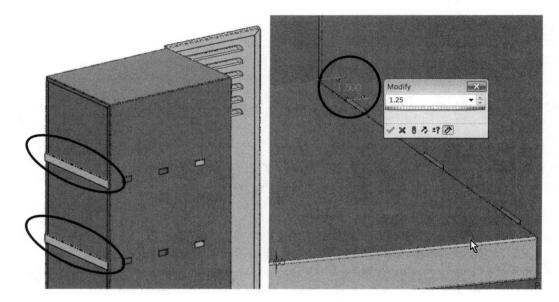

**303. –** The last thing to do is to add a series of holes to hold the back with rivets or screws. We can add the holes to one part, and then make the holes in the other part using in-context relations. In this case, the holes will be added *while* editing the assembly, *not* a part, and will be added to multiple components at the same time using an **Assembly Feature**.

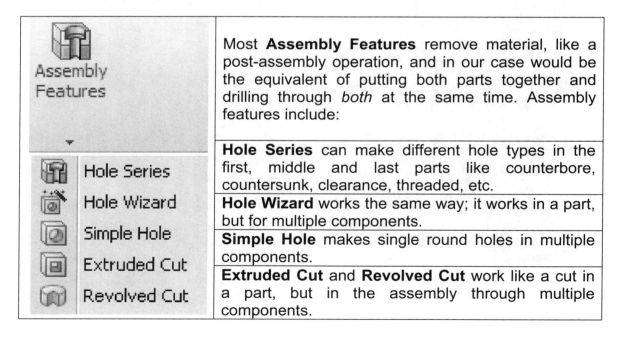

| | |
|---|---|
| **Assembly Features** | Most **Assembly Features** remove material, like a post-assembly operation, and in our case would be the equivalent of putting both parts together and drilling through *both* at the same time. Assembly features include: |
| Hole Series | **Hole Series** can make different hole types in the first, middle and last parts like counterbore, countersunk, clearance, threaded, etc. |
| Hole Wizard | **Hole Wizard** works the same way; it works in a part, but for multiple components. |
| Simple Hole | **Simple Hole** makes single round holes in multiple components. |
| Extruded Cut | **Extruded Cut** and **Revolved Cut** work like a cut in a part, but in the assembly through multiple components. |
| Revolved Cut | |

**304.** – Select the "**Hole Wizard**" option from the "**Assembly Features**" drop-down icon. We'll use 1/8" rivets to secure the back to the locker. Turn the locker to see the upper left back corner; select the simple hole, and make it 1/8". Make the hole's end condition "Blind" with a depth of 0.25". (It will be deep enough to go through both parts.)

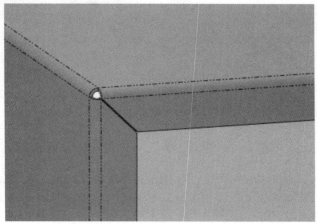

Select the "Positions" tab and locate a single hole as indicated. We'll make a linear pattern to add the rest. Click **OK** to complete.

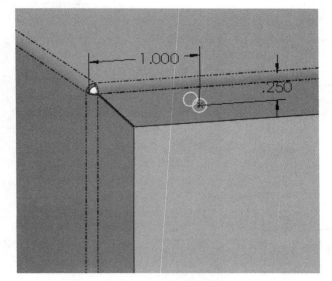

Note an additional options box at the bottom titled "**Feature Scope**." This is where we define which parts will be affected by this feature and if we want the feature to be propagated to the individual parts. If we leave the "**Propagate feature to parts**" option unchecked, the holes will only exist in the assembly and not in the parts. This is useful when making post-assembly operations. If the option is checked, the holes will be visible in the parts *and* the assembly like any regular feature, and will be added as an external reference.

A hole is added to both parts. Since the feature was not propagated to the parts (the option "**Propagate feature to part**" is unchecked), opening either part will not show the hole.

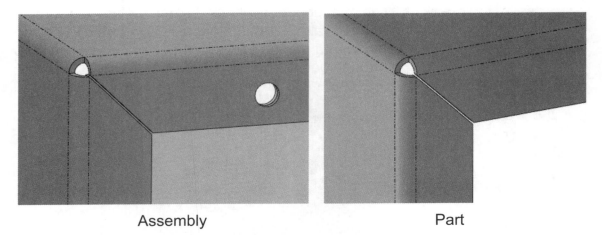

Assembly                                    Part

**305. –** When assembly features are added, the "**Assembly Features**" drop-down icon is expanded to include feature patterns including linear, circular, table and sketch driven. Select the "**Linear Pattern**" and make a horizontal pattern with 6 holes spaced 1.625″.

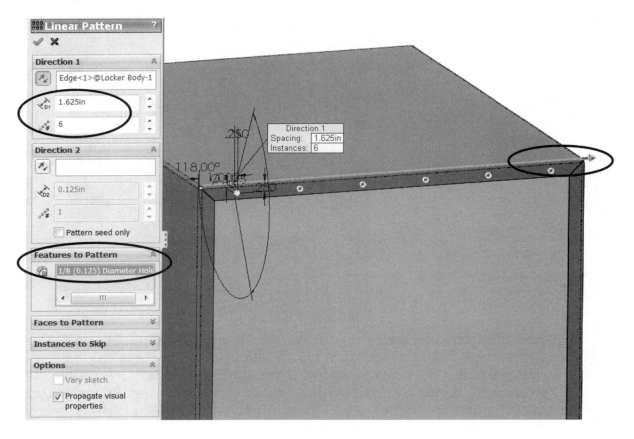

**306.** – Make similar assembly features and patterns in the other three flanges to finish the assembly. (Hint: Edit the Hole Wizard in the top to add a second hole in the bottom and pattern both holes together; use the same approach for the sides.) Save and close the assembly.

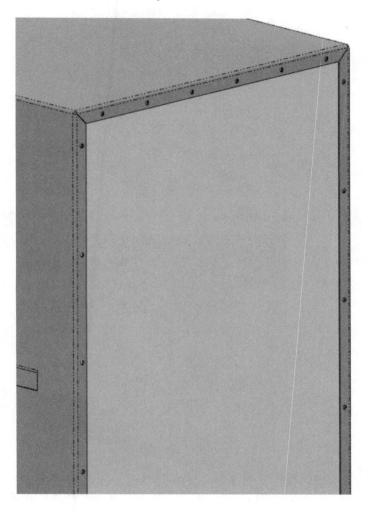

**CHALLENGE EXERCISES:**

1: Change the locker's body to be the same size as the base. Edit the *Locker Body*'s first sketch and add external references.

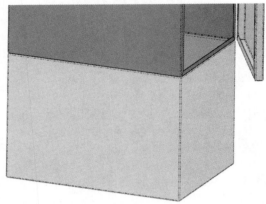

2: Change the locker's base dimension to 12″ wide x 14″ deep x 14″ high.

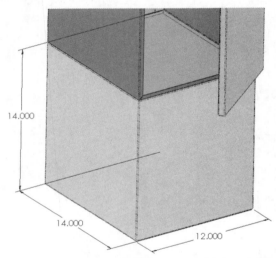

3: Add assembly features using the Hole Wizard to attach the locker's body to the base like we did for the rear *Locker Back* panel.

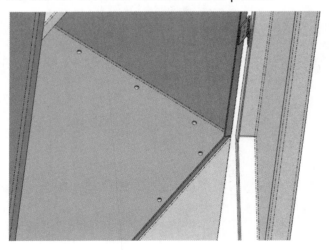

4: Add equations in the assembly to make the *Locker Door*'s width 7/8″ narrower than the *Locker Base* and the *Locker Door*'s height 7/8″ smaller than the *Locker Body*.

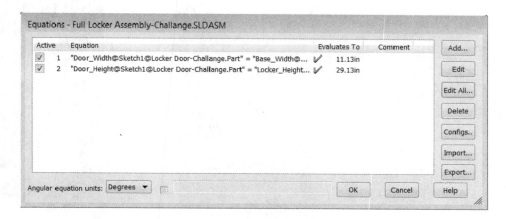

5: Make the *Locker Door* flush with the front face of the *Locker Body*. Modify the front miter flange in the *Locker Body*. Edit the miter flange sketch as shown.

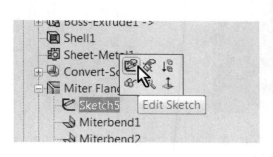

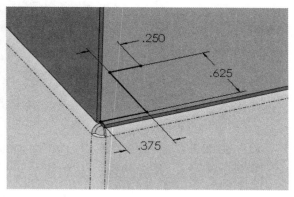

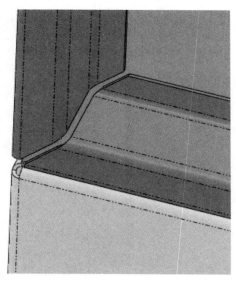

6: Change the *Locker Door* and hinge's mates to make it flush with the front of the *Locker Body*.

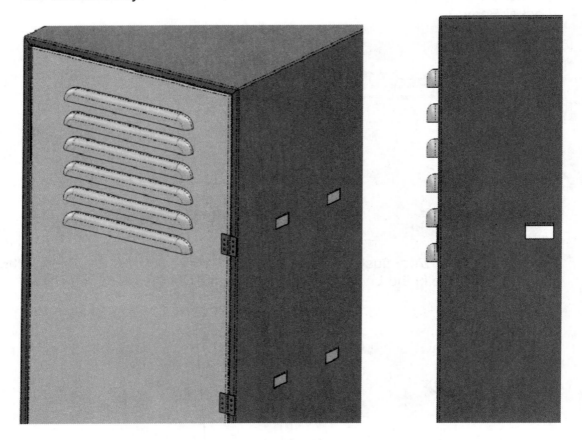

7: Make detail drawings of all parts including a flat pattern and an assembly drawing with an exploded view and bill of materials.

**Extra Credit**: Design a suitable lock for the door and incorporate it into the assembly.

**Review and Questions:**

a) Name the different options available in SolidWorks to calculate sheet metal bend allowances.

b) How is the Relief Ratio calculated (Rectangular and Obround reliefs)?

c) What is and how is the K-factor calculated?

d) Which external references state will propagate changes immediately in an assembly (In-Context, Out of Context, Broken, Locked)?

e) How can external references be temporarily "frozen"?

f) What does the option "Merge faces" do in a sheet metal component?

g) What is the "Link to thickness" option and what does it do?

h) What is the extension used for library features?

i) What is the option "Flexible" in a subassembly used for?

j) Explain the difference between a Miter Flange and Edge Flange?

**Answers:**

a.- Bend allowance, Bend Deduction, K-Factor

b.- It's the relation between the sheet metal thickness and the width of the relief.

c.- It's the relation between the distance from the inside bend radius and the neutral plane to the thickness.

d.- In Context.

e.- Locking them using under "List External References".

f.- It eliminates all the bend lines and bend regions in the flat pattern making it a single surface.

g.- It's an option available when adding extrusions and cuts to sheet metal parts to make the extrusion (or cut) the same depth as the sheet metal's thickness.

h.- *.SLDLFP

i.- If a subassembly has mates that permit motion, the motion will be available at the top level assembly.

j.- In an Edge Flange, the width and shape of the flange can be changed but not its profile; in a Miter Flange, only the profile can be edited.

**Notes:**

## *3D Sketch and Weldments*

A 3D sketch, as its name implies, exists in 3D space and is not limited to a plane. Common uses for a 3D sketch include path and guide curves for sweeps and lofts, as the "centerline" for structural profiles (weldments), as a reference to create auxiliary geometry, etc.

Weldment refers in general to a multi body part that is made from profiles extruded (or swept) along a 2D or 3D sketch. It is particularly useful when designing structures, welded components, tubular parts, etc. and has special features to represent welding processes, manufacturing annotations like weld types, calculating a list of members to be cut of each type of profile used (very much like a Bill of Materials) and more trade specific tools to fully design and document a welded structure.

**Notes:**

## *3D Sketch*

To learn how to make a 3D sketch, we'll build a tubular frame for a chair. We'll need two sweeps, each using a 3D sketch as a path.

**307.** – Before making the 3D sketch, we'll make a 2D sketch and an auxiliary plane to help us draw the 3D sketch. Draw a 14″ construction line in the Right plane, and exit the sketch.

**308.** – Switch to an Isometric view and select the "**Reference Geometry, Plane**" icon. We'll create an auxiliary plane at 20 degrees from the Right plane. Select the "Right" plane in the "**First Reference**" selection box and the sketch line we just drew in the "**Second Reference**" selection box. Make the plane 20 degrees to the left (you may have to "**Flip**" the direction). Click **OK** to finish.

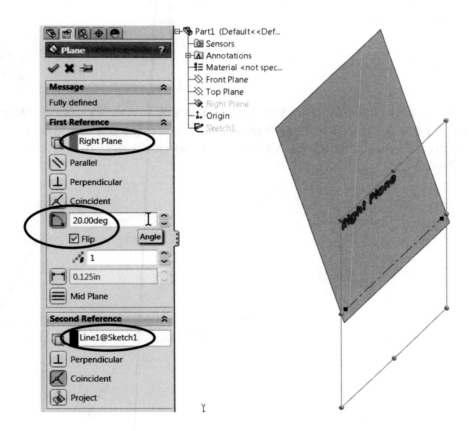

**309.** – Now select the menu **"Insert, 3D Sketch,"** or the **"3D Sketch"** icon (not in a toolbar by default). We'll make the first path for the tubular frame. When we start, the only difference from a regular sketch is that we get "3DSketch1" in the FeatureManager, status bar and window title.

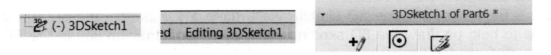

**310.** – After selecting the **"Line"** tool, we immediately see a bigger than usual sketch origin, aligned parallel to the **"Front"** plane and an "XY" label next to the mouse pointer. This is to let us know that, when we draw the line, we'll be working in a 'plane' parallel to the Front plane (XY-plane in the 3D Sketch). Click in the origin to start drawing a line; move towards the right and align with the 'X' direction. The yellow inference icon is somewhat small, but visible.

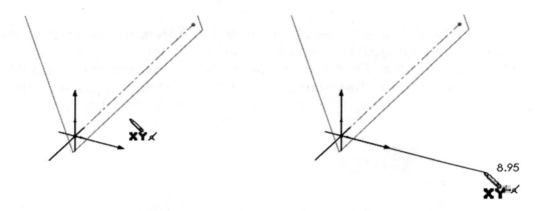

**311.** – For the second line, go down and right, but still in the XY-plane. Notice the origin moves to the start of the new line to alert us of the plane's orientation we are working on. Repeat the same two lines at the other end of the construction sketch we drew first.

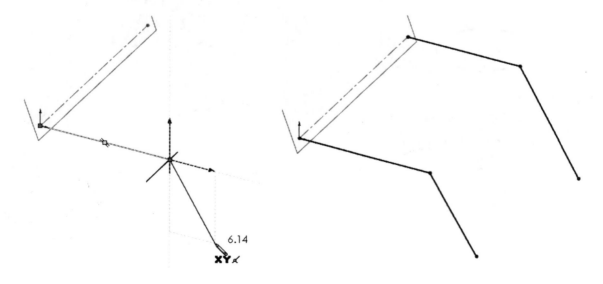

**312.** – When we work in a 3D sketch, besides the usual geometric relations available, now we have more options to help us fully define our design.

| Relation: | Between entities: | Result: |
|---|---|---|
| Along X | Line or two points | Line or endpoints aligned along the global X axis. |
| Along Y | | Line or endpoints aligned along the global Y axis. |
| Along Z | | Line or endpoints aligned along the global Z axis. |
| Normal | Line and Plane or flat face | Makes the Line perpendicular to the plane or face. |
| On Plane | Plane or flat face and Line or point | Makes the line or point Coincident to the plane. |
| ParallelYZ | Plane or flat face and Line | Makes the selected line parallel to the YZ plane. |
| ParallelZX | | Makes the selected line parallel to the ZX plane. |

**313.** – The first thing to do is to add the relations we know we want to have so far.

Select both lines along the X axis and add an **Equal** relation (same length).

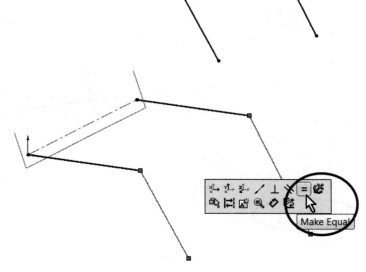

Select both angled lines and add an **Equal** relation (same length).

**314.** – Add an **On Plane** relation between the first diagonal line and the Front plane. By adding this relation, the line will not 'move' along Z.

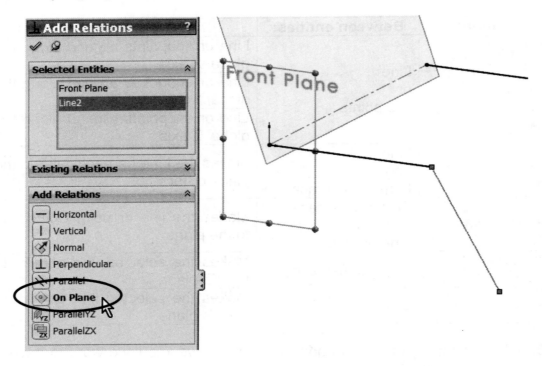

**315.** – Add a Parallel relation between the two diagonal lines.

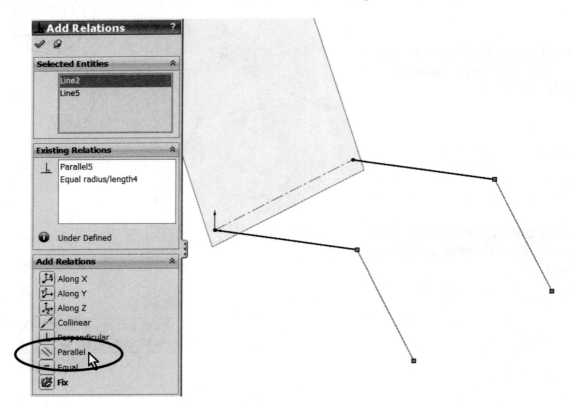

**316.** – Now add dimensions. The sketch should be fully defined up to this point.

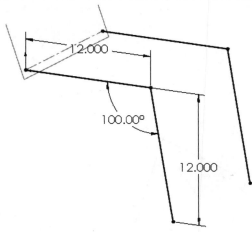

- Dimension the horizontal line 12″ long.

- Add the angular 100° dimension between the two lines.

- Add the vertical dimension between the horizontal line and the endpoint at the bottom. If you select the lower line only, you'll dimension it's length, not the distance from the horizontal.

**317.** – The next step is to add the backrest part of the chair. The plane we added at the beginning will help us align the 3D sketch's X, Y and Z axes directions about it. Select the "**Plane1**" and then click to turn on the **Line** tool. The sketch origin and the local directions will now be temporarily aligned to **Plane1**.

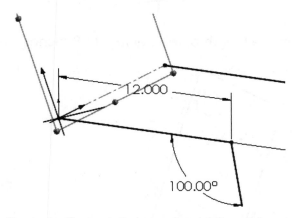

**318.** – Draw a new line starting at the part's origin going 'up' along the plane, then to the 'right' and 'down' to the start of the other line to make them Coincident (don't worry if it's not parallel).

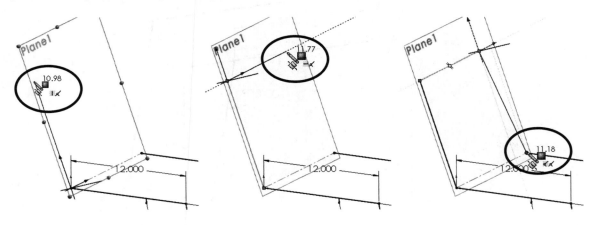

**319. –** Turn off the **Line** tool. Add a **Parallel** relation between the two lines aligned with *Plane1*.

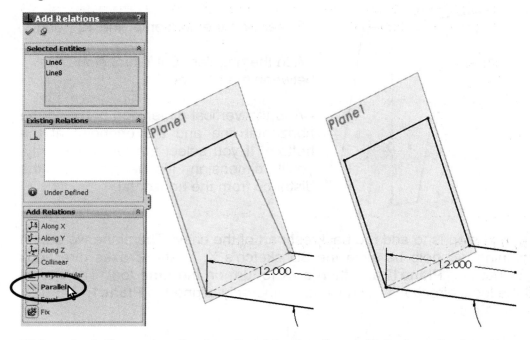

**320. –** And dimension the length of the backrest 18 inches (its length, not height).

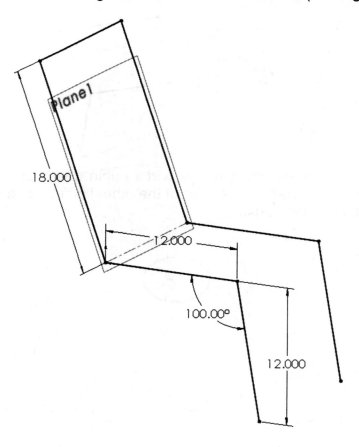

**321.** – To finish the sketch, select the "Sketch Fillet" tool and round all sharp corners with a 2″ radius. When adding the fillet we are warned about segments with equal relations; keep adding fillets until done. Since we are rounding all segments, they will still be equal at the end. Click Yes to continue when asked.

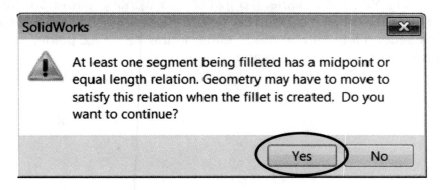

Click **OK** to finish the sketch fillets. Exit the sketch when finished.

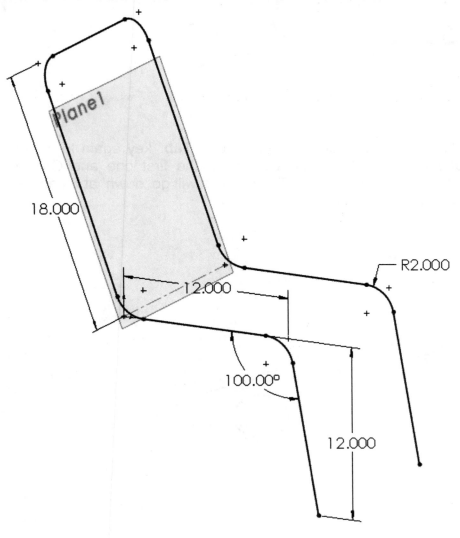

**322.** – The next part of the chair will be done similar to the first one. Start a new 3D Sketch (rotate the model as needed for clarity). Start a line close to the origin Coincident to the construction sketch along the X axis. Notice we are working in the XY plane; now we want to go along the Z axis and because of that we need to change to the YZ or XZ plane. To switch the working plane on-the-fly, press the "**Tab**" key (just once; no need to hold it) to rotate through the other work planes. The second line can be made either in the YZ or XZ plane. In the second picture we are working in the YZ plane.

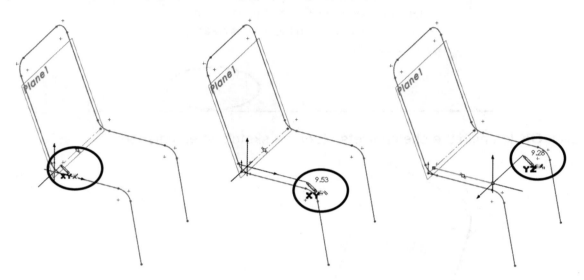

**323.** – Add the second line and press the "**Tab**" key again to switch to the XY plane and draw the third line parallel to the first one and Coincident to the construction sketch as shown. The last line will go 'down' at an angle for the rear leg of the chair.

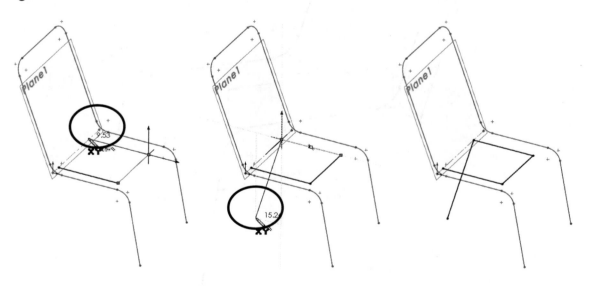

**324.** – Add a similar line to the other side.

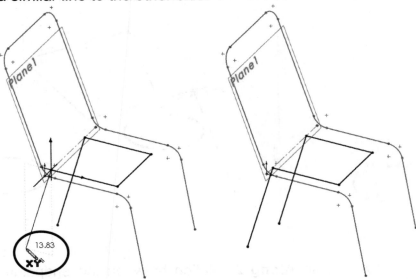

**325.** – Dimension the lines 0.75" from the endpoint of the construction sketch, the angle between the two lines and the length of the seat as shown.

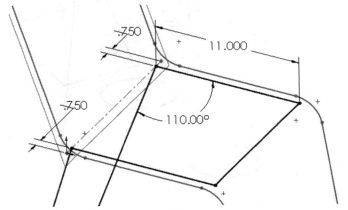

**326.** – Now we need to add some relations. Select the endpoints at the bottom of the legs on one side of the chair and add an **Along X** relation; this way we'll make them lie on the same plane and axis.

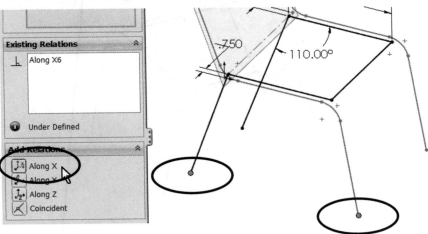

**327.** – Repeat the same relation for the end lines on the other side of the chair.

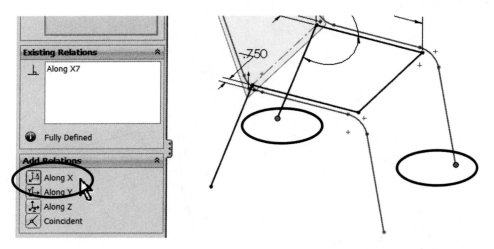

**328.** – And finally, add an **Along Z** relation between the endpoints of the two lines in the back to fully define the sketch.

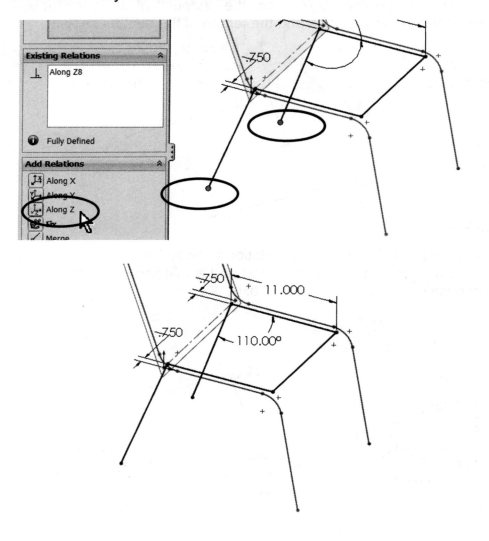

**329.** – To finish the second 3D Sketch, add a 2″ sketch fillet to all corners as we did in the first sketch. Close the sketch to finish.

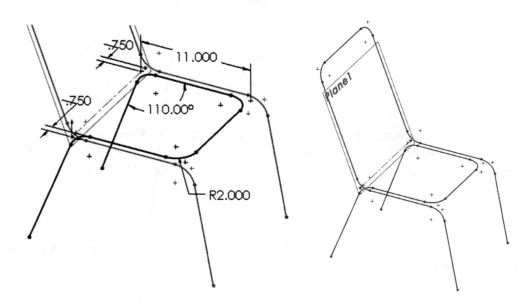

**330.** – To make the tubes, we need a plane at the endpoint of a leg for the sweep's profile. Add an auxiliary plane Parallel to the Top plane ("First Reference") and Coincident to the endpoint of the chair's leg ("Second Reference").

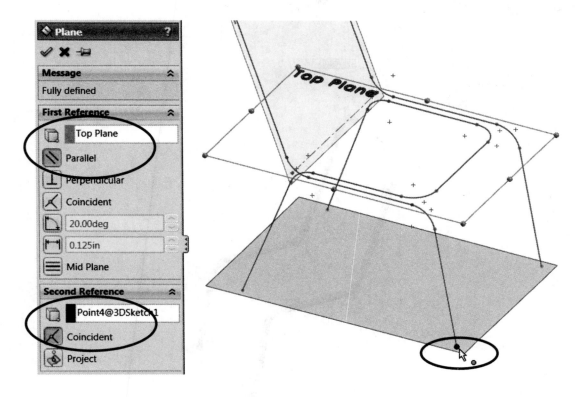

**331.** – When the new plane is finished, add a new 2D sketch in it. Be sure to make the circle Coincident to the endpoint of the 3D sketch and then exit the sketch.

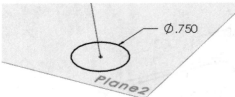

**332.** – Make a sweep using this last sketch as the "**Profile**" and the first 3D sketch as the "**Path**." We'll use the "**Thin Feature**" option in the Sweep to make the wall 0.07″ thick with the material going inside. Click **OK** to finish the first tube.

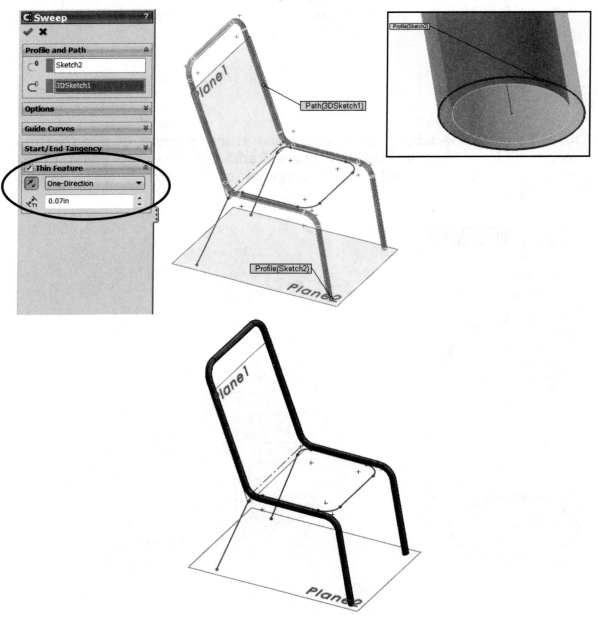

**333.** – To make the second sweep we need a new profile sketch. Since we want both profiles to be the same, we'll use a function called "**Derived Sketch**" to make the second profile exactly the same as the first one. Using this approach, if the first profile sketch changes, the second one updates, too. To add a derived sketch <u>we have to pre-select</u> the sketch we want to derive *and* the plane/face where we want to put it. Expand the "**Sweep-Thin1**" feature, select the profile sketch, hold down the "**Ctrl**" key and select "**Plane2**" in the FeatureManager or the graphics area. Now, select the menu "**Insert, Derived Sketch**" (if we don't pre-select them, this command is unavailable).

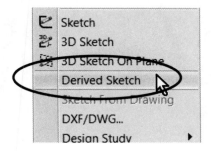

Immediately after selecting "**Derived Sketch**" we are editing the new sketch. Notice that most sketching tools are disabled except for dimensioning and relations. In a derived sketch the geometry cannot be modified; it can only be located. The only thing left for us to do is to make the circle Coincident to the other 3D sketch. The derived sketch will be right on top of the first sketch; we dragged the circle away from it for clarity. Add a Coincident relation between the circle's center and the 3D Sketch endpoint as shown. When done, exit the sketch.

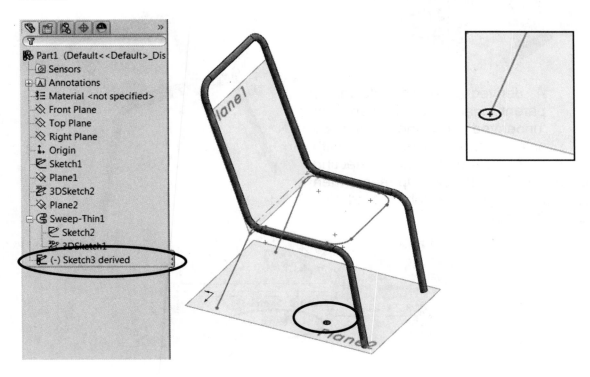

Make the second sweep with the same options as the first one. Hide planes and sketches. Save and close.

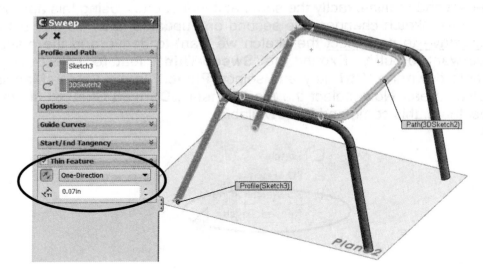

**334.** – Now that the chair's frame is finished, here's a challenge: make the necessary changes to make the uneven legs on the right side flat to the bottom and maintain the original height (Yes, I knew there was a problem. I was saving it for the reader to fix ☺).

A derived sketch's link to its parent can be broken, or 'underived' from the original by selecting the derived sketch with the right mouse button and selecting **"Underive"** from the pop-up menu, then we can edit the sketch. Underive cannot be undone.

Another way to make the path to sweep the frame of the chair is by using a **"Projected Curve."** By drawing the desired curve's projections in the Front and Top planes, we can combine them into a 3D curve and use it as a sweep path.

**335. –** Open a new part and add the following sketch in the Front plane. The sketch's origin is at the end of the 18″ line. Exit the sketch when done.

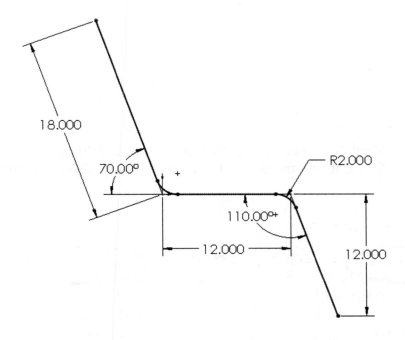

**336. –** Make a new sketch in the Top plane as shown and exit the sketch when done. Add geometric relations to the previous sketch endpoints to make it exactly the same size.

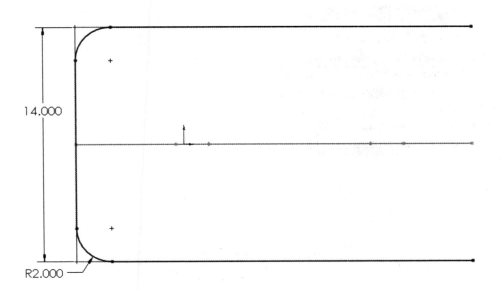

This is what the two sketches look like in an isometric view:

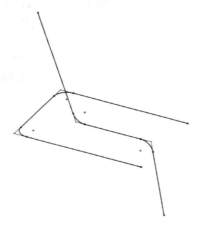

**337. –** Now, select the "**Projected Curve**" command from the "**Curves**" drop down menu in the Features toolbar or the menu "**Insert, Curve, Projected**."

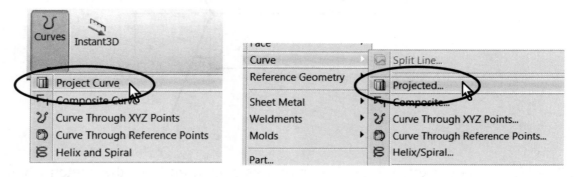

Select the "Sketch on Sketch" option and pick both sketches previously made. Click **OK** to finish.

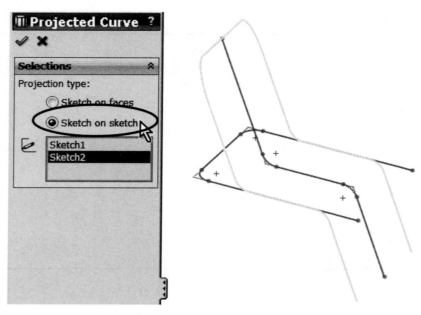

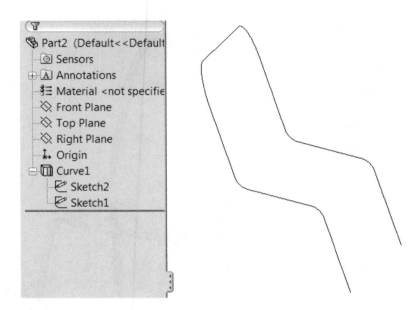

Now we can use the projected curve as a path for the sweep operation.

 Note that, when projecting curves, the radius may not be correctly projected, as is the case with the upper curves in the backrest. In this case it's better to model this part with a 3D sketch, but it was also a good option to show how a projected curve works, and some of its limitations.

**CHALLENGE EXERCISE:** Create the second curve for the chair's frame using a "Projected Curve" and add the two sweep features.

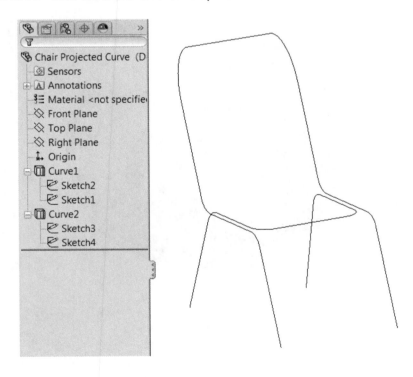

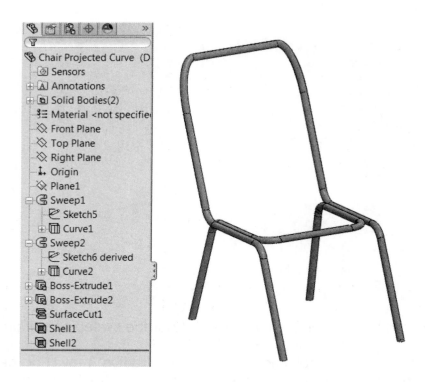

 Download a more extensive "Projected Curve" tutorial from our website: http://mechanicad.com/tipstricks.html

## Weldments

A welded structure can be defined as a part whose elements are long and thin and which can be made with standard structural members. The weldments environment in SolidWorks allows us to design welded, modular or similar structures made from constant cross section elements (i.e., round or square tubing) easily, including weld beads, gussets and end caps in a multi body part. Detail drawings of weldments usually include material cut lists with length and cut angles ready for manufacturing.

Besides including a library of structural members in both metric and standard sizes, SolidWorks allows us to add our own structural member profiles to the built-in library.

When we work with weldments, the first thing we need to do is to make one or more 2D and/or 3D sketches that will serve as the structure's 'skeleton,' defining the structure's centerline, inside, or outside dimensions, just like in sheet metal. In a weldments part, each sketch line will be used to locate one element of the structure.

 A weldments part is probably one of the few instances where it's efficient to use a part file instead of an assembly to represent multiple 'parts.'

To learn how to use the weldments environment, we'll make the following conveyor structure using 2″ x 2″ welded steel.

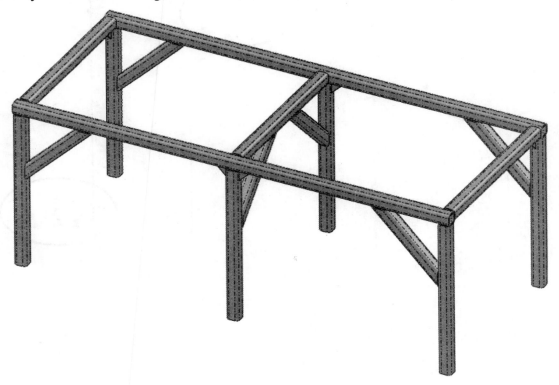

**338.** – The first thing we need to do is to make a 3D sketch (or a combination of multiple 2D sketches) that will be the *skeleton* for our welded structure. Just as with sheet metal, we need to decide if the sketch dimensions will represent inside, outside or centerline dimensions of the welded structure. In our case, the conveyor's legs will be the centerline, and the top will be outside dimensions; in other words, the width and length are not as important, but the height is. Open a new part and start a 3D sketch (menu "**Insert, 3D Sketch**"). Select the "**Line**" tool and press the "**Tab**" key to switch to the "**YZ**" plane. By default, 3D sketches always start in the "**XY**" plane.

TAB key once…

To make the 3D sketch directions easier, the reader will be directed to go along the X, Y and Z axes in the positive or negative directions.

Start the sketch line in the origin, go up in **Y**, negative **Z**, and negative **Y** and stop. Don't worry about the size; we'll dimension it after adding relations.

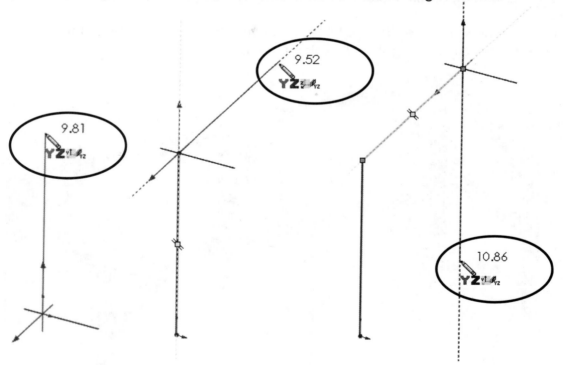

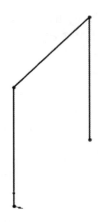

**339. –** Still with the "Line" tool active, start in the upper left and right corners and draw two lines going in the **X** direction. Press the "**Tab**" key if needed to switch to the **XY** or **XZ** plane; either one works in this case.

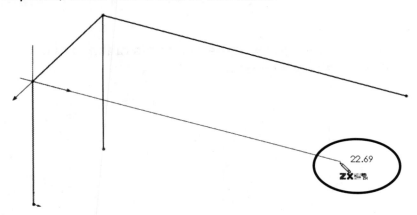

**340. –** An advantage of working in a 3D sketch is that we can 'snap' to other geometric elements even if they are not in the same plane we are working on. Draw the next four legs, adding **Midpoint** and **Coincident** relations to the two long lines as shown. Switch planes if needed by pressing the "**Tab**" key.

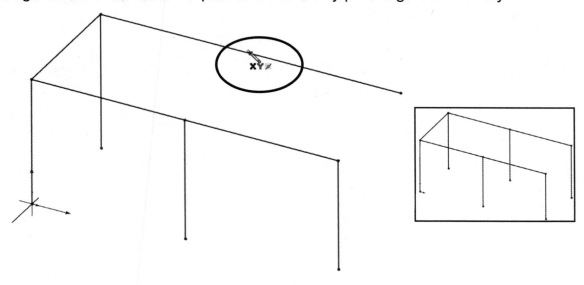

**341.** – Draw the next two lines along the **Z** direction to complete the geometry. Snap to the endpoints, even if the lines are not exactly in the **Z** direction.

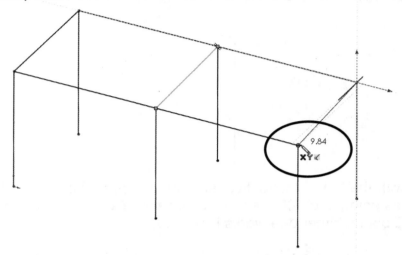

**342.** – Add **Along X** relations to the three endpoints of the legs on each side, one side at a time, *or* make all six legs **Equal**.

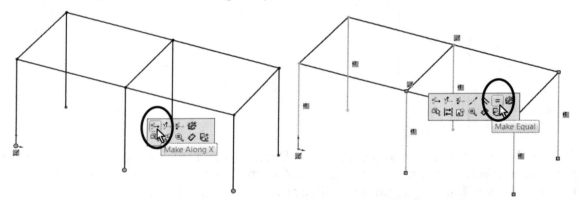

**343.** – Since we 'snapped' two of the transversal elements, we need to make them either **Along Z** *or* **Parallel** to the first one.

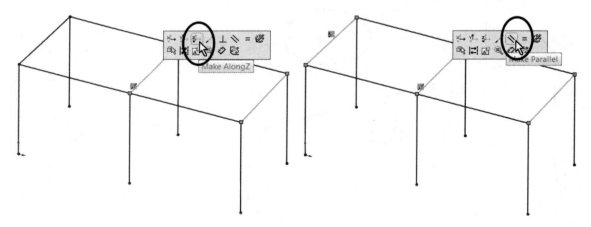

**344.** – Add the following dimensions (we only need one 36″ dimension because we added a **Midpoint** relation to the long line):

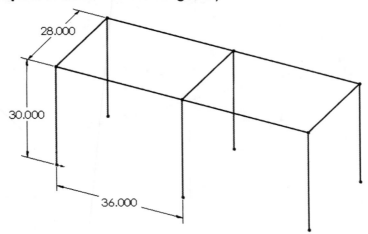

**345.** – Add corner reinforcements and dimension one as shown. Draw the lines by 'snapping' to the existing lines. Make all the reinforcement lines **Equal**.

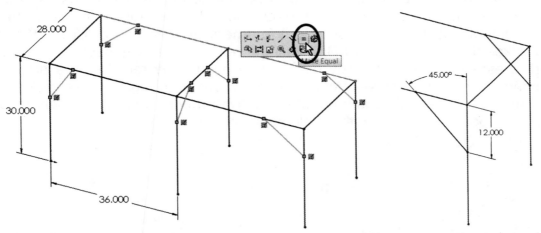

**346.** – Make the lower three endpoints on one side **Along X**, then the other side, and finally **Along Z** on one end to fully define the sketch.

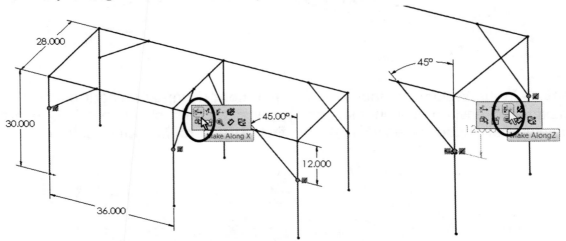

**347.** – The finished sketch now looks like this. Exit the sketch to continue.

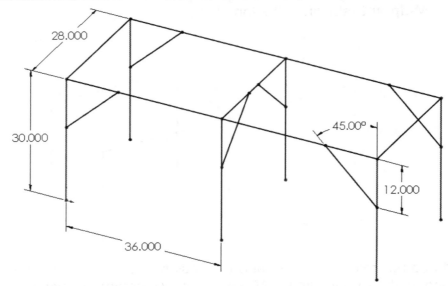

**348.** – Weldments work similarly to sheet metal in the sense that a special feature is added to the FeatureManager that enables the weldments environment, which in this case is a "**Weldment**" feature and a "**Cut list**" folder that takes the place of "**Solid Bodies**"; the reason for this is because a welded part is essentially a multi body part, where each body represents a structural member. Make sure the weldments toolbar is enabled. Right mouse click in the CommandManager's tabs and activate the "**Weldments**" tab, and/or right mouse click in a toolbar and turn on the Weldments toolbar.

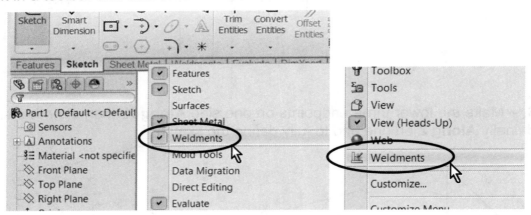

**349.** – In the Weldments toolbar is a "**Weldment**" icon; selecting it enables the weldments environment in the part but, just as with sheet metal, it is also automatically added when we make the first "**Structural Member**" feature.

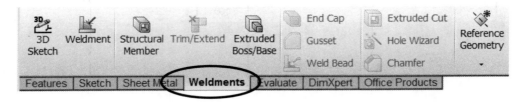

To start, select the "**Structural Member**" icon. From the "**Selections**" options, select "ansi inch" in "**Standard**", "square tube" in "**Type**" and "2x2x0.25" in "**Size**."

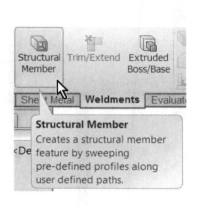

**350.** – The first group of structural members to be added will be the 'legs.' As we start selecting them in the screen, we see a preview of each one with the selected profile centered in each line (we'll talk about locating the profile later).

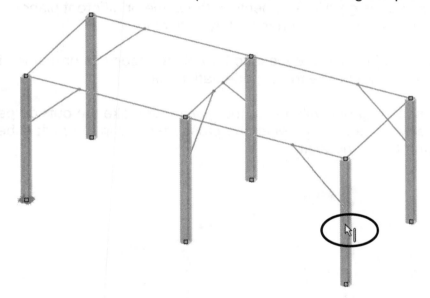

**351.** – Since we'll be adding more members and the legs are just the first group, click in the "**Keep Visible**" option and then **OK** to create them. By doing this we can continue adding more groups.

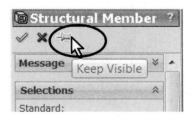

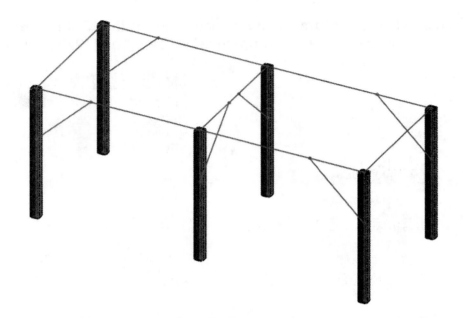

When selecting sketch lines to add Structural Members to a group, remember that the lines in group can be:

    a) Discontinuous <u>parallel</u> segments in the same or different planes, or

    b) Continuous segments connected by endpoints.

 The idea of having groups is to be able to modify its properties in a single operation, like profile to use, orientation, etc.

**352. –** The second group will be the four lines that make the outside perimeter at the top. We won' be able to select the cross member in the middle because it's not connected to an endpoint.

**353.** – Before clicking OK, we need to make a few modifications to how this group will be located, and how the corners will be trimmed. Zoom in a corner (the one with the sketch of the member's profile is a good option, but any one works). For this group we'll use the "**End Miter**" corner treatment. By using this option, all the connecting elements in this group will get this treatment. The different options for corner treatments available are:

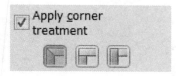

The preview is translucent; these images are the end result for clarity.

 The first distance box after corner treatments is used to specify a gap between the connected segments of the same group, and the second to add a space between one group and the previous. This is usually done to add a space to weld the structural members together.

Also, for "**End Butt**" corner treatments, we can have a simple cut or a coped cut end condition.

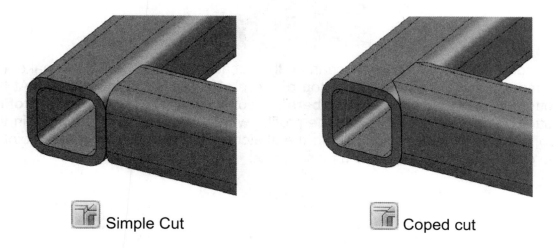

We can change the type of corner treatment individually by clicking in the pink point at the corner of the preview and selecting a different option of corner treatment, including weld gaps.

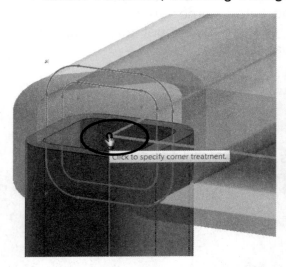 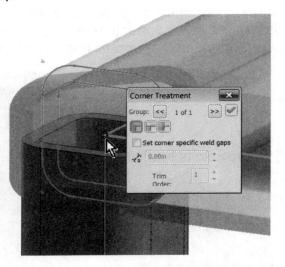

**354. –** By default, when adding new members, the sketch line pierces the profile's origin automatically. If we remember, the conveyor must have a height of 30″; if we don't change it, it will end up being higher than needed by one half the profile.

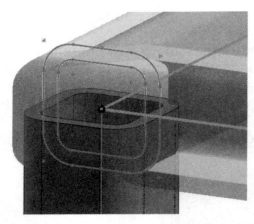

To correct this we have to change the location of the profile to make the element's sketch line pierce the top of the profile instead of the center. At the bottom of the "**Structural Members**" options, click on the "**Locate Profile**" button. The part will zoom into the profile, where we can select the point in the profile's sketch to be Coincident to the sketch line. Any vertex or sketch point in the profile can be selected as a pierce point.

**355.** – Select the top, middle point as indicated; the preview will update the profile's location to the desired position. Click **OK** to add the group and continue. Do not worry about the members intersecting each other; we'll trim them as soon as we finish adding the last group.

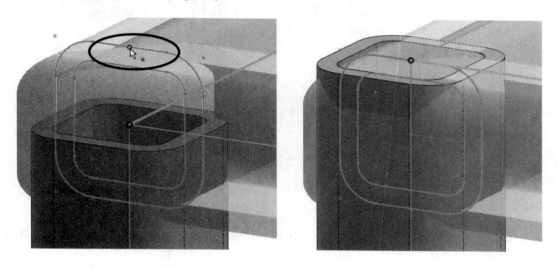

**356.** – For the next group, select the middle line, and change the profile's location as we did in the previous step. Click **OK** to add the next group.

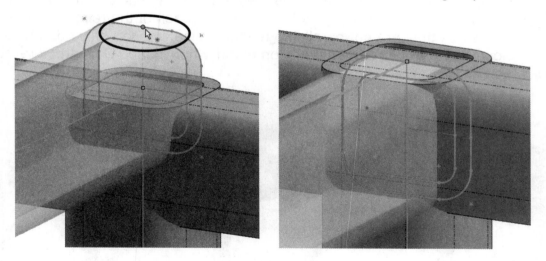

**357.** – For the next group, select two reinforcements (since only two are in the same direction, we can only do two at a time). When we select them, we notice the profiles are not correctly aligned. They are in the centerline, but rotated. To rotate the profile, scroll down to "**Rotation Angle**" and enter "**45**" degrees.

 Other options to orient the profile include selecting a line or edge in the "**Alignment**" selection box and aligning the horizontal or vertical axis. We can also mirror the profile horizontally or vertically if needed.

**358.** – Repeat the same process with the reinforcements on the other side (another group of two) and finally make a group for each of the reinforcements in the center; since they are not parallel to anything else, we can only add one at a time. Close the "Structural Member" command when done. Our structure now looks like this:

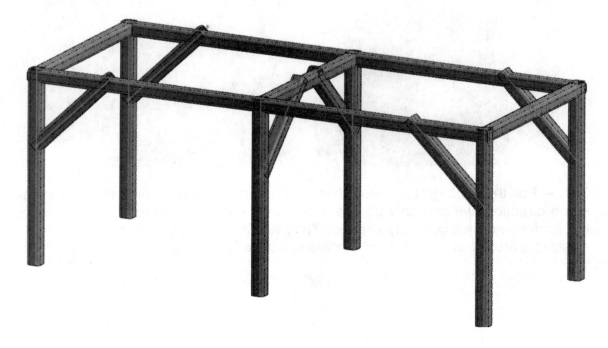

**359.** – Since the structural members are intersecting, the next step is to trim the excess material. From the "**Weldments**" toolbar, select the "**Trim/Extend**" command. We have the option to trim elements with one or more faces/planes, or other bodies. In our example, we'll trim the bodies using a face. Select the "**End Trim**" option to cut the bodies at the selected surface. In the "**Bodies to be Trimmed**" selection box, select two or four elements to trim at a time (we can select all bodies to trim, but the screen will be cluttered with "keep" or "discard" labels).

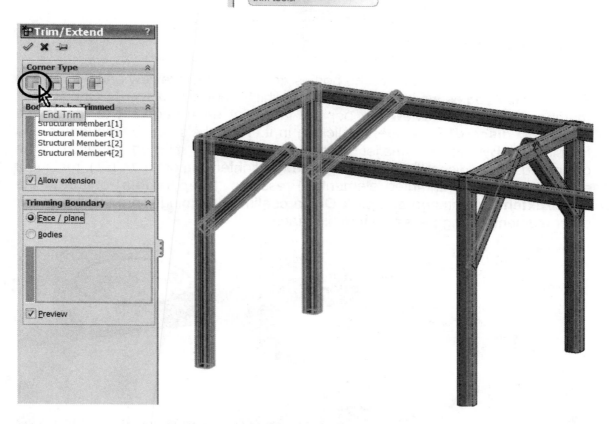

**360.** – In the "**Trimming Boundary**" selection box, select the "**Face/Plane**" option and pick the face under any of the top members to be the trim boundary. Rotate the model to select the correct face.

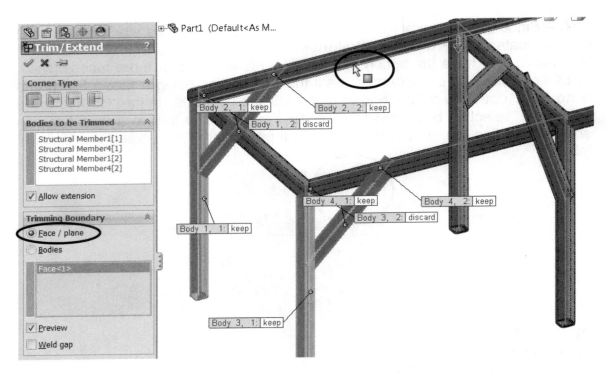

**361. –** After selecting the face, the bodies are 'cut' in the preview and we have to review which bodies we want to keep and which bodies to discard. Check each member being cut. Review the pop up labels of each segment to toggle the **"keep"** or **"discard"** message by clicking in it. The labels can be moved around for clarity. By default, smaller segments are usually marked correctly to be discarded. The "discard" elements preview is lighter (almost invisible), making it easier to identify untrimmed elements. Press the "**Keep visible**" button in the "**Trim/Extend**" command and click **OK** to continue trimming. Trim the top of the other elements using the same trimming face.

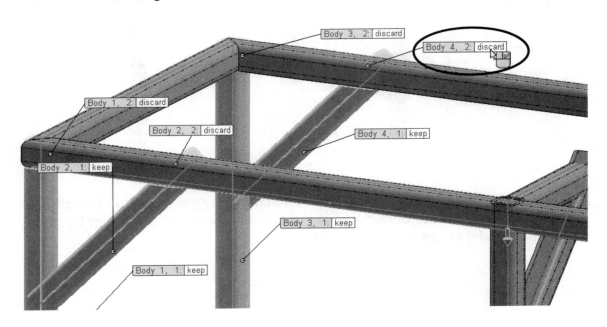

 If we had elected to trim all the legs at the same time, the screen would have been cluttered with "keep/discard" labels.

**362.** – Trim the corner reinforcing elements on both sides and the middle ones using the faces indicated.

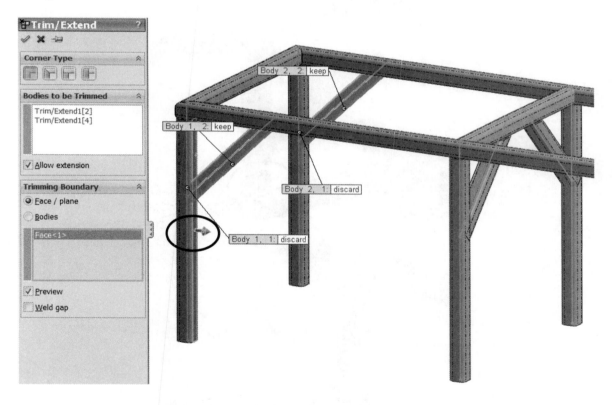

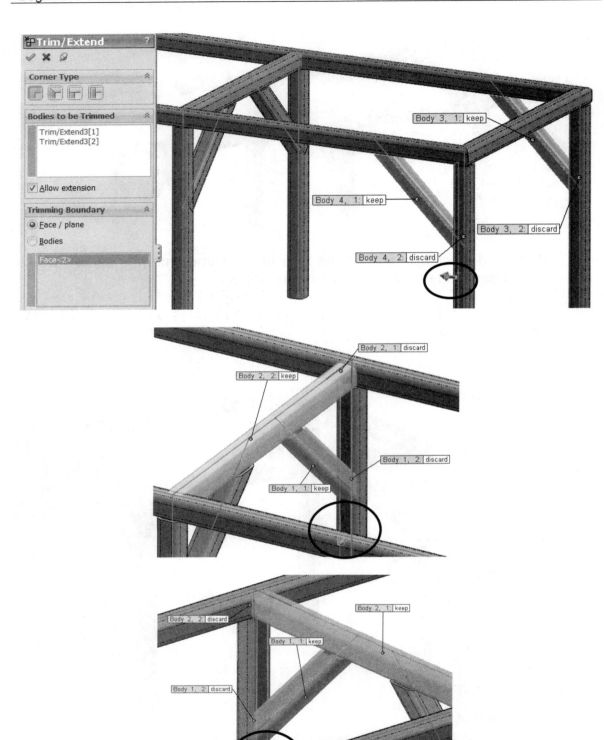

Our part is now completely trimmed and no bodies intersect each other.

**363.** – The next step is to add gussets to our structure. Gussets are steel plates used to add strength and support at the intersections of structural components; they can be either bolted or welded. For our example, we'll add gussets in the corners, and weld beads after that. To add a gusset, click on the "**Gusset**" icon. To add it, we need to define the faces that will be reinforced, their dimensions and location. Zoom in one corner looking at it from the bottom up to select the faces as shown. First, select the two faces indicated in the "**Supporting Faces**" selection box to get a preview.

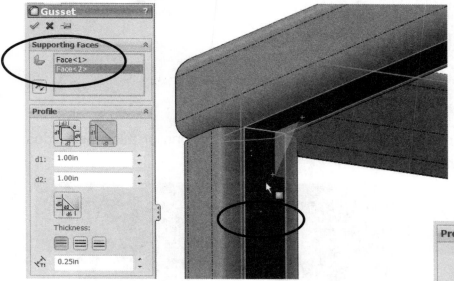

**364.** – We can make polygonal or triangular gussets. In our example we'll use the triangular option, and dimension it 2″ x 2″ (measured from the corner). Polygonal gussets have more dimensions, marked *'d1'* to *'d4'* and *'a1'* (For angle 1).

*'d5'* and *'d6'* are the chamfer's dimensions in the inside corner. A chamfer is usually added to allow space for a weld bead. Make the chamfer 0.5″ x 0.5″. Chamfers can also be defined by one dimension and an angle (*'a2'*).

The gusset's thickness can be added on one side, the other side or both sides. We'll make our gusset 0.25″ thick mid-plane ("**Both Sides**").

Finally the "**Location**" of the gusset can be set on one side of the face, the center, the other side, or offset from any of them. We'll make ours in the center.

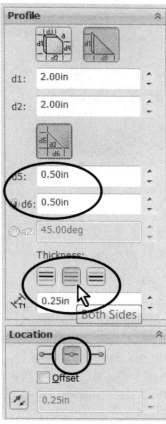

Gusset location options can have all possible combinations of thickness sides, location and even an offset if needed.

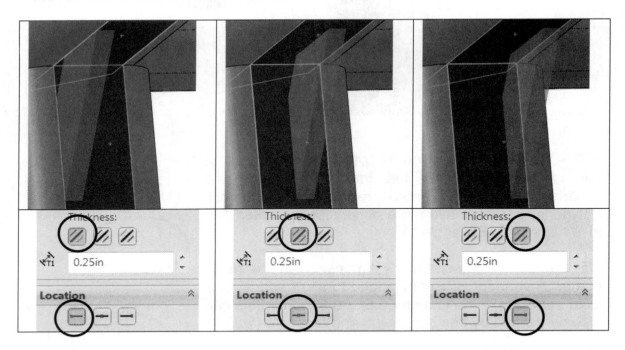

**365. –** Press the "**Keep visible**" icon and add the remaining gussets to the rest of the inside corners that don't have a diagonal member. Click OK to finish when done. SolidWorks remembers the settings, and we only have to select a set of faces and the gusset is automatically positioned, we only click OK to continue to the next one until we are done.

After adding all gussets, our conveyor looks like this (gussets highlighted):

**366.** – Another feature unique to weldments is the "**End Cap**". An end cap will add a cover to close the open end of a structural member. Rotate the part to look at it from below and zoom at the end of one leg. Click on the "**End Cap**" command in the Command-Manager and select the end face of a leg. The thickness will be set to 0.125 inches **inward** (because we want to maintain the 30 inches height). The "**Offset**" option refers to the distance measured from the edge of the end cap to the edge of the structural member. It can be set using a ratio of the structural member's thickness or a specified distance turning off the "**Use thickness ratio**". Set the offset ratio to **0.5** (half the structural element's thickness), and activate the option "**Chamfer corners**" with a value of **0.125"**.

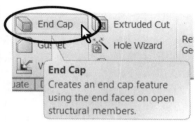

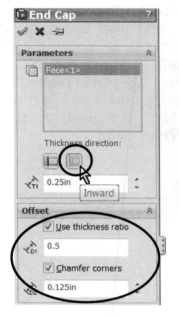

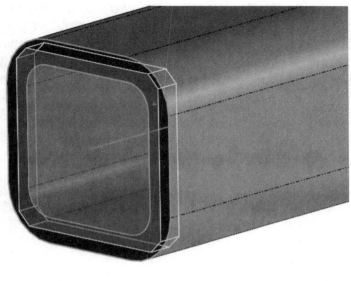

A note about "Thickness direction:" If we make the end cap going 'Outward', its thickness will be added to the length of the structural member. If we make it 'Inward', the structural member will be shortened by the end cap''s thickness, as in this case.

Select the six legs' end faces to add all end caps with one command (a selection filter for faces will be automatically activated while we finish the command).

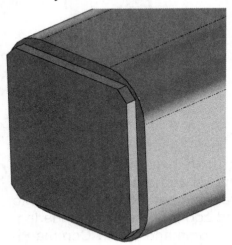

 An important detail to keep in mind when working with weldments is that the "Merge result" option in all features that add material is turned 'Off' by default. If we add an extrusion (any type) and want it to be merged to one or more bodies, we have to turn the "Merge result" option 'On'.

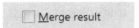

**367.** – To complete our structure, we'll add weld beads and the correct welding annotations. SolidWorks 2011 adds a new way to add weld beads using a simplified weld bead that is easier to use, lightweight and removes certain limitations of previous versions, like allowing bodies with gaps and the capability to handle all types of geometry. It also adds new features like weld properties in drawings, association of weld beads to welding symbols, a new weld folder and a user-definable weld path. Select the "**Weld Bead**" command from the Weldments toolbar or the menu "**Insert, Weldments, Weld Bead**".

**368. –** Zoom in one corner, looking at it from the bottom. There are two ways to add a weld bead: selecting faces or using the Smart Weld Selection Tool. First, select the two faces indicated in the inside corner; notice the preview with the intersection of the faces to be welded. Set the weld bead size to **0.25"**.

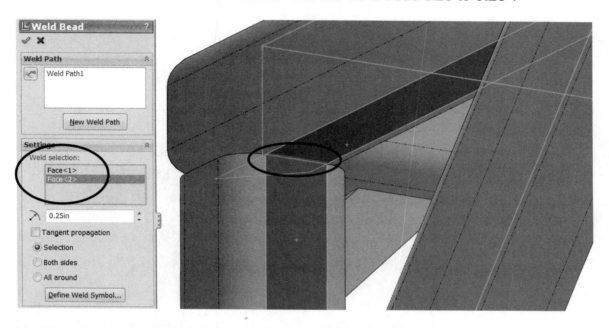

In this case we want the weld to go around the sides, so we'll turn on the "Tangent Propagation" option. Notice the preview goes around the tangency where both bodies touch. It doesn't go all the way around because the body on top is trimmed with a miter cut.

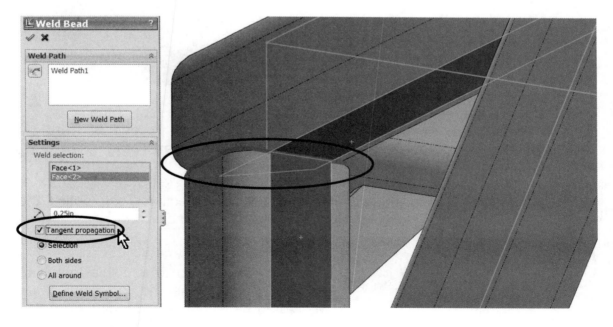

**369.** – To add the rest of the weld bead, select the "**New Weld Path**" button, rotate the part, and select the faces on the other side as indicated. Notice the weld bead settings remain the same. If we continue adding all the required weld beads that share the same settings, they will be grouped together.

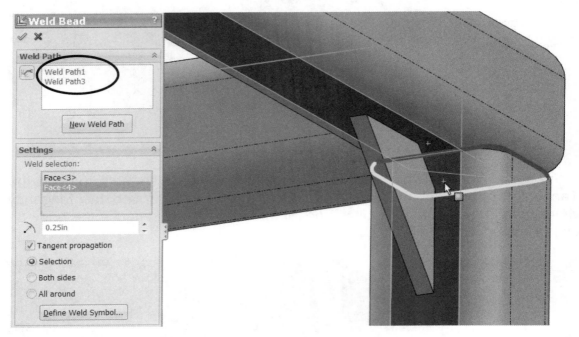

**370.** – Click in the "**New Weld Path**" to continue adding the rest of the weld beads. Move to the opposite corner to continue. Instead of selecting faces manually, we'll use the **Smart Weld Selection Tool**.

Activate the Smart Weld Selection Tool; notice the mouse pointer changes to a pencil icon.

What we need to do to use this tool is to click-and-drag across the intersection we wish to add a weld bead to, going from one face to the other.

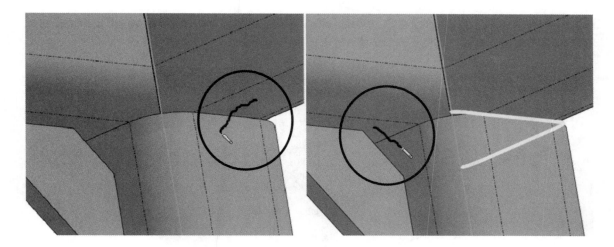

Notice that as we make a new selection, a new 'Weld Path' is automatically added to the list.

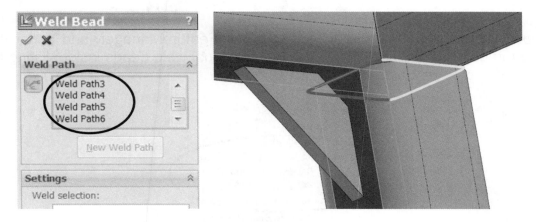

**371.** – Add the rest of the weld beads between all structural members and click OK to finish. We'll add weld beads to the gussets next.

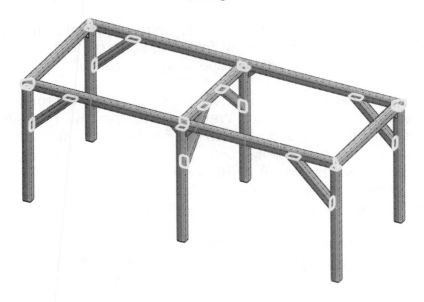

**372.** – Right after finishing the 'Weld Beads', the corresponding weld beads and annotations are added to the weldment.

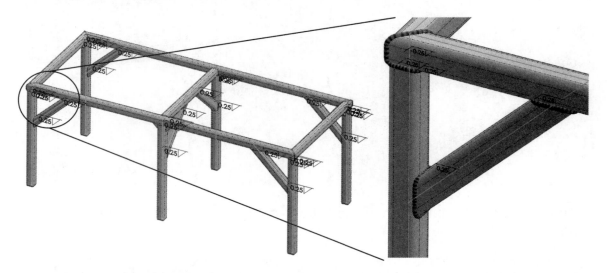

A new "**Weld Folder**" has been added to the FeatureManager, and under it is listed the new '0.25in Fillet Weld' with the individual weld beads inside, listing the length of each weld bead.

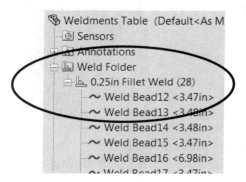

 To turn off the cosmetic weld beads and/or the weld annotations, right mouse click in the "Annotations" folder and turn off "Display Annotations"; or in the "Weld Folder", select "Hide Cosmetic Welds".

**373.** – To add the weld beads to the gussets, we'll use a different option. Select the "**Weld Bead**" command from the Weldments toolbar and zoom in one of the gussets (annotations have been turned off for clarity). Select the two faces indicated to weld the gusset to the structural element; make the bead size **0.125″** and in this case select the option "**Both sides**" under "**Settings**". Notice a new weld bead is added to the opposite side of the gusset, saving us time (similarly, if we select "**All around**", the entire loop is selected).

 When adding weld beads using the Smart Weld Selection Tool, click and drag <u>starting in an unselected face</u>; otherwise it will get unselected and you'll have to re-select again to add a weld bead.

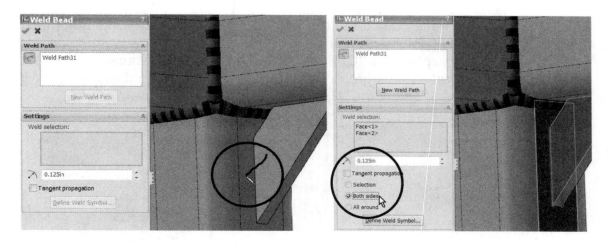

In these pictures it's easier to see the reason why we added the chamfer in the gusset is to allow the weld bead to pass through it.

 Weld Bead options include defining a starting offset and bead length, and an intermittent (optionally staggered) weld bead.

**374.** – Add weld beads to all the gussets using the same settings as before and click OK to finish.

 Every time weld beads are added, the part's annotations are displayed again. Turn them off to avoid a busy screen.

**375.** – Now that we have completed the welded structure, SolidWorks automates the creation of the 'cut list' by grouping structural members of the same type and size together. If we expand the "**Cut list**" folder in the FeatureManager, we'll see a long list of solid bodies. To group them together, make a right mouse click in the "**Cut list**" folder and select the "**Update**" option from the pop-up menu.

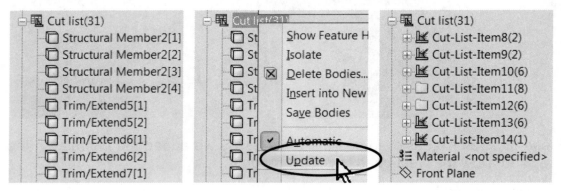

If desired, the "Cut-List-Item" folders can be reordered; the reason to do this is because this is the order in which they will be listed when we import the cut list into the drawing. A good idea is to reorder the elements by type and size, and leave the gussets and end caps at the end. To reorder the items, simply drag-and-drop them up or down as needed.

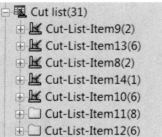

**376.** – Save the part as *Weldments Table* and make a new drawing with an isometric view; shaded with edges and tangent edges removed will work fine for this example. Import the model dimensions to this view.

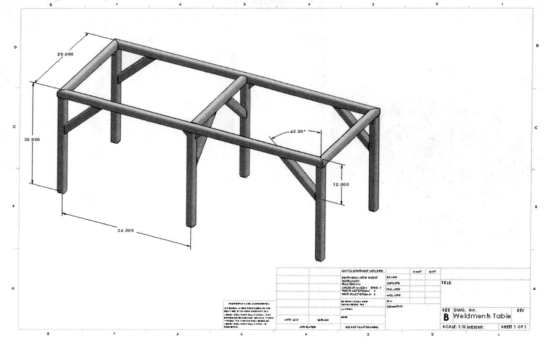

**377. –** Select the view, and from the right mouse click menu, select "**Tables, Weldment Cut List**", or from the menu "**Insert, Tables, Weldment Cut List**". Accept the defaults for the table and click OK. Locate it in the upper right corner. Adjust the view's scale if needed.

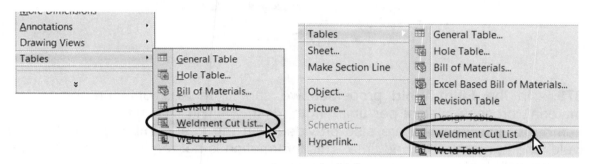

| ITEM NO. | QTY. | DESCRIPTION | LENGTH |
|----------|------|-------------|--------|
| 1 | 2 | TUBE, SQUARE 2.00 X 2.00 X .25 | 74 |
| 2 | 6 | TUBE, SQUARE 2.00 X 2.00 X .25 | 27.75 |
| 3 | 2 | TUBE, SQUARE 2.00 X 2.00 X .25 | 30 |
| 4 | 1 | TUBE, SQUARE 2.00 X 2.00 X .25 | 26 |
| 5 | 6 | TUBE, SQUARE 2.00 X 2.00 X .25 | 14.73 |
| 6 | 8 | | |
| 7 | 6 | | |

The empty rows in the list correspond to the gussets and end caps. To fill in the correct information in the description, go back to the part file; in the "**Cut list**" folder select the corresponding folder with a right mouse click and select "**Properties**". In the "**Cut List Summary**" tab we can see all the properties for each group of elements, or we can select the "**Properties Summary**" tab to see a list of properties with the values of each group. Fill in the appropriate descriptions for the groups missing one. Click OK to complete.

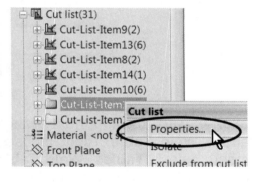

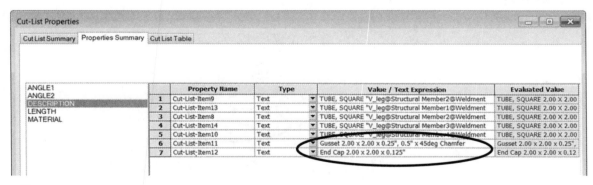

You *may* have to fill in the "MATERIAL" property of all cut list items for the table to properly update in the drawing.

**378.** – While in the part, expand the "**Weld Folder**"; right mouse click in each of the "Fillet Weld" items and select "Properties" from the pop-up menu.

**379.** – In the **Fillet Weld** properties we can fill in additional properties like material, process, weight per unit length, cost, welding time per unit length and number of passes. We are also provided with the total number of welds, total weld length, mass, cost and time. This information is not required, but is useful if we add weld tables to our weldment drawing.

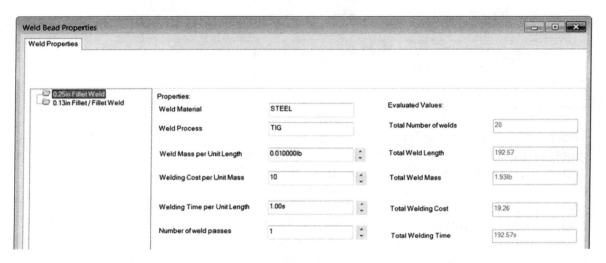

**380.** – Switch back to the drawing. Our cut list will be updated and now we can add a **Weld Table**. Right mouse click in the isometric view; from the pop-up menu, select "**Tables, Weld Table**". Turn on the "**Combine same weld type**" option. Click OK and locate the table in the drawing. Change the table's font and size as needed.

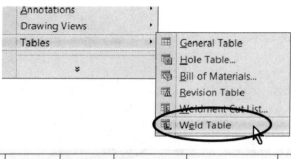

| ITEM NO. | WELD SIZE | SYMBOL | WELD LENGTH | WELD MATERIAL | QTY. |
|---|---|---|---|---|---|
| 1 | 0.25 | △ | 192.56 | STEEL | 1 |
| 2 | 0.13 | △ | 96 | STEEL | 1 |

**381.** – Add the identification balloons to identify each structural element using the "**Auto Balloon**" function. Select the "**AutoBalloon**" command from the Annotation toolbar, or the menu "**Insert, Annotations, Auto Balloons**". In the "Balloon Layout" options, select "**Balloon Faces**" to attach balloons to the structural members' faces. Under "Balloon Settings" select the "**Circular Split Line**" style, and pick "**Quantity**" in the "**Lower text**" selection list. Arrange the balloons as needed.

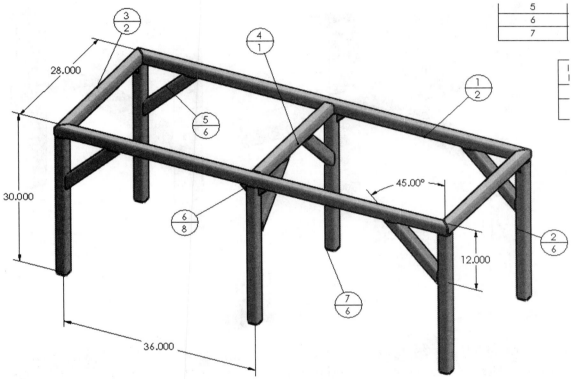

In the "**Balloon text**" or "**Lower text**" selection lists, we have the option to select "**Custom Properties**"; if we do, a new selection list is revealed where we can select any property including cut list properties.

**382. –** To identify the welds, select the "**Weld Symbol**" command from the Annotation toolbar or the menu "**Insert, Annotations, Weld Symbol**".

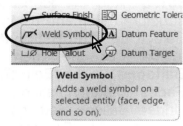

In the Weld Symbol properties window we can add all the necessary specifications for the welding instruction sheet, or we can click in the Weld Beads and the symbol is automatically filled. Click to select a weld bead, locate the symbol in the sheet and repeat as needed.

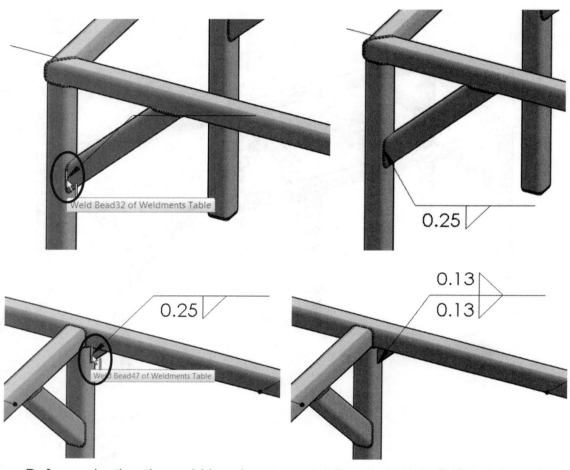

Before selecting the weld bead          After the weld bead is selected

 When adding more Weld Symbols, the last type used is remembered. When a different weld bead is selected, the symbol is updated to reflect the currently selected bead. Close the Weld Symbol properties window when done.

**383.** – Save the drawing and close.

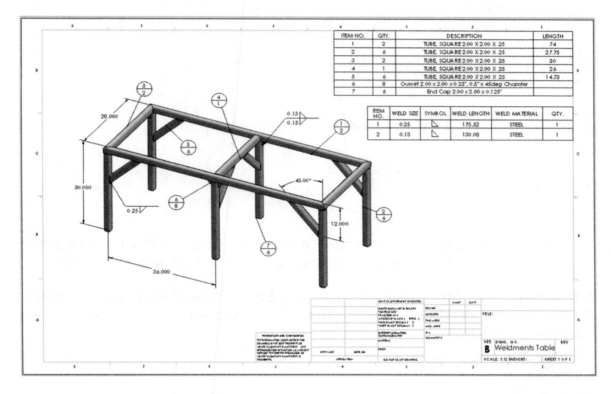

**384.** – To review more weldments options, make the following (2D) sketch in the Top plane. The center of the arc is coincident to the origin; this will save us from making an auxiliary plane for the next step. We can only use circular arcs and straight lines for weldments. Exit the sketch when finished.

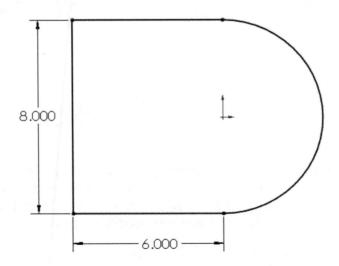

**385.** – Switch to an isometric view; add the following sketch in the Right plane and exit when done.

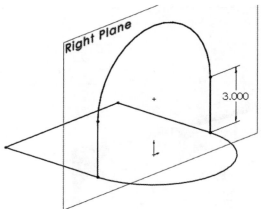

 As an alternative (or challenge), make a 3D sketch with all the lines and exit when done. It makes no difference when we work with weldments.

**386.** – Select the "**Structural Member**" icon from the Weldments toolbar. Select the "ansi inch" standard, "pipe" type and "0.5 sch 40" size. Pick the lines indicated in the preview.

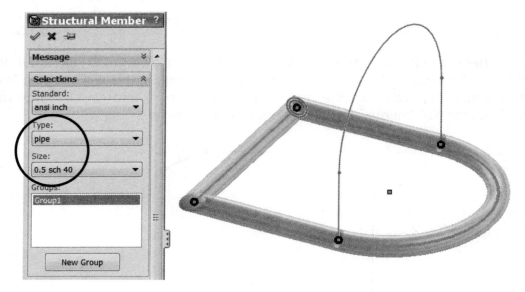

For "**Corner treatment**" instead of applying a global option, we'll manually select the treatment for each connection. When using circular arcs in the structure, we have the option to either merge the arc member to the adjacent segment globally by checking the option "**Merge arc segment bodies**", or on an individual basis.

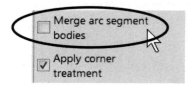

**387. –** Click on the point in the corner and select the following corner treatments:

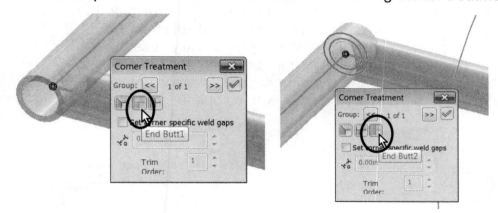

💡 The option "**Set corner specific weld gaps**" will add the indicated gap between the connecting elements for welding.

**388. –** In the case of the joint between a straight line and an arc, changing the corner treatment gives us the option to merge the segments into a single element. In our example we'll leave this option unchecked.

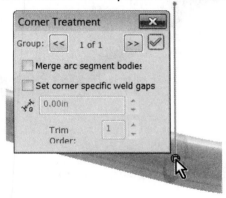

**389. –** Click OK and add the rest of the structural elements with the same settings.  Leave the default corner treatment as "**Miter**".  Click OK to complete. Save the part as *Welded Frame*.

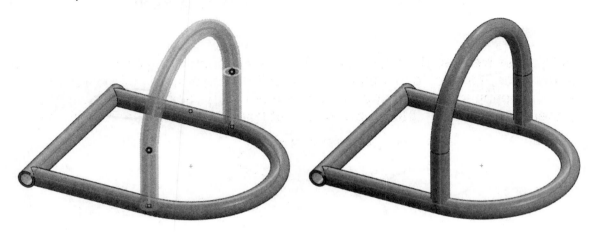

**390. –** Now select the "**Trim/Extend**" command to trim overlapping elements. Select the "**End Trim**" corner type option. Select the vertical elements in the "**Bodies to be Trimmed**" selection box. In "**Trimming Boundary**" use the option "**Bodies**" and select the straight and curved members. Make sure the trimmed segments are correctly marked "**keep**" or "**discard**". Click OK to complete.

**Trim/Extend**
Trims or extends structural members using adjoining structural members as the trim tools.

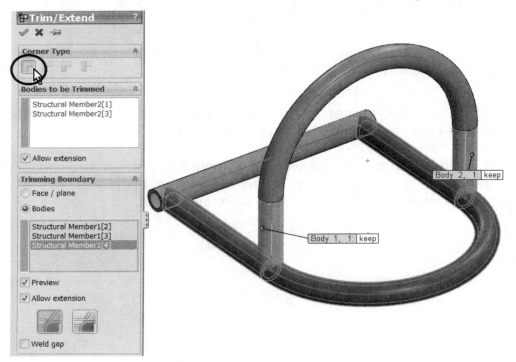

 After the structural members are completed we can hide the sketch(s) used.

**391. –** Right mouse click in the "**Cut list**" folder and select "**Update**" from the menu to group elements together. Remember that we can preview the cut list by selecting "**Properties**" from the cut list item's right mouse menu.

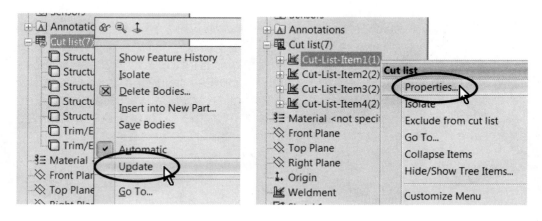

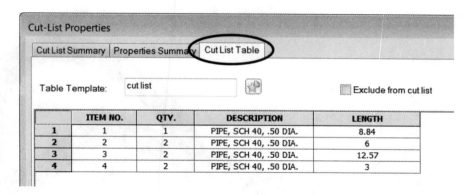

**392.** – When working with multi body parts (like weldments), we can save each body to a new part file and make a new assembly with those parts at the same time. To save <u>a single body</u> as a new part, it can be selected from the "Cut-List-Item" folder or the graphics area with the right mouse button and select "**Insert into new part…**" from the pop-up menu. But….

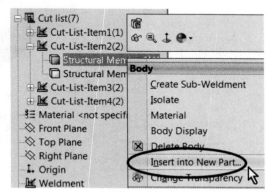

…what we want to do is to save <u>all of the bodies</u>, each to a part, *and* make an assembly at the same time using those parts. Right mouse click in the "**Cut list**" folder and select "**Save Bodies**".

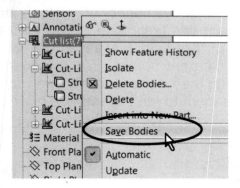

**393.** – In the "**Save Bodies**" command, we can select one or more bodies to save as a part. In our example we'll name them 'Body 1' to 'Body 7' by clicking in the label attached to each body or double-clicking in the row for each body. The option "**Consume cut bodies**" removes the bodies from the part after saving to an external file. We'll leave this option unchecked. Since we also want to make a new assembly, select the "**Browse…**" button in the "**Create Assembly**" option box and name it *Welded Frame Assembly*. Click OK to finish.

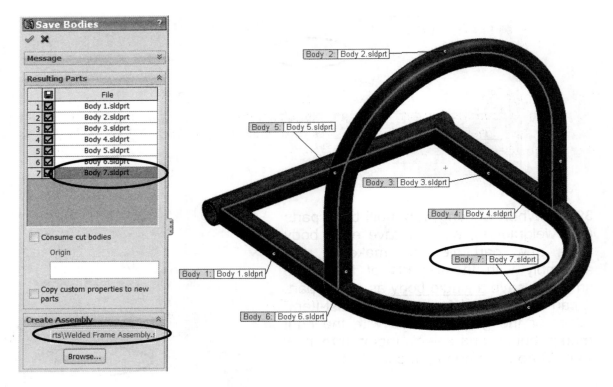

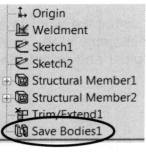

**394.** – A new feature called "**Save Bodies**" is added to the FeatureManager; a new part file is generated for each body saved as well as the new assembly which is already open. Go to the menu "**Window**" and switch to the new assembly just made. An inconvenience of making an assembly from bodies using this technique is that all the parts will be automatically "fixed" in the assembly, and identical parts are given different names. We could skip duplicate parts when saving the bodies, but then we have to manually add and mate them to the assembly. Your choice.

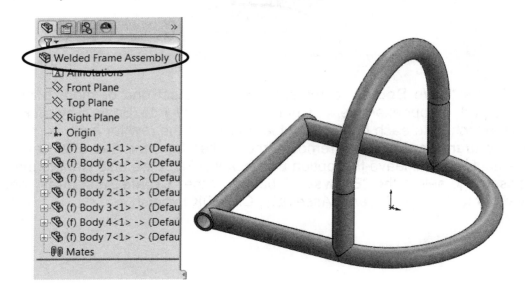

The parts have external references to the original welded part. In this case, the reference status is "In context" because the welded part is open and loaded in memory.

**395.** – Opening one of the assembly parts shows the only feature is a saved body from a multi body part, listed as "**Stock-*part-name***". From this point on, we can add more features to a part if needed, and these changes will be reflected in the assembly, but not in the original multi body part (weldment part in this case).

 If we add a feature to the welded <u>multi body part</u>, like a cut across multiple bodies, the changes will be propagated to the saved parts <u>only</u> if the feature is added BEFORE the "**Save Bodies**" feature.

**Notes:**

## *Structural Member Libraries*

A word about structural profile members: SolidWorks includes a small number of profiles pre-loaded in the "**Structural Member**" library. To add more profiles we have to make a new part, draw the desired profile and save the sketch as a library feature part in the folder defined for structural members.

**396.** – Make the following sketch in a new part. We can use any plane. Units are in millimeters (mm). Don't forget the sketch points in the middle of each side; they can be used as pierce points when we locate the profile in a weldment. Exit the sketch when done.

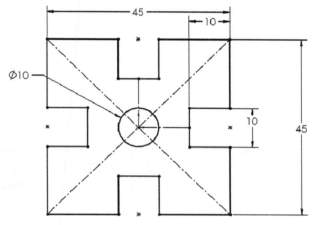

**397.** – Pre-select the sketch in the FeatureManager and save the file as a Library Feature Part (Lib Feat Part *.sldlfp). The default folder for weldments profiles is "*<SW_Install_Folder>*\**data**\**weldment profiles**". Here we can select a Standard and Type folder to save our library, or create our own. Save the library as "**45 x 45**" in the folder "*<SW_Install_Folder>*\data\weldment profiles\iso\square tube". Now this profile is available for structural members.

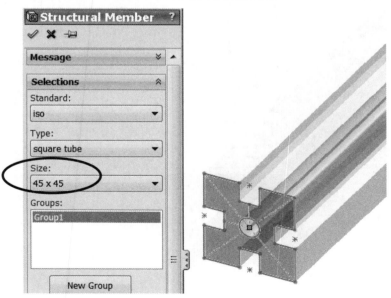

**398.** – To add more weldments profile library folders, go to the menu "**Tools, Options**". Under the System Options tab, select "**File Locations**" and pick "**Weldment Profiles**" from the drop down list. The folders we add will be listed under "Standard" in the Structural Members command.

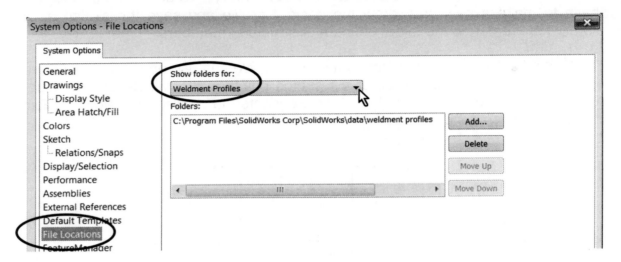

 SolidWorks Toolbox has a considerably larger list of profiles, but unfortunately they cannot be used directly in weldments. They would have to be converted to library feature parts first, following the procedure just described.

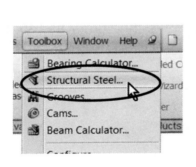

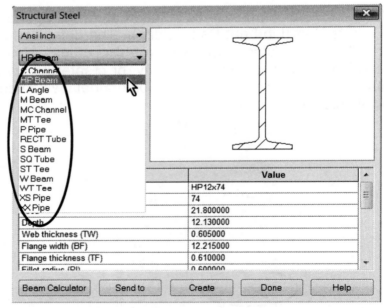

**Review and Questions:**

a) Name three geometric relations available in a 3D sketch that are not available in a 2D sketch.

b) Describe how to create a Derived sketch.

c) What is the difference between using a 2D or a 3D sketch for weldments?

d) Name the conditions to be able to select multiple sketch segments at the same time for a structural member group.

e) Can multiple gussets and end caps be added at the same time?

f) How can we generate a cut list to include the structural member's type, length and cut angles?

g) If welded part bodies are saved to an assembly, are identical bodies saved as one file or multiple files?

**Answers:**
a - Along X, Y, Z, On-Plane, Normal, ParallelYZ, ParallelZX.
b - Pre-select the sketch to derive and the plane/face to place the derived sketch and click in the menu "Insert, Derived sketch".
c - None. They both work the same.
d - They must be parallel or continuous connected by an endpoint.
e - Gusset's have to be added one at a time, end caps can be added multiple at a time.
f - Right mouse click in the "Cut list" folder and select "Update". Then import the Cut List table to a drawing.
g - Each body, even identical ones, are each saved to a different file always.

**Notes:**

# Surfacing and Mold Tools
## Surface Modeling

So far we have been working with single and multi body solid parts, and now we'll start working also with surfaces. By including surfaces in our models, we are able to create increasingly complex designs that would otherwise be very difficult to model with solids. Working with both solids and surfaces is called 'hybrid modeling', as we incorporate both solid and surface bodies in the same model. When we work in a hybrid model, the surfaces are usually used as support geometry, as stopping or trimming boundaries for solids and/or other surfaces, etc.

Background and a little bit of history:  The first computer models used for design (over 40 years ago) were wireframe models capable of defining the edges of a part and had severe limitations, especially when it came to defining a three dimensional surface, as it could only be approximated using a mesh of lines with little detail.  Think of a wireframe model as a 'stick figure'. A wireframe model is basically what we are able to do now with a 3D sketch – just lines.

Some years later, surface models were developed that allowed more definition of a component, including curved faces and were a huge improvement over the wireframe models, but still had limitations when it came to calculate a part's volume, weight, etc.  When we talk about a surface model, think of a parade's floating balloon.  It has the surfaces (fabric) and the wireframe (stitches), and is essentially empty.  Similarly, it's safe to say that a surface model *may* have imperfections, like faces not matching correctly creating gaps or overlapping faces (think of the balloon with an opening at a corner).  This would create a problem if we wanted to calculate volume, weight, etc., or use it for manufacturing.

Later, in the 1980's (give or take a few years…), solid models became available, but (just like surface modelers) were difficult to use, required special training and were available in high end workstations.  A design station's cost, complete with hardware and software, would be in the tens of thousands of dollars, affordable only by big corporations or government agencies. Design tools were greatly improved, producing better results faster, and making it easier to integrate with computer numerical controlled (CNC) manufacturing.

Some years later (circa 1990's), solid modelers became available in the Windows operating system, making them considerably more affordable to mainstream designers, and being native Windows applications made them easier to learn and use. These solid modelers incorporate all the advantages surface and solid models offer, including better integration with manufacturing, analysis, animation and many other downstream applications.

At present, with the advances in technology making computers faster than ever before (and no limit in sight), now we are able to take advantage of it and create bigger, ever more complex designs in record time, helping us bring product designs faster to market.

A word about hybrid modeling: It is not uncommon to see that dedicated surface modelers can generate superior and better looking surfaces for automotive, aerospace and consumer product design than many solid modelers (like SolidWorks), and they can also make changes easier and faster maintaining the intended shape. This makes creating highly complex surfaces easier. With that said, it is common in these industries to generate the complex surfaces in one software package and then import them into solid modelers to complete the rest of the design process.

When we talk about surface modeling, we are referring to creating models using mainly surfaces, or the 'skins' of parts, and afterwards converting them into a solid or using them to build solids. The tools available include almost all the solid features like extruded, revolved, swept and lofted surface…

plus a few more specific to surface modeling, most of which will be covered in this book.

To start surface modeling, we'll make a hair dryer using a few simple surfaces and then we'll convert them into a solid model. After finishing, we'll split the model to make a file for each of the different parts to practice and learn more about multi body parts.

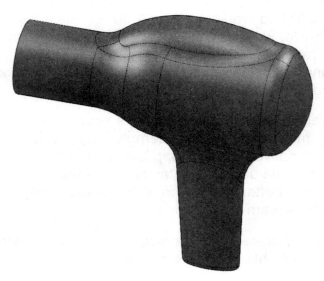

If the Surfaces toolbar is not visible, activate it by right mouse clicking in a CommandManager's tab, and select "**Surfaces**", and/or the menu "**View, Toolbars, Surfaces**".

**399.** – To save time and focus on the surfacing functionality, download the file *Hair Drier.sldprt* from www.mechanicad.com/download.html and open it. It has a number of sketches and planes already made.

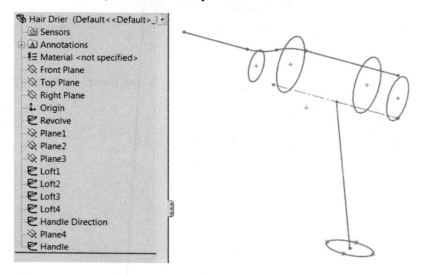

**400.** – The first feature will be a revolved surface. Select the sketch named *Revolve* in the FeatureManager and click on the "**Revolved Surface**" command, or menu "**Insert, Surface, Revolve**". The sketch's centerline is automatically selected.

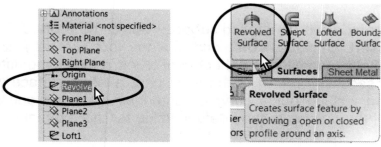

The revolved surface will be made 360 degrees. Click OK to complete it.

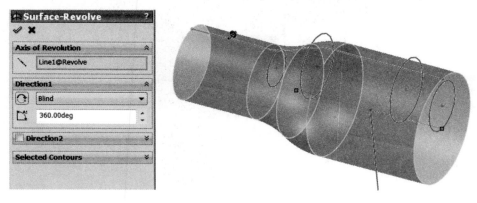

As opposed to when we work with solids, when the first surface body is created, a "**Surface Bodies**" folder is added to the FeatureManager, and it works like the multi body solids.

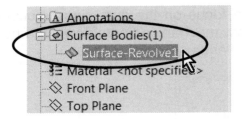

The 'Surface-Revolve1' we just made is only a surface. It has no thickness, volume or mass; it's only a surface.

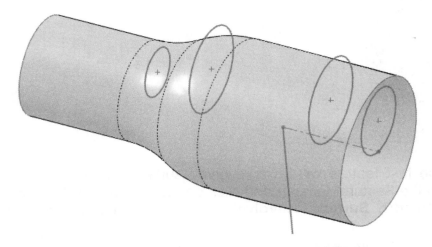

**401. –** The next feature will be a lofted surface. Select the "**Lofted Surface**" icon or the menu "**Insert, Surface, Loft**", and pick the four sketches named 'Loft1' through 'Loft4'. Select them left to right or right to left, it makes no difference; just pick them in consecutive order. For the most part, a lofted surface works like a solid loft; we can include guide curves, centerline, start and end constraints. Leave the rest of the options to their default value for this example and click OK to complete it.

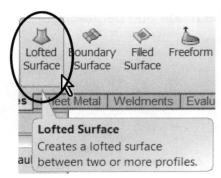

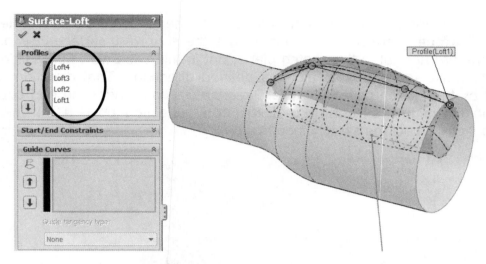

Now we have two surface bodies. Note that surfaces do not 'merge' automatically as solids do; they simply intersect each other but remain separate bodies.

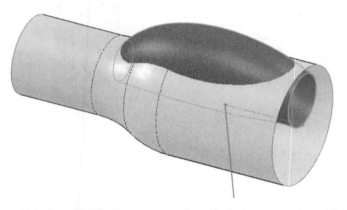

 The main difference between a lofted surface and a solid body loft is that in a lofted surface we can use open *or* closed sketches, curves, edges, etc., to create irregular, complex surfaces.

**402.** – The next feature will be the handle. We'll make an extruded surface with a draft along a defined direction. Select the sketch named 'Handle' in the FeatureManager and click in the "**Extruded Surface**" icon, or the menu "**Insert, Surface, Extrude**".

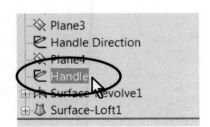

The end condition for the extrusion will be up to the revolved surface. Select the "**Up to Surface**" end condition and select the revolved surface. By default, extrusions are normal to the sketch plane, but in this case we'll use a little used option to make the extrusion along a defined direction. That direction will be defined by the sketch called *'Handle Direction'*. Right under the end condition selection list is the "**Direction of Extrusion**" selection box. Click inside to activate it and select the sketch line shown.

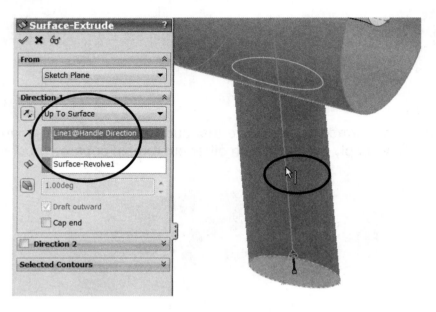

 The "**Direction of Extrusion**" option is also available for extruded boss and cuts in solid bodies.

**403. –** Another option we'll use in the extrusion is the option to add a draft as we extrude. Adding a draft makes the body (surface or solid) grow out or shrink with a defined angle. To turn the draft option on, click in the "**Draft On/Off**" icon; the angle box will be activated as well as the "**Draft outward**" checkbox. For our example, type an angle of **3 degrees**, and check the "**Draft outward**" checkbox.

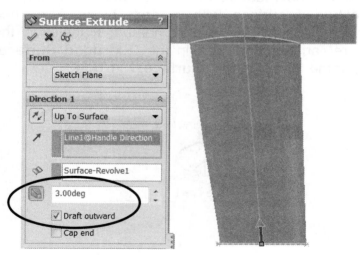

Now we have three surface bodies. You can hide the *Handle Direction* sketch; we will not need it anymore.

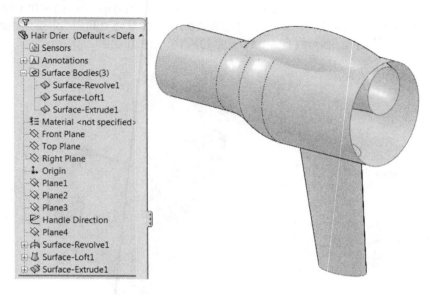

**404.** – The next step is to trim the surfaces to make them match exactly. By trimming the surfaces, we are looking to make all surfaces touch each other at the edges only, with the ultimate goal to form a single, closed, continuous surface that will be converted into a solid body. There are several ways to trim surfaces. We can use other surfaces, planes, or a sketch. First, trim the revolved surface

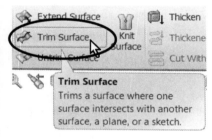

with the handle. Select the "**Trim Surface**" icon from the CommandManager, or the menu "**Insert, Surface, Trim**". Under "**Trim Type**" select "**Standard**"; this means that we'll use a trim tool (Sketch, Plane or Surface) to cut *other* surfaces; add the handle surface under the "**Trim tool**" selection box.

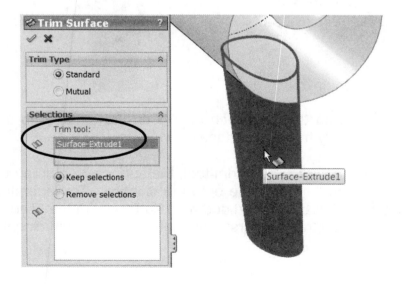

**405.** – Select the "**Keep selections**" option and in the "**pieces to keep**" selection box, pick the revolved surface anywhere but the area where it meets the handle surface, as this is the part we want to keep after trimming. Alternatively, if we use the "**Remove selections**" option, we have to select the elliptical surface inside to remove it. Use either approach and click OK to complete.

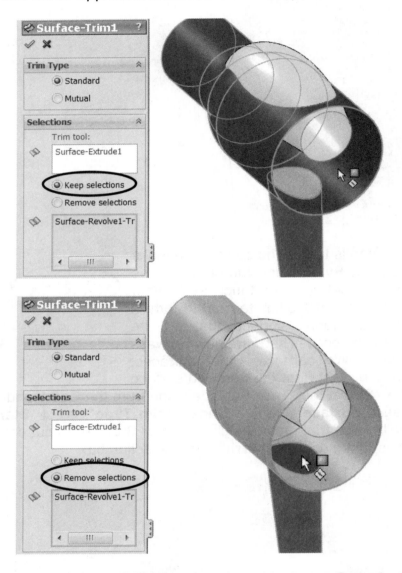

Trimming surfaces using this approach only cuts one surface. In the next step we'll see how to mutually trim two surfaces.

When we use a sketch as a trim tool, the surface is trimmed by projecting the sketch normal to its plane onto the surface. To understand it better, think of the sketch being extruded as a surface with the "Through All" end condition in both directions first, and then used as a trimming surface.

This is the resulting trimmed surface, and we still have three surface bodies.

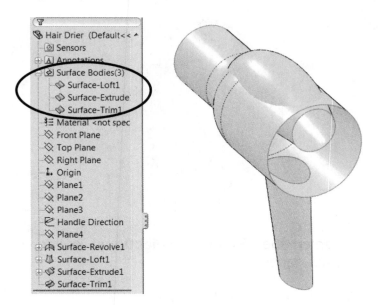

**406. –** For the next feature, we'll trim two surfaces at the same time. This means that we'll select two (or more) surfaces, and they will be cut at their intersection(s); then we can select which bodies we want to keep or delete. Select the "**Trim Surface**" command, and use the option "**Mutual Trim**". In the "**Surfaces**" selection box, pick the revolved and lofted surfaces. With the "**Keep selections**" option chosen, select the outside faces for both of them in the "Keep selections" box. They will change color when selected. Click OK to finish.

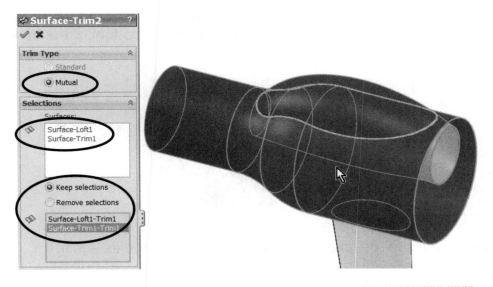

 When we trim two surfaces using the "**Mutual Trim**" option, the resulting surfaces are merged into a single surface.

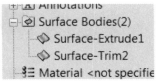

Our resulting model now looks like this:

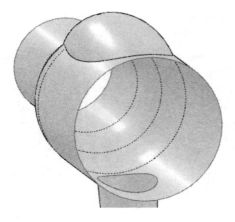

 If we had selected the "**Remove Selections**" option, we would have selected the inside faces.

**407.** – Since we need to make a fully closed surface before we can convert it into a solid, we'll need to close the openings with surfaces. We have a couple of options to close them. For the opening at the bottom of the handle, we'll make a flat surface. Select the "**Planar Surface**" command from the Command-Manager or the menu "**Insert, Surface, Planar**".

To make a planar surface, we can select a set of closed edges or a closed sketch. Turn the model over and select the edge at the bottom of the handle and click OK to finish.

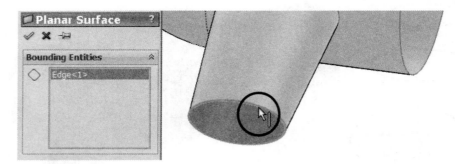

We added a new surface, and now have three surface bodies again.

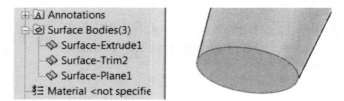

**408.** – For the front of the hair drier we'll use a different command. Select the **"Filled Surface"** command from the Command-Manager or the menu **"Insert, Surface, Fill"**. This command is more flexible than the planar surface; it allows us to use planar or non-planar sketches, edges or curves, make the new surface tangent to adjacent faces, or constrain the surface to one or more curves giving us control over the resulting surface. For the first part of this command

**Filled Surface**
Constructs a surface patch within a boundary defined by existing model edges, sketches, or curves.

we'll select the front open edge of the hair drier in the **"Patch Boundary"** selection box. In the **"Curvature Control"** selection list pick **"Contact"**. Using this option, the new surface is made to only touch the edges selected. Click OK to complete this surface.

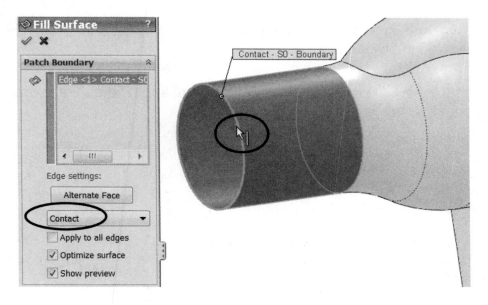

This will be our fourth surface.

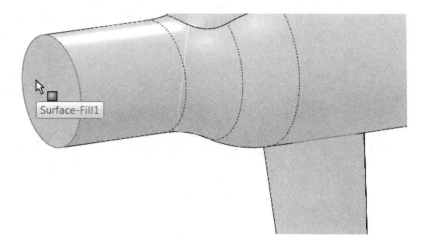

**409.** – The only place left to close is the back of the hair drier. Before we close it, we'll add two sketches that will be used in a **"Filled Surface"** command. Select the Front plane and add the following sketch. Use a **3 Point Arc** or a **Centerpoint Arc**. Be sure to add "Pierce" relations between the endpoints of the arc and the surface edge. Exit the sketch when done.

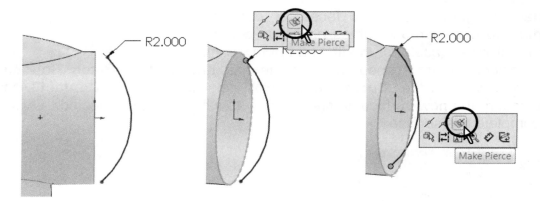

**410.** – Add a new sketch in the Top plane and add "Pierce" relations to both surface edges as we just did.

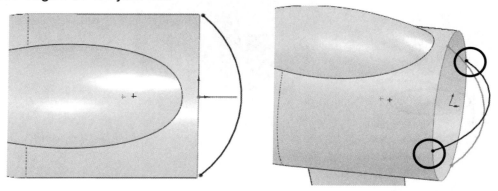

To make the arc coincident to the previous sketch, add a **"Sketch Point"** to its midpoint, and then a **"Pierce"** relation between the point and the previous sketch. Exit the sketch when done.

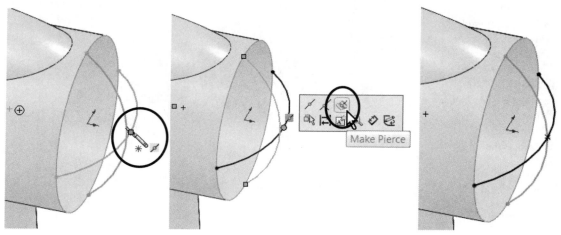

**411.** – Select the "**Filled Surface**" command from the Surfaces toolbar. Select the open edge in the back of the hair drier in the "**Patch Boundary**" selection box, and both of the sketches we just made in the "**Constraint Curves**" selection box. The surface will conform to the curves and match exactly with the edge. Since we are adding constraint curves, changing the curvature control will make no difference in this case. Be sure to check the option "**Merge result**" at the bottom; this way the new surface will be merged with the revolved surface.

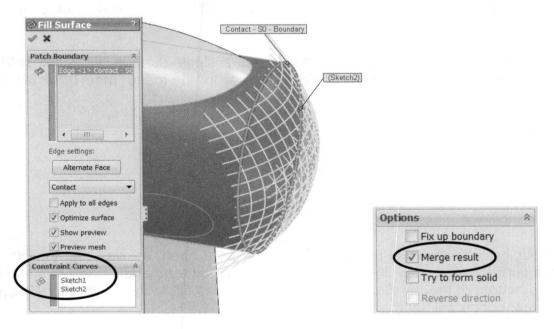

It would now appear that we have a closed surface to convert into a solid, but we need to do one more step before, and that is to merge all four surfaces into a single surface body using the "**Knit Surface**" command.

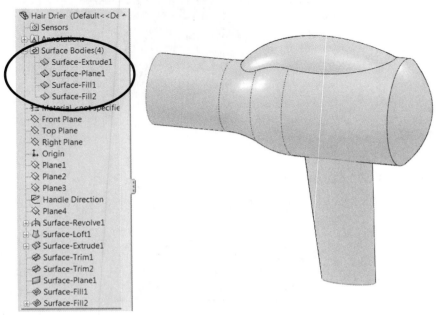

There are basically two ways to convert the surfaces to solid models:
   **a)** We can thicken an open or closed surface, giving the surface a specified thickness.
   **b)** We can convert a closed surface into a solid, but it can only be done with a single, closed surface.

When we refer to a *closed surface*, we are talking about a *water tight* surface. In other words, it has to be a completely enclosed volume, like a balloon.

**412.** – To merge the necessary surfaces into a single surface body, select the "**Knit Surface**" command in the Surfaces toolbar, or the menu "**Insert, Surfaces, Knit**".

For our hair drier we will ultimately leave the front open, so we'll knit the other three surfaces into one. In the graphics area, select the handle, the flat surface at the bottom of the handle, and the second surface fill. In this case, the "**Merge entities**" option will not make any difference.

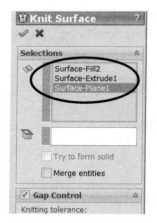
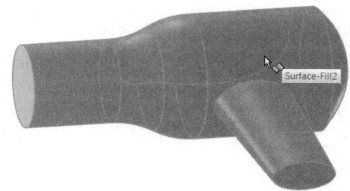

Now the model has two surface bodies.

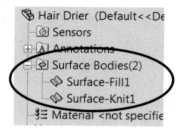

**Things to keep in mind when knitting surfaces:**

- Surfaces must be touching at the edges.
- Surfaces must not overlap.
- Surfaces knitted will be absorbed into a new surface body.
- If the surfaces selected form a closed volume, they can be turned into a solid body that will absorb the surface bodies.

**413.** – Before thickening the surface, we want to add fillets to our hair drier. We can add fillets to a surface similarly to a solid body. Select the "**Fillet**" command and add a 0.25 inch fillet to the back of the drier and a 0.125 inch fillet at the bottom of the handle.

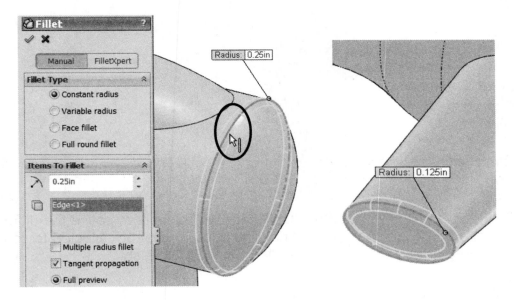

**414.** – For the top of the drier, add a 1 inch fillet. Make sure the "**Tangent propagation**" option is turned on.

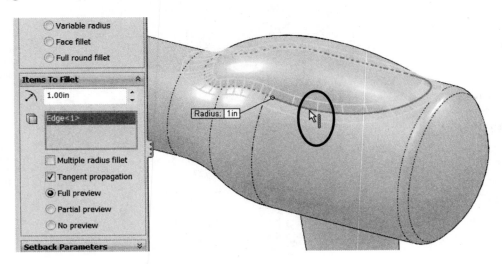

**415. –** For the last fillet, if we use a regular fillet with constant radius, we get a fillet that covers a large surface. Select the "**Fillet**" command again, but in this case select "**Face Fillet**" in the "**Fillet Type**" option and pick the two faces indicated, one in each selection box.  We may need to click on the "**Reverse Face Normal**" option to make the arrows in the faces point to each other in order for the Fillet command to work.  Make the fillet 1″ radius.

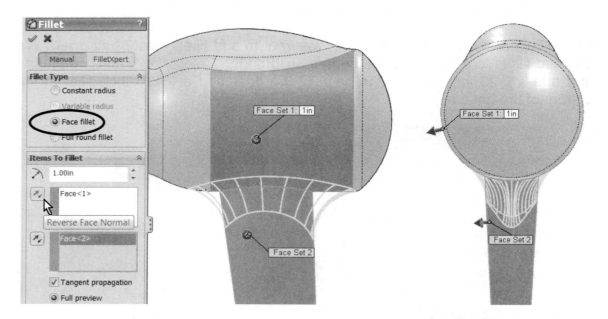

In the "**Fillet Options**", select the "**Constant width**" option; notice the difference in the fillet's preview.  The option "Trim and attach" must be selected to correctly trim and merge the surfaces and the fillet. Click OK to finish.

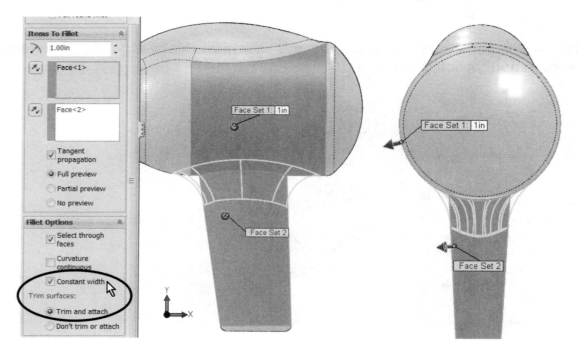

**416.** – Now we are ready to convert the knitted surface body into a solid. Hide the "**Surface-Fill1**" body to see the effect of thickening the surface better. Select it in the graphics area or the FeatureManager and click on the "**Hide**" icon.

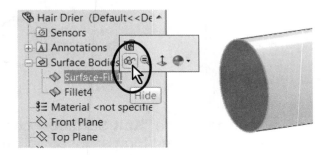

**417.** – The first method to make a solid is to thicken a surface. Select the "**Thicken**" command in the Surfaces toolbar, or the menu "**Insert, Boss/Base, Thicken**". In "**Surfaces to Thicken**", select the surface '*Fillet4*'. When we thicken a surface, we can add material to one side or the other, or 'mid plane' (in both directions). For our example, we'll make the

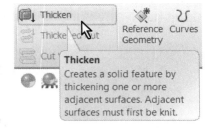

surface 0.1" thick inside to keep our dimensions as outside dimensions. Notice the preview when we change the side to thicken. Click OK to finish.

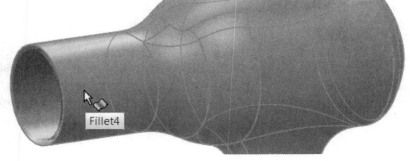

Now we have a solid body.

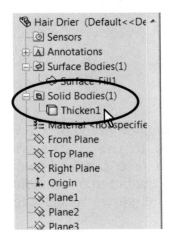

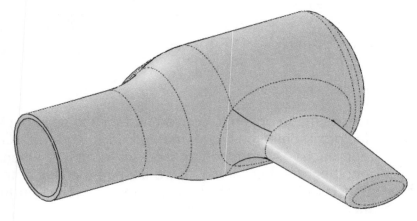

**418.** – To show the second method to convert surfaces to solids, delete the '**Thicken1**' feature, and show the surface that we had hidden before.

**419.** – With the surface visible, select the "**Knit Surfaces**" command, and select both surfaces. When the surfaces knitted form a closed volume, the option "**Try to form a solid**" is enabled. Check this option and click OK to finish. Now we don't have any surface bodies and our model is a solid body.

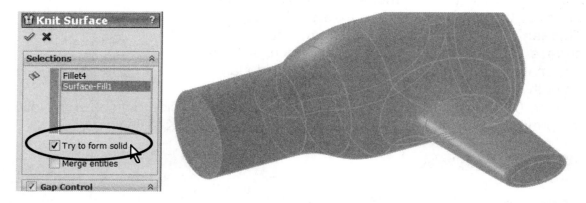

From this point on we can treat our model as a regular solid body; we don't have any surface bodies left and only one solid body. Make a 0.1″ shell feature and remove the front face of the hair drier to complete the model.

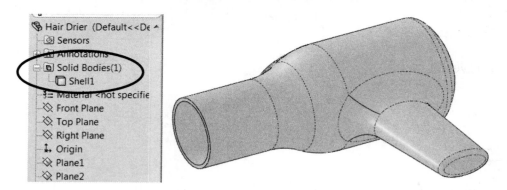

Choosing an option to convert surfaces to solid depends on many different factors; sometimes one method fails and we have to use a different approach. A common reason for errors is when a face overlaps with another after thickening. If we change the fillet at the bottom of the handle to a 0.5 inch radius, the "Thicken" command will fail. In this case we would add the fillets *after* thickening the surfaces.

When we make a design that is made of multiple parts that need to maintain an overall given shape, like our hair drier, we use a technique called *Master Model*, where we start with a part that has the overall shape and size of the complete assembly, and is later split into individual components. The master model has all the features that are common to all the components, usually the outside shape; it is then split, the bodies are saved to individual parts, and each part is finished with the features unique to each one.

The first body we are going to split from the hair drier's master model will become the back cover. To split a solid into multiple bodies, we can use a plane, a surface that crosses the entire model or an open or closed sketch.

**420.** – Add a sketch in the Front plane and draw a line 0.125″ to the left of the origin as shown. When using an open sketch to split a model, the sketch *must* cross the model, and the split will be made by projecting the sketch normal to the sketch plane.

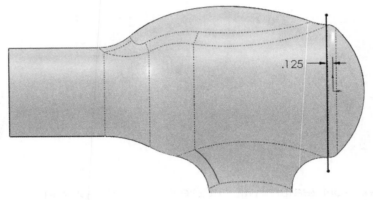

**421.** – Select the "**Split**" command from the menu "**Insert, Features, Split**" while still editing the sketch. The current sketch will be added to the "**Trim Tools**" selection box. Click on the "**Cut Part**" button to divide the body.

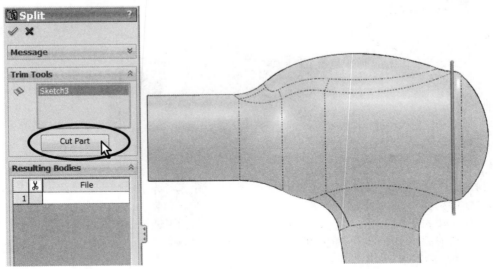

295

**422.** – After cutting the part we have two bodies listed in the "**Resulting Bodies**" list. With this split operation, we'll save the back cover. Select its body and double click in *<None>* to name the new file. Save this body as *Hair Drier Cover*.

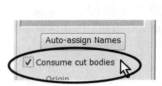

Before finishing the "**Split**" command, turn on the "**Consume cut bodies**" option. By doing this the body we are saving will be deleted from the master file. Click OK to finish.

A "Split" feature is added to the FeatureManager, the master model is now cut, and the cut body is added to the new part file.

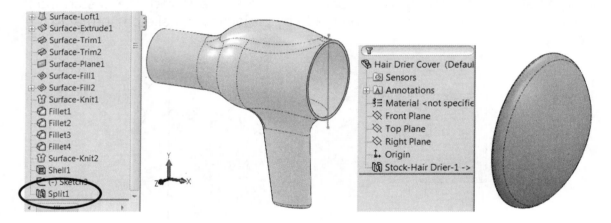

**423.** – The next split feature will cut the remaining body in two parts using the Front plane of the part. Select the "**Split**" command again; select the Front plane in the "**Trim Tools**" selection box and cut the part. Save both bodies and name them *Hair Drier Left* and *Hair Drier Right*. Check the "**Consume cut bodies**" option and click OK to finish.

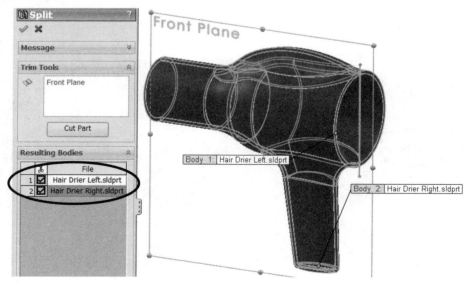

The "Split" command can use multiple surfaces, planes or sketches at the same time.

After completing the second "Split" command, there are no more bodies in our master part and the two bodies have been added to new files. It is not necessary to use the "Consume bodies" option; the split bodies can remain in the master part. We used this option to show the reader its effect.

From this point on we can add more features to each part and then add them to an assembly to finish the design.

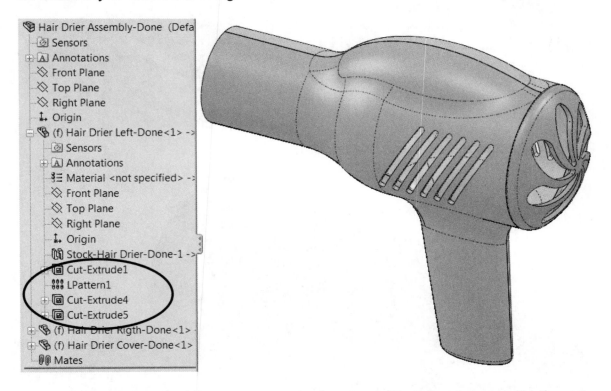

 When *re-assembling* components from a split part, we can add them to the assembly's origin and they will be fixed in the same place they were in the part before they were split.

## CHALLENGE EXERCISE:

Using the hair drier files, add the following features. Select the best place to add them: in the master file before splitting the part *or* in the split bodies (after saving them to a part).

Hint: Features present in more than one part can be added in the master file; features unique to each part can be added in the master file or the split part.

- Add vents to the cover and sides (this is your chance to be creative ☺).
- Add a lip and cut extrusion to assemble the left and right parts, and between both halves and the cover.

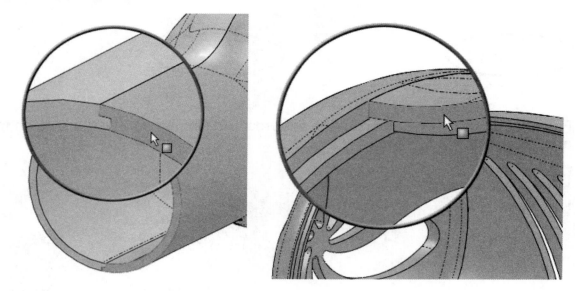

- Add cutouts for a switch and power cord.

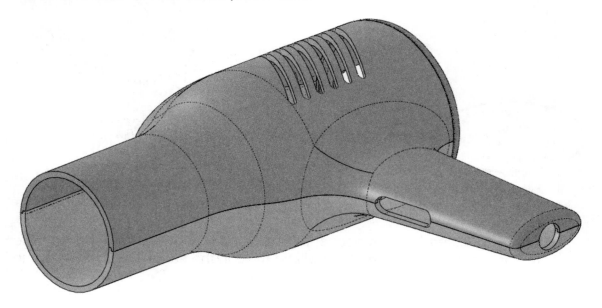

For the next example, we'll design a bucket using surfaces and, at the end, convert to a solid model. The process followed here to build the bucket is not the most efficient way to build a bucket, but it will show the reader how to use several surfacing tools.

**424.** – Make a new part and add the following sketch in the Front plane. Don't forget the vertical centerline at the origin.

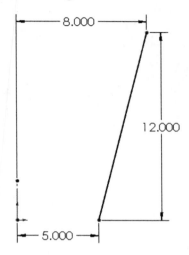

**425.** – Select the "**Revolved Surface**" command from the Surfaces toolbar, or from the menu "**Insert, Surface, Revolved**". Make the revolved surface 360 degrees. The surface will be revolved about the centerline.

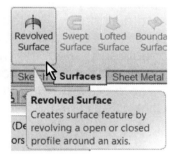

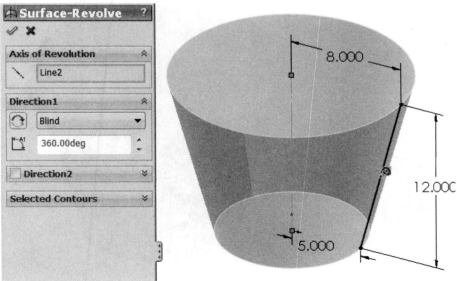

**426. –** Add the following sketch in the Front plane and make a second revolved surface. The top of the line is horizontal with the top edge of the first surface.

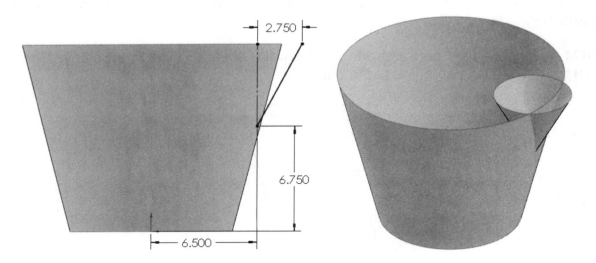

**427. –** After creating both surfaces we have to trim them. Select the "**Trim Surface**" command from the Surfaces toolbar, or the menu "**Insert, Surface, Trim**". In this step we'll use the "**Mutual**" trim type option; this means that both surfaces will work as a trim surface. In the "**Surfaces**" selection box, pick both surfaces. Activate the "**Keep selections**" option and select the main body of the bucket and the outside face. Notice how the surfaces change color to preview the part of the surface that is kept. Click OK to finish.

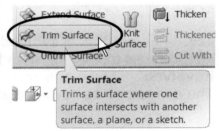

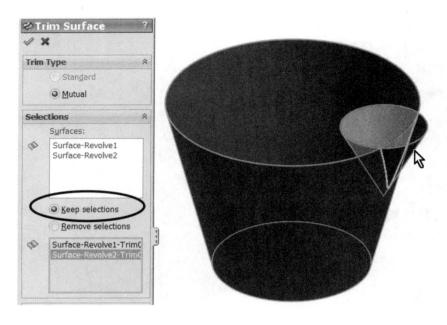

The resulting trimmed surfaces are merged into a single surface body. By default open surfaces have a light blue color on the open edges. Note in our surface the upper and lower open edges of the surface are blue and the edge where we trimmed the surfaces is black.

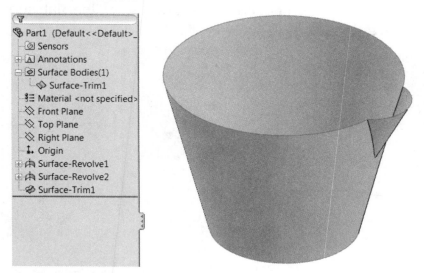

**428.** – Now we'll fillet the edge where both surfaces meet. Select the "**Fillet**" command, and add a 1″ radius fillet.

**429.** – We need to add a lip to the top of the bucket, but instead of creating a plane at the top of the bucket and making a sketch for the planar surface, we'll make a planar surface with the open edge, extend it and trim it. Select the "**Planar Surface**" icon from the Surfaces toolbar or the menu "**Insert, Surface, Planar**".

**430.** – To make a planar surface, we need to select a sketch that defines a closed area, or a closed loop of edges. To select the top edges (which are all tangent to each other), right mouse click on one edge and select the option "**Select Tangency**". This option automatically selects all tangent edges, which in our case are all the edges needed. The preview of the flat surface will be automatically shown. Click OK to complete it.

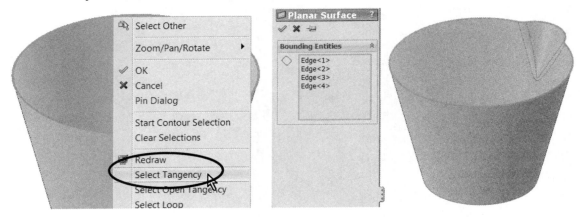

**431.** – The planar surface we just made will be an intermediate step. What we'll do now is make this surface bigger to build the lip at the top of the bucket, and then we'll fillet and trim the surfaces at the same time. Select the command "**Extend Surface**" from the "Surfaces" toolbar, or the menu "**Insert, Surface, Extend**". The "**Extend Surface**" command helps us to make a surface bigger,

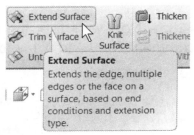

extending its edges by a given distance, up to a point or another surface. In case of curved a surface, we can extend its edges continuing the same surface, or linearly. Select the planar surface we just made and enter a 0.875″ distance. Since this is a flat surface, using the "Same surface" or "Linear" option makes no difference. Make sure the preview is going out and click OK to complete the surface.

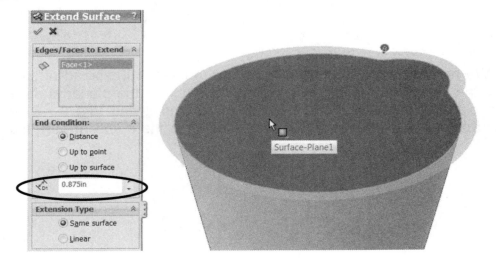

**432. –** Click in the "**Fillet**" command and select the "**Face fillet**" type. Enter a 0.375" radius and select the planar face in the "**Face set 1**" and the bucket's body in the "**Face set 2**" selection boxes. If a fillet preview is not visible, click on the "**Reverse Face Normal**" buttons next to the selection boxes to make both arrows point towards each other. Under "Fillet Options" make sure the "**Trim and attach**" option is selected; this option will trim the unused surfaces and knit the fillet with the other surfaces automatically.  Click OK to complete.

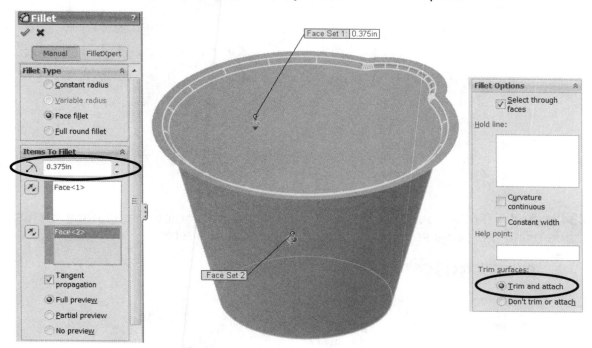

After completing the fillet, the inside face is trimmed, the fillet is blended along the perimeter of the bucket, and all surfaces are merged into a single body.

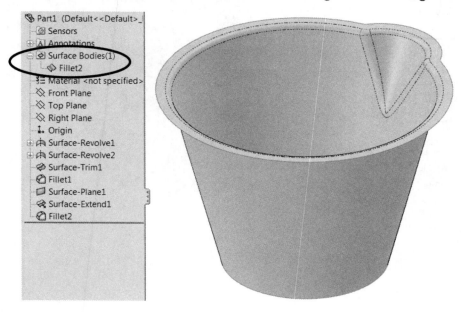

**433. –** Add a new planar surface at the bottom of the bucket using the "**Planar Surface**" command and selecting the round edge. We'll have two surface bodies after this command.

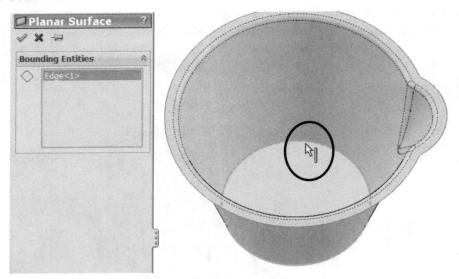

**434. –** Add a 0.625" face fillet between the bucket and the bottom surface we just made using the same settings we used for the fillet at the top.

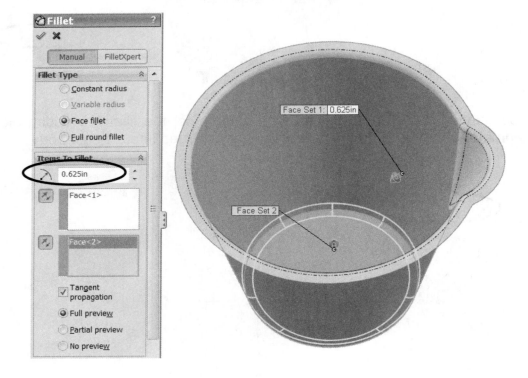

Now the bucket's surface is complete.

**435.** – To convert the surface to a solid, select the "**Thicken**" command from the Surfaces toolbar, or the menu "**Insert, Boss/Base, Thicken**".

Make the surface 0.125″ thick, going *inside* the bucket; click OK to finish.

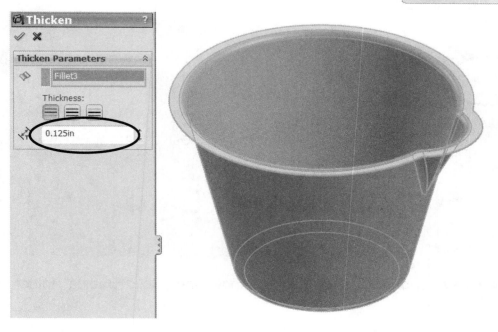

 Now our part is a single solid body (no "Solid Bodies" folder) and the surface body was absorbed by the "**Thicken**" command (also, no "Surface Bodies" folder).

**436.** – To complete the bucket's design, we'll add a couple of attachment points for a handle. To make the first extrusion we'll use the "**Extrude From**" option. Switch to a Front view and make the following sketch in the Front plane. Notice the sketch is in the middle of the part.

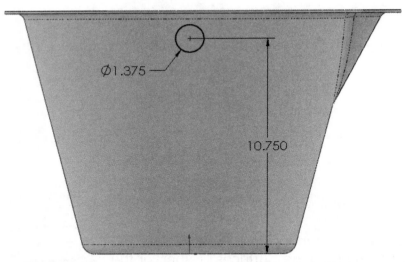

**437.** – Select the "**Extruded Boss**" command. In the "**From**" selection box, pick "**Offset**" and type **8.25″**. In the "**Direction 1**" option box, select "**Up To Next**" and reverse the direction if needed. Clear the "**Merge result**" checkbox, as we'll model this feature as a multi body. Click OK to finish.

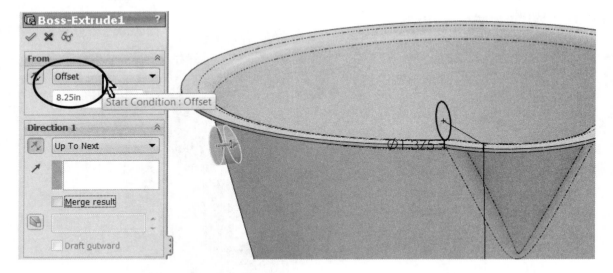

Now we have two solid bodies listed under the "Solid Bodies" folder in the FeatureManager.

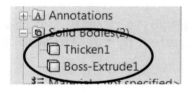

**438.** – Add a new sketch in the front face of the boss we just made with a concentric circle 0.625″ in diameter. Make an Extruded Cut with a "**Through All**" option. Before finishing the cut extrude, under the "**Feature Scope**" options, clear the "**Auto-select**" checkbox and select the body made in the previous step, as we only want to affect this solid body with the cut and not the entire bucket. Click OK to finish.

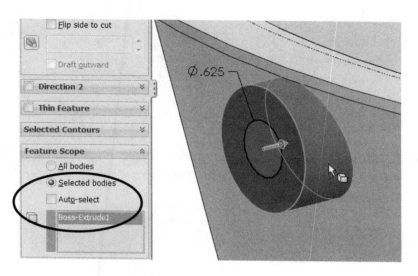

**439.** – In the next step we'll make a mirror of this body to have two attachment points for the bucket's handle. Select the "**Mirror**" command, and using the Front plane as the mirror plane, select the "**Cut-Extrude1**" body to be mirrored in the "**Bodies to Mirror**" selection box. Do not merge the bodies at this time; we'll do that in the next step. Click OK to finish.

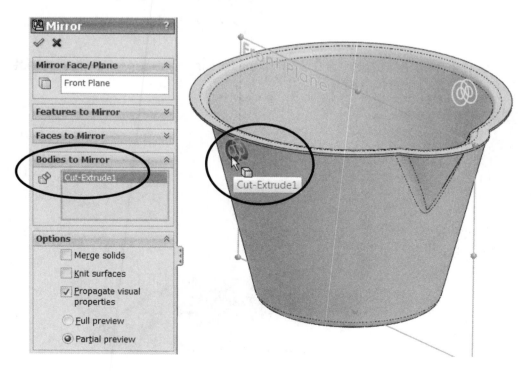

**440.** – At this point we have 3 solid bodies, and what we need to do now is to combine them into a single one. Select the menu "**Insert, Features, Combine**" or select all three bodies in the "Solid Bodies" folder and right mouse click to select the "**Combine**" option.

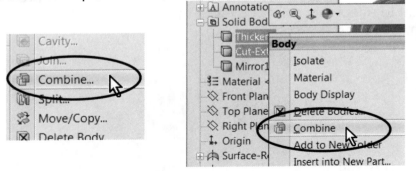

**441.** – Select "**Add**" under the "**Operation Type**" options and click OK to complete. This will merge all three bodies into one.

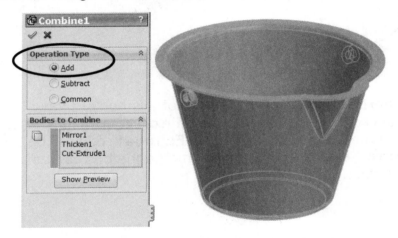

**442.** – The last step is to add a 0.375″ fillet to the bosses. We can select the face of the bucket or the two edges.

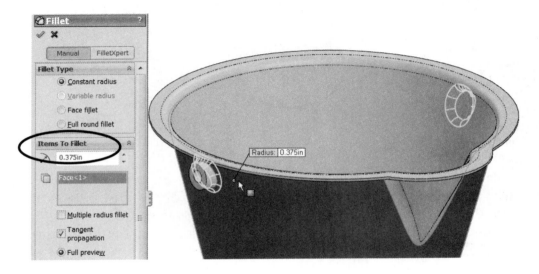

**443. –** Save the part as *Bucket* and close it. Our finished part looks like this:

### More About Surfaces

When modeling more complex shapes, we may have to resort to surfaces in order to create auxiliary geometry as support for our models in the form of trim surfaces, start or end conditions for extrusions and cuts, to generate guide curves, etc. In the next model, we'll use a couple of surfaces to generate a curve that will be used for a sweep. Look at the following image of a sword's grip.

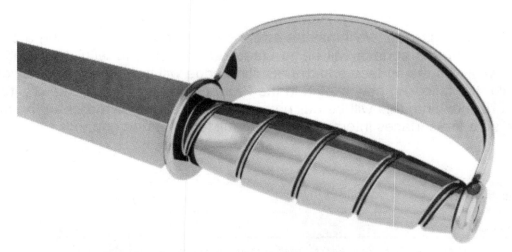

At first glance it seems to be a simple enough model; but when we think about it, the groove in the grip is going in a spiral around an uneven surface, which makes for an interesting challenge and which we are going to show in the next few steps.

**444.** – The first thing we are going to do is to define the profile of the grip. Start a new part and make the following sketch in the Front plane. The vertical and horizontal lines are centerlines (construction geometry), and the top is an arc.

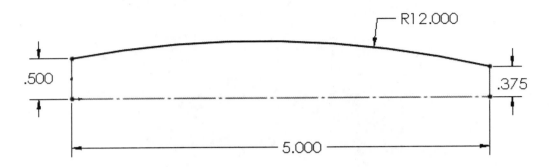

**445.** – Select the "**Revolved Surface**" command and make a 360 deg. revolved surface.

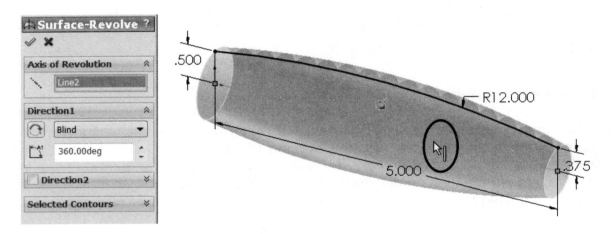

**446.** – For the next step, we'll make a swept surface that will twist along a path. The purpose of this surface will be to create an intersection with the revolved surface; we'll trim the surface and the resulting edge will be the path for a sweep cut. Make the following new sketch in the Front plane and exit the sketch. It's a single horizontal line; this will be our path. Make the sketch longer than the part to make sure the surfaces intersect along the full length of the grip.

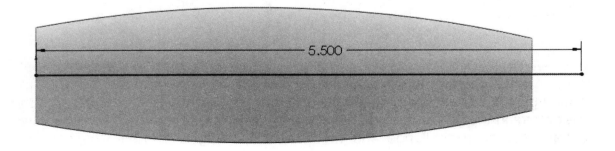

**447.** – Make another sketch in the Front plane; this time it will be a vertical line as shown. Be sure to make this line higher than the revolved surface. Exit the sketch when done.

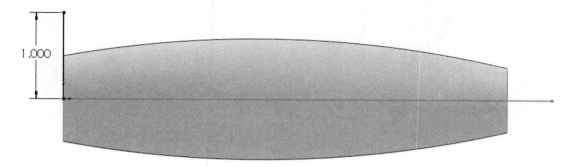

1.000

**448.** – Select the "**Swept Surface**" command from the Surfaces toolbar or the menu "**Insert, Surface, Sweep**". Select the vertical line sketch as the Profile, and the horizontal line sketch as the Path. Under the "**Surface Sweep**" options select "**Twist Along Path**" under the "Orientation/Twist" selection list, and in the "Define by:" selection list pick "**Turns**"; enter a value of **4**. The Profile sketch will twist along the length of the Path sketch 4 turns. Click OK to finish.

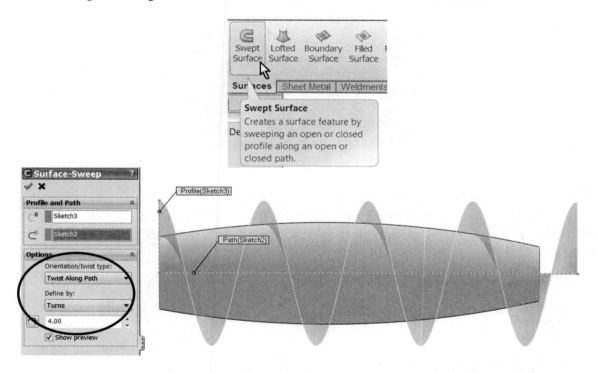

**449.** – What we are interested in is the curve along the intersection of both surfaces, so we'll trim the swept surface with the revolved surface, and use the edge as a path for a swept cut. Select the "**Trim Surface**" command; using the "Standard" trim type, select the revolved surface in the "**Trim tool**" selection box, activate the "Keep selections" option, and select the outside of the swept surface to keep it. Click OK to finish.

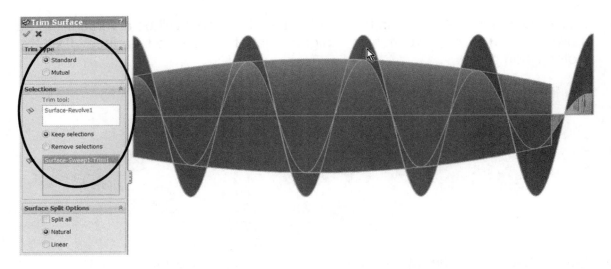

Select the revolved surface in the graphics area (or the FeatureManager's "Surface Bodies" folder) and hide it.

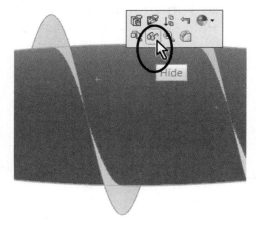

**450. –** Now we need to make a solid body for the grip. Show the sketch in the "Surface-Revolve1" and start a new sketch in the Front plane. Select all the lines of the revolved surface sketch and use "**Convert Entities**" to project them into our new sketch.

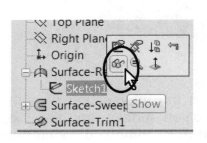

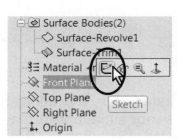

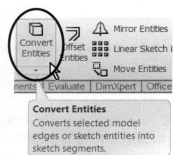

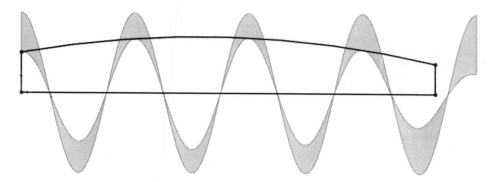

**451. –** Select the "**Revolved Boss/Base**" command from the Features toolbar (this is a solid feature), and select the horizontal line to make the revolved feature about it. Click OK to complete it. Now we have a solid body and two surface bodies in our part. We can hide the revolved surface sketch when done.

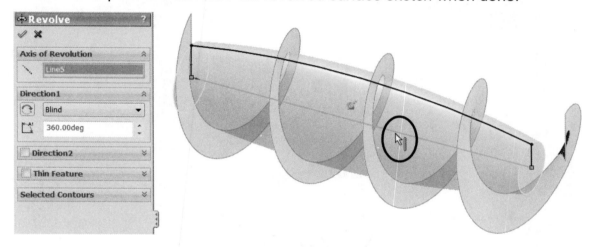

**452. –** Now we need to make the profile for a Sweep Cut. Add a new sketch in the Front plane, close to the left of the swept surface, and draw it as shown. Draw an equilateral triangle (hint: make all three lines equal) and add the two construction lines as indicated, then add a "Pierce" relation between the endpoint of the horizontal construction line and the swept surface edge. Exit the sketch when done.

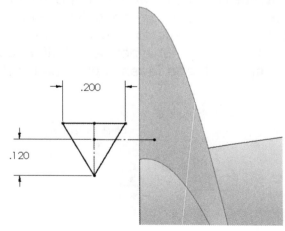

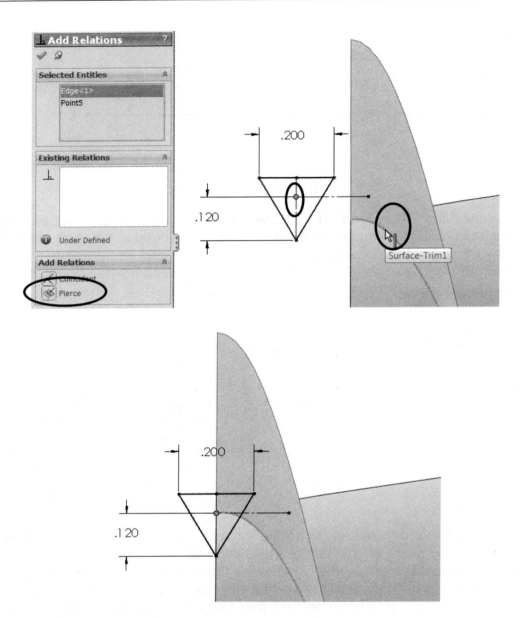

**453. –** Select the "**Swept Cut**" command from the Features toolbar or the menu "**Insert, Cut, Sweep**", and select the triangular sketch for the Profile and the inside edge of the trimmed surface for the Path. In the "**Options**" box, select "**Follow Path**" in "Orientation/Twist type:" and "**All Faces**" in "Path alignment type:". Turn off the "**Align with end faces**" option and click OK to finish.

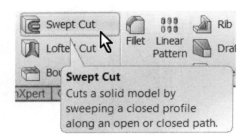

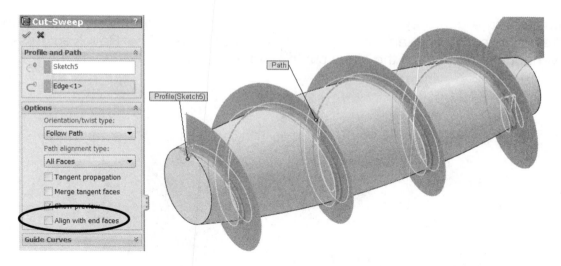

**454.** – Hide the trimmed surface to view the resulting cut in the solid body.

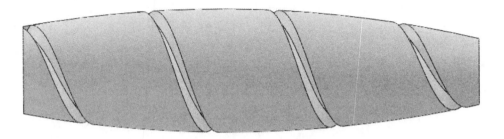

**455.** – Add a 0.035″ radius fillet at the bottom of the swept cut

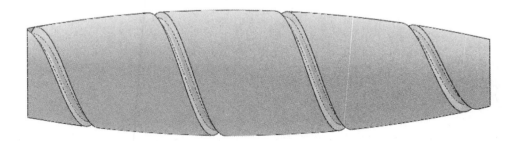

**456.** – Add a 0.075″ radius fillet to the two outer edges of the swept cut.

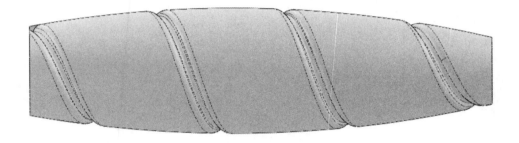

**457.** – Add a guard and pummel to the grip using a revolved boss. Add a new sketch in the Front plane and make a revolved boss. The Revolved Boss is overlapping the ends of the spiral cut to cover the ends.

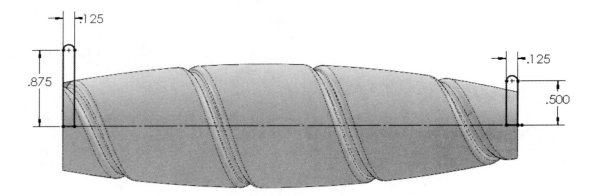

Save the file as *Sword Grip* and close it.

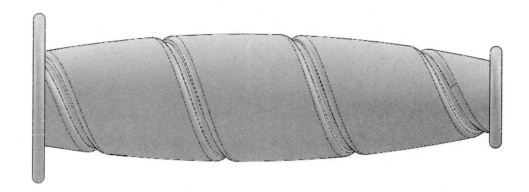

## CHALLENGE EXERCISE:

Add a hand guard to the sword grip and a blade to your sword. Here is just a suggestion.

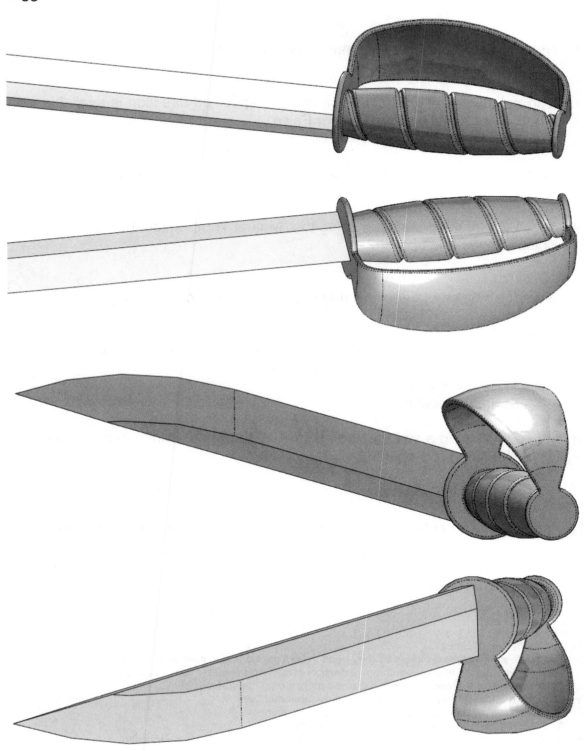

**Review and Questions:**

a) What is the thickness of a surface?

b) When two surfaces intersect each other, they merge. True or False.

c) The option to make an extrusion along a specified direction is available **only** when extruding a surface. True or False.

d) Name two types of elements that can be used to trim a surface.

e) When we trim two surfaces using the "Mutual Trim" option, how many surface bodies do we end up with?

f) Name two types of geometry that can be used to create a planar surface.

g) Which of the following is a requirement to knit two or more surfaces:
   A - Surfaces must be touching at the edges.
   B - Surfaces must be open.
   C - Surfaces must be closed.

h) When thickening a surface, the option "Try to form a solid" can be used if:
   A - The surface is open.
   B - The surface is closed.
   C - The surface is a loft.

i) Name two elements that can be used to split a part into multiple bodies.

**Answers:**
a - Zero, it has no thickness.
b - False. When two surfaces intersect they need to be trimmed and knitted to be merged.
c - False. This option is available with any extrusion or cut feature, either solid or surface.
d - Another surface, a Plane or a sketch that will project onto the surface.
e - One, the mutually trimmed surfaces are merged automatically.
f - A closed 2D sketch or a group of closed edges on a plane.
g - A. Surfaces cannot be knitted if they are not touching at the edges.
h - B. When thickening a closed surface the option "Try to form a solid" will be enabled.
i - A Plane, a surface or sketch that extends past the solid body.

## *Mold Tools*

After completing a part it is common to have to design a mold for it if the part is going to be made by plastic injection or forge. Mold making is a manufacturing specialty where experience plays as big a role as preparation and study, and it's not an easy trade to master.

When designing a mold, a large number of factors must be taken into consideration, including: the shape and size of the part, the material to be used (plastic, resin, metal, etc.), the process, the tooling necessary to make the mold, etc. In other words, it's a complicated process.

The purpose of this chapter is not to teach mold making, as that by itself is enough to fill several books and there would still be much more to learn. The intent is to show the user the tools available in SolidWorks for mold making, understand how to use them and briefly touch on design considerations that can affect manufacturing of a molded part, like draft and parting line selection.

Be aware that a complete mold design includes a large number of components starting with a mold base; from there we have to design cooling lines, runners, gates, add hardware components (springs, nuts, bolts, ejection pins, dowels, O-rings, slides, lifters, etc.). Our focus in this chapter will be limited to showing how to create the core and cavity, side cores and inserts. Many times these are the most difficult tasks; adding the rest of the components and design elements to a complete mold design is just what we were talking about.

In this chapter we'll learn how to make molds for a few of the parts we have previously made and a couple others where we'll learn different techniques. This will give the reader a good idea of what needs to be done and, more importantly, how it can be done in different situations. More complex parts will require additional steps, multi part molds, inserts, sliders and such, but that's precisely where the skill and knowledge of the designer comes into play. We are only showing how to use the most common tools available for that purpose.

**458.** – We'll start by making a simple mold for a business card holder. Download the file *Card Holder* from mechanicad.com/download.html and open it.

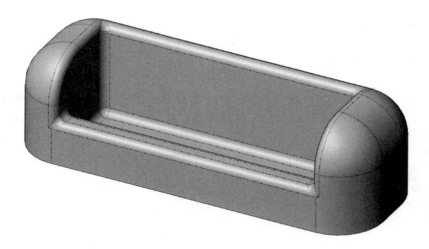

**459.** – One of the most critical and important details when making a mold is to know if we can get it out of the mold. The first thing we need to do is to make a "**Draft Analysis**". A draft analysis will tell us if we have the required draft in the 'vertical' faces to eject the part from the mold. By 'vertical' we are referring to the faces parallel to the direction the part will separate from the mold or 'direction of pull'. Picture it this way: when we make a cake or a pie, the mold's vertical walls have an inclination, or "**Draft**" angle, to facilitate releasing the cake from the mold. If the walls were truly vertical, it would be very difficult to get the cake out of the mold in one piece. Even worse would be to have the walls inclined inside; this is a condition known as a negative draft, and the cake would never come out complete.

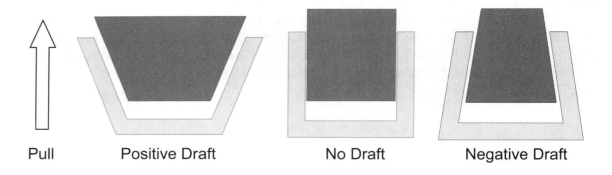

Pull          Positive Draft          No Draft          Negative Draft

The required draft to easily separate the part from the mold will vary depending on the part's size, the material to be used, whether the part has texture or not, the process used, etc. What we know for sure is that we <u>always</u> want to have a positive draft and as much as possible. If our part's design forces us to have a negative draft in one or more faces, we have to use a different approach, like a multi part mold, side cores or a combination of both. Later in this lesson we'll cover how to deal with this situation.

**460. –** To start, make sure the "**Mold Tools**" toolbar is open in the Command-Manager. (Right mouse click in a tab and select "**Mold Tools**" or turn on the **Mold Tools** toolbar.)

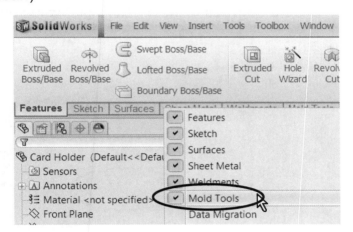

**461. –** In the Mold Tools toolbar we have some commands available in other toolbars, for example, from Features, Surfaces, Evaluate tools and a few mold specific tools.

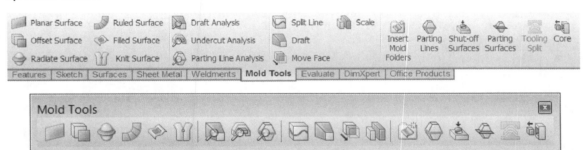

 When we design a mold, surfaces are used to create the Core and Cavity. A Core is defined as the 'male' half of the mold, and the Cavity as the 'female' half of the mold. Some molds only have either a core or a cavity.

**462. –** The first step is to analyze our part to make sure we have at least 3 degrees of draft in the vertical walls. This is an arbitrary value that we'll use for our example. Select the "**Draft Analysis**" command from the Mold Tools toolbar or from the menu "**View, Display, Draft Analysis**".

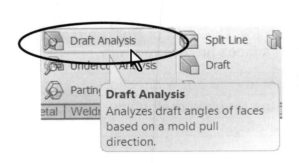

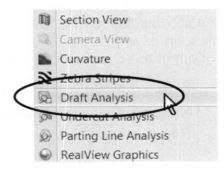

For the "Draft Analysis" tool we have to select a face or plane <u>perpendicular</u> to the desired direction of pull or an edge along the direction of pull. In our case, we'll use the bottom of the *Card Holder* for our direction of pull (we could also use the Top plane). Enter **3 degrees** in the "Draft Angle" value box.

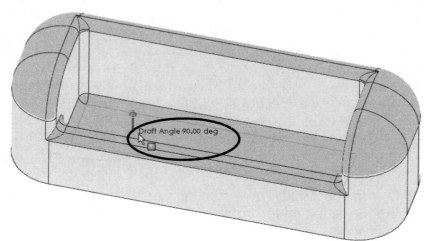

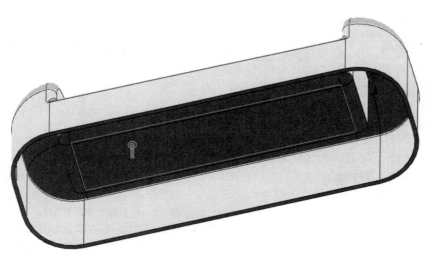

 Note that as we move the mouse around the part, the angle to the direction of pull is displayed next to the mouse pointer.

As soon as we select the reference for "Direction of Pull", in this case the bottom of the *Card Holder*, our part's faces are colored with:

| | |
|---|---|
| **Green** | Positive draft, indicated by the arrow direction |
| **Yellow** | Faces with less than the required draft angle |
| **Red** | Faces with negative draft |

"**Positive**" and "**Negative**" are only telling us what side of the mold a face will be made with, and can be reversed using the "**Reverse Direction**" icon next to the "**Direction of Pull**" selection box. When we have a Core and Cavity mold, "Positive" faces will be on one side, "Negative" faces will be on the other. In our case the green faces will be made in the Cavity, and the red faces in the Core. What we are interested in are the yellow faces that need to be given a draft to properly release from the mold, and these are the ones that have to be modified to be either "Positive" (green) or "Negative" (red). Once we have identified the faces that need to be drafted, cancel the "Draft Analysis" tool. If we click OK, the draft analysis colors remain visible and we can see which faces need to be modified as we edit the part. The first feature to be modified will be the 'Boss-Extrude1'. Select it in the FeatureManager or the graphics area and edit it.

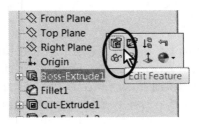

 To turn off the Draft Analysis view, click on its icon again.

**463.** – In "Direction 1", activate the "**Draft On/Off**" option and enter **3 degrees**. You will see the faces in the preview 'leaning in' the part. Click OK to complete.

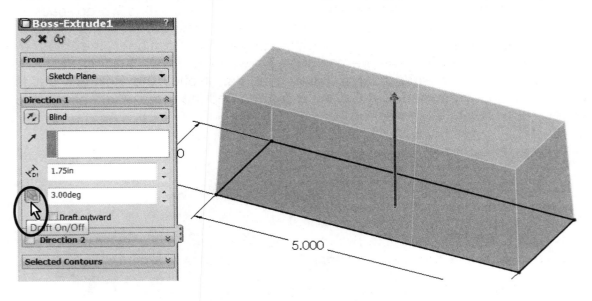

*DRAFT ANALYSIS VIEW:* After completing this change we can see that only a few faces still require draft and are still yellow, some in the top (Cavity side) and some in the bottom (Core side).

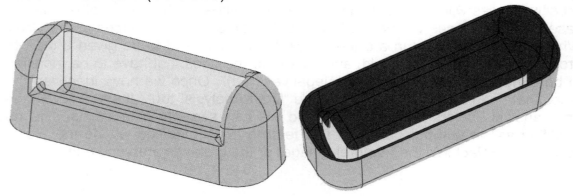

**464. –** Since not all faces can be given a draft at the time a feature is created, we have to add it as a secondary operation. To add a draft to the remaining faces

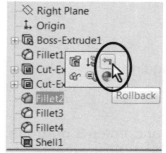

that need it, we'll use the "**Draft**" command. Faces to be drafted must not be connected to a fillet or the draft will fail. Analyzing our model, we can see that we have a few operations, then fillets and a shell at the end to make the part hollow. What we need to do is to 'rollback' the model to just before the 'Fillet2' feature to be able to add the draft. Since the part is shelled at the end, fixing the faces in the top (Cavity side) will also take care of the faces in the bottom (Core side). Select the 'Fillet2' feature; from the pop-up menu select "Rollback". By doing this we go *'back in time'* in the FeatureManager, to right before the fillets and the shell are created. By doing this, we are able to add a new feature at this position in the Feature-Manager; when we are done we can "Roll Forward" to finish building the part, essentially un-suppressing the remaining features. Notice the Rollback bar is now located just below the 'Cut-Extrude2' feature and the remaining features are grayed out under it ('Suppressed').

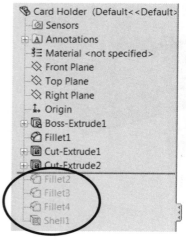

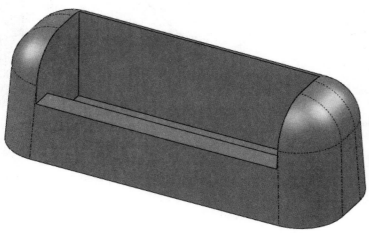

**465.** – Select the "**Draft**" command from the Command-Manager or the menu "**Insert, Features, Draft**". The "**Draft**" command is available in the Features or Mold Tools toolbars. (To make selection easier, the "Draft Analysis" view is off.)

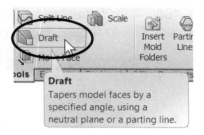

The faces we need to draft are the inside area, where business cards will be placed.

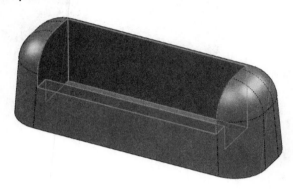

In the "**Draft**" command, select "**Neutral Plane**" in the "Type of Draft" selection box. The "Neutral Plane" is a reference flat face or plane that will be used to measure the draft against. This is also where the faces to be drafted will start to *'incline'*; think of it as a hinge where the face starts to move. Select the bottom face of the cavity as the "Neutral Plane" and enter **3 degrees** in the "Draft Angle" value box. Notice the arrow in the corner of the selected face is pointing up; this is the "**Direction of Pull**" we want.

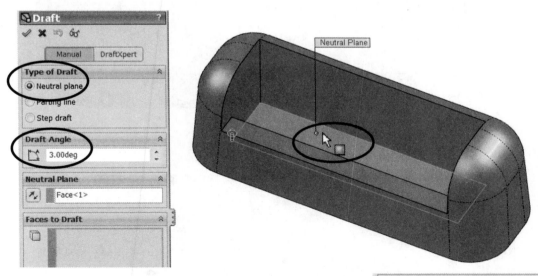

 The draft's "Direction of Pull" can be reversed using the "Reverse Direction" icon next to the "Neutral Plane" selection box.

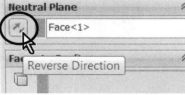

**466.** – Add the four vertical faces inside the "Faces to Draft" selection box and click OK to finish. Notice the faces moving after completing the draft.

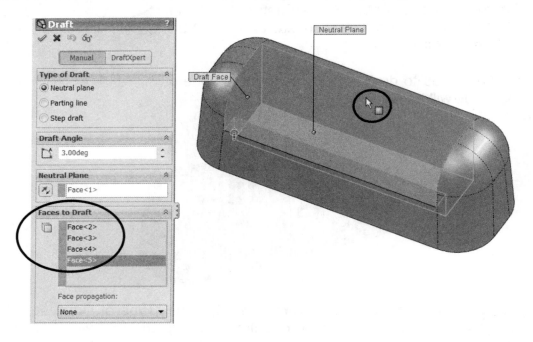

Top view before the draft…

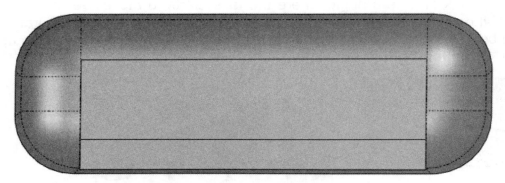

… and after the draft.

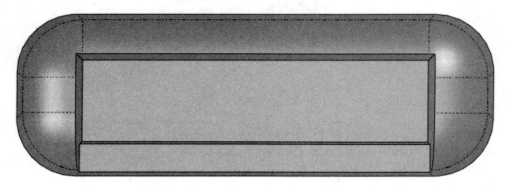

**More on "Neutral Plane":**

The plane we select as the "Neutral Plane" will define how the drafted faces will be inclined.  Look at the following images and the neutral plane selections. In all cases the "Direction of Pull" is pointing up.

The difference between the different "Neutral Plane" selections is that the faces to be drafted are projected to the "Neutral Plane" and at this point is where they will be the 'hinged' and start to incline.

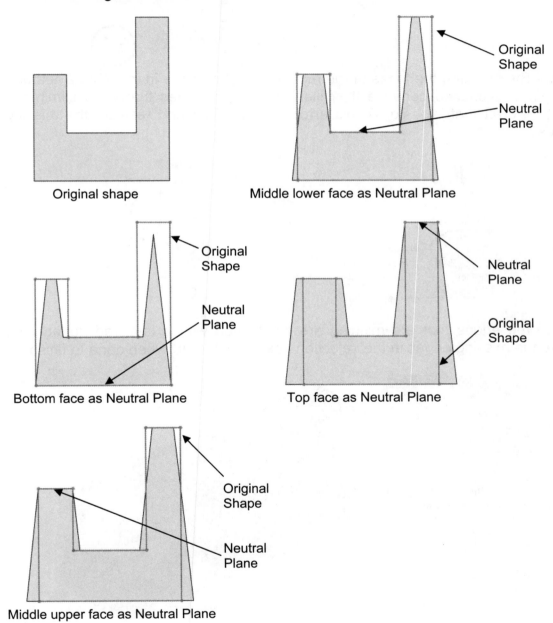

Original shape

Middle lower face as Neutral Plane

Bottom face as Neutral Plane

Top face as Neutral Plane

Middle upper face as Neutral Plane

Depending on the desired result, we may have to make multiple "Draft" features with different "Neutral Plane" selections.

**467. –** Back to our part. Select the "Rollback bar" and drag it all the way to the bottom. If you get an error message, close it for now.

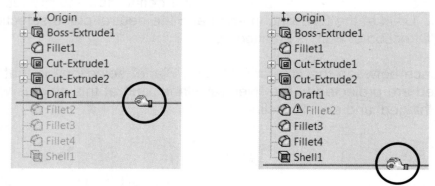

**468. –** By changing the faces of the model we get an error in the 'Fillet2' feature. The error is caused because this fillet cannot find edges that were eliminated with the draft feature. To fix this error, edit the fillet and reselect the missing edges.

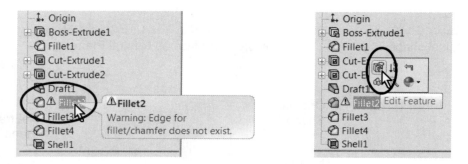

Notice the edges that are missing are highlighted with a faint red dotted line. Erase the missing edges in the selection box and click OK when done to finish.

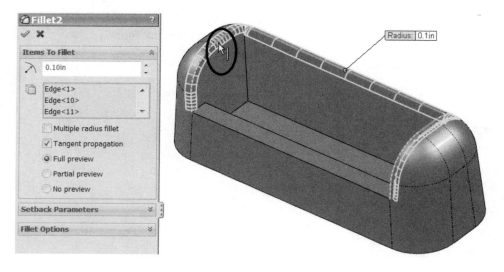

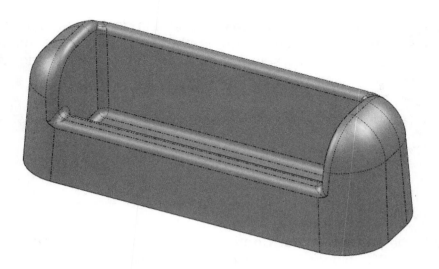

**469. –** Use the "**Draft Analysis**" view and verify all faces have the required three degrees of draft to continue. One side is now completely green ("Positive" draft), the other side is completely red ("Negative" draft) and no yellow faces. Click Cancel to continue (if we press OK we'll keep the "Draft Analysis" view colors).

**470.** – When we make a mold for a plastic part, the design part is usually scaled up to compensate for part shrinkage in the mold when the melted plastic solidifies. To scale the part, select the "**Scale**" command in the Mold Tools toolbar or the menu "**Insert, Features, Scale**".

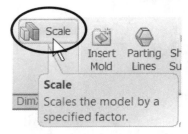

**471.** – Scale the part about the "**Centroid**" using a scaling factor of **1.03**; this will make the part 3% bigger to compensate for mold shrinkage. Click OK to complete. Notice the part is slightly bigger when complete and a "Scale" feature is added to the FeatureManager.

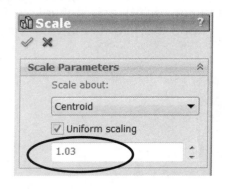

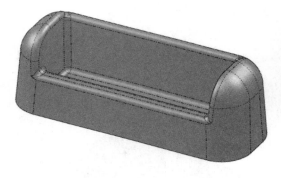
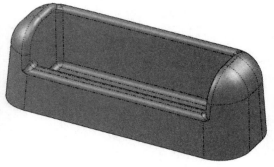

See the difference? Roll back and forward the 'Scale' feature to see the change. Subtle, but visible.

Shrinkage value varies depending on the material used and the part's geometry. If a part is elongated, it may shrink differently along one axis than the other. In this case, a non "Uniform scaling" option is used.

**472. –** After scaling the part, we are ready to make the mold. The process to make a mold in SolidWorks is:

- Define a Parting Line.
- Create Shut-off Surfaces to close holes in the part (If needed).
- Create a Parting Surface to split the mold.
- Make a Tooling Split to generate the Core and Cavity.
- Make additional side cores and inserts (If needed).

**473. –** A **parting line** is formed by the edges where the two halves of the mold meet. An easy way to identify the parting line is using the "Draft Analysis". In simple terms, the parting line will be the edges where the faces with "Positive" draft (green) meet the faces with "Negative" draft (red). In simple two piece molds (a single core and cavity) like this, the parting line is usually automatically found and selected. Select the **"Parting Line"** command from the Mold Tools toolbar or the menu "**Insert, Molds, Parting Line**". The command

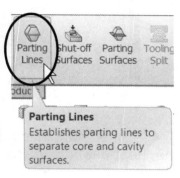

works similarly to the "Draft Analysis", with the addition of some options and a selection box. In the Mold Parameters selection options, select a plane or flat face for a "Direction of Pull" (like the "Draft Analysis"). Select the same flat face inside the *Card Holder* or the Top plane (your choice); set the draft angle to **3 degrees** and press the "**Draft Analysis**" button.

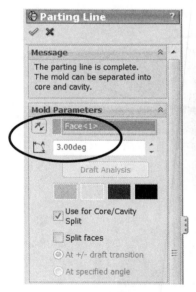

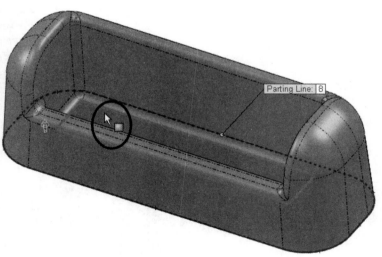

Make sure the "**Use for Core/Cavity Split**" option is checked. This option will automatically generate surfaces for Core and Cavity (we'll see them later). In the "Parting Line" selection box the edges that make up the parting line are already selected, and the message "The parting line is complete" is highlighted in green at the top. Click OK to finish.

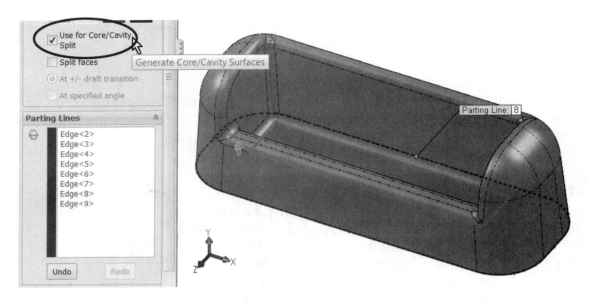

**474.** – After completing the parting line, a new feature 'Parting Line1' is added to the FeatureManager, and in the "Surface Bodies" folder two sub-folders are created, each with a surface for the Core and Cavity. These surfaces are automatically created with the "Parting Line" command. In this example, the "Cavity Surface Bodies" are the faces with a "Positive" draft (green) and the "Core Surface Bodies" are the faces with a "Negative" draft (red). The parting line remains visible on the screen (it can be hidden just like other features if wanted).

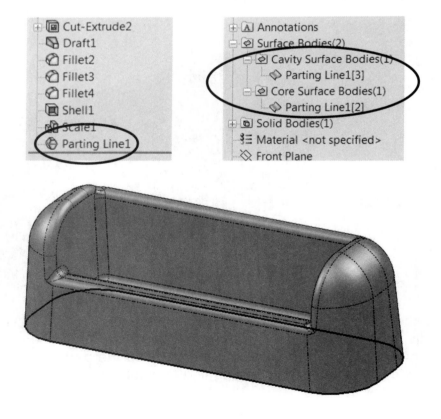

The next step would be to close any holes with "Shut Off Surfaces", but since our part has no holes, this step is not necessary.

**475. –** Now we need to generate the parting surface. In general terms, the parting surface has to be generated manually or automatically to serve as a boundary to separate the mold into core and cavity along with the Core and Cavity surfaces previously generated. The parting surface is connected to the parting line and generally radiates away from it perpendicular to the "Direction of Pull". Select the "**Parting Surfaces**" command from the Mold Tools toolbar or the menu "**Insert, Molds, Parting Surfaces**". In this part, the parting line lies in a flat surface, and this makes it easy to generate. Select the option "**Perpendicular to pull**" – the parting line is automatically selected – and enter a value of **1″** for the "Parting Surface" distance value. The option "Knit all surfaces" automatically merges all the faces generated into one. Click OK to finish.

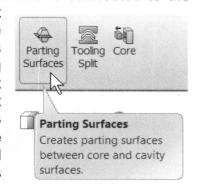

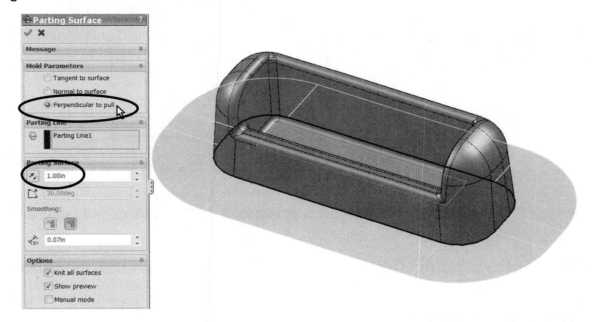

After generating the parting surface, a new folder is added to the "Surface Bodies" folder called "Parting Surface Bodies" and the new surface is listed here.

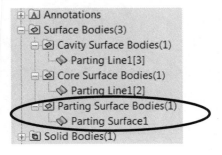

**476. –** The next step is to generate the tooling split. In this step we make the solid bodies for the core and cavity. To make these bodies, we need to make a sketch perpendicular to the "Direction of Pull" that fits inside the parting surface. The generated core and cavity will be defined by this sketch. We can make the sketch first and then make the tooling split, or start the "Tooling Split" command and make the sketch at that time. In this example, we'll make the sketch first. Select the parting surface and add a new sketch in it. Select the surface and use the "**Convert Entities**" command to project the surface edges and exit the sketch.

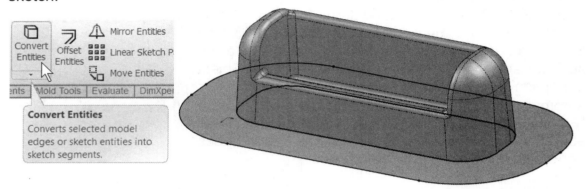

**477. –** Now, select the "**Tooling Split**" command from the Mold Tools toolbar or the menu "**Insert, Molds, Tooling Split**".

 The "Tooling Split" command is unavailable until a parting line feature is added to the model.

**478. –** When we use the "Tooling Split" command, we are first asked for a plane or flat face to add a sketch, or an existing sketch (if the sketch we just drew is pre-selected, this step is skipped). Select the sketch we just made in the graphics area or the FeatureManager.

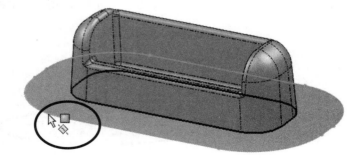

**479. –** After selecting the sketch, we can enter the "Block Size" for the core and cavity measured from the sketch plane. In the "Core", "Cavity" and "Parting Surface" selection boxes, the corresponding surface bodies are automatically selected. This is the reason why the surfaces are listed under the "Surface Bodies" sub-folders; alternatively we can manually select the surfaces, if needed. Enter a block size big enough to completely enclose the *Card Holder* part; in our case 2.25″ up and 0.5″ down will work. Click OK to finish.

 Knowing the size of the mold base that will be used, or the sizes available, usually helps when deciding how big to make the blocks. This way they are big enough to fit in the mold base and not bigger than needed.

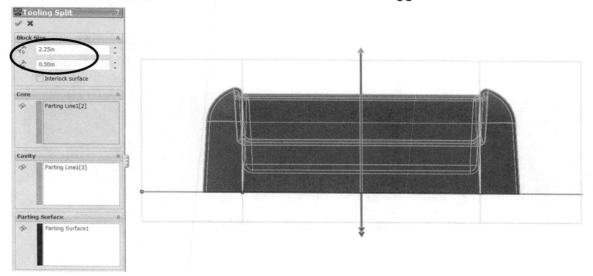

**480. –** Now the core and cavity are finished. Hide the 'Parting Line' feature by selecting it and clicking in the "Hide" command. In the "Solid Bodies" folder we now have three bodies: one is the part, one is the core and the third is the cavity. At this point, the core and cavity bodies can be inserted into a new part file to continue designing the mold and adding the rest of the mold specific features, like cooling lines, injection ports, ejector pins, etc., using the same approach we used when working with a master model. To finish our design, save the core and cavity bodies to a part as '*Card Holder Core*' and '*Card Holder Cavity*'.

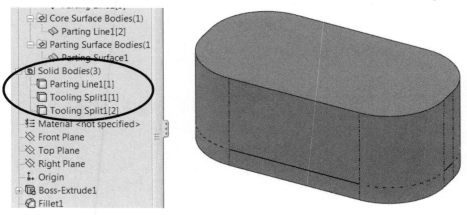

Our finished *Core* and *Cavity* parts look like this:

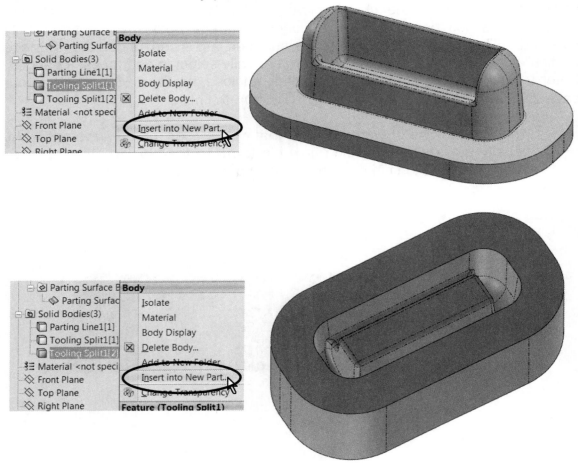

 In the original part, the solid bodies can be hidden to see the result without having to save the bodies to a new part file.

**481.** – For the second mold exercise, download the file *Hair Drier Cover-Mold* from www.mechanicad.com/download.html and open it.

 *This part's external references have been broken to avoid potential conflicts with user generated files.*

**482.** – This part is similar to the previous one in the sense that it can be made with a simple two-part mold, but this one has vents that the previous part did not. This will help us learn how to work with a part that has holes in it. The first thing we need to do is to verify if our part's faces have at least three degrees of draft. Select the **"Draft Analysis"** icon from the Mold Tools toolbar and select the Right plane as the "Direction of Pull".

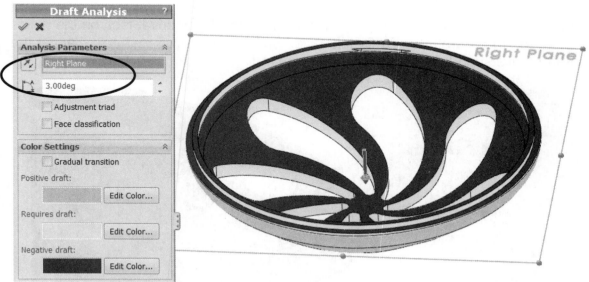

From the analysis we can see that the ventilation holes and the extrusion built to assemble the cover ('Extrude-Boss1') don't have the required three degrees of draft, and therefore we need to fix them before we can continue. Click Cancel to continue (if we click OK, the Draft Analysis colors will remain visible).

**483.** – Select the 'Boss-Extrude1' feature and edit it.

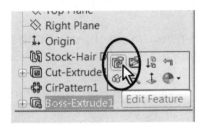

**484.** – Activate the "Draft On/Off" option under the "Direction 1" group and enter a value of **3 degrees**. Click OK to finish.

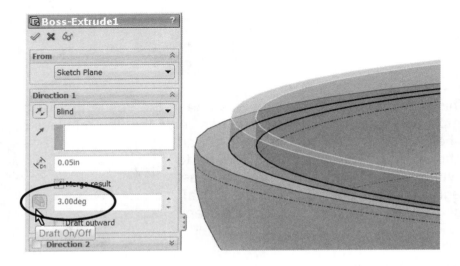

**485.** – Making a "Draft Analysis" again reveals a small cylindrical face on the inside that needs to be drafted.  To fix this face, we'll use the draft feature.  Cancel the "Draft Analysis" and select the "**Draft**" command.

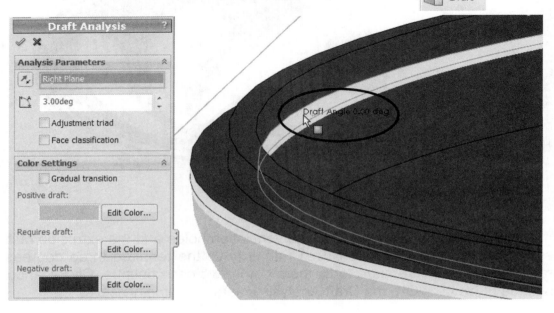

**486.** – Upon closer examination we can see that there are a couple of smaller faces also along the surface that needs to be drafted.

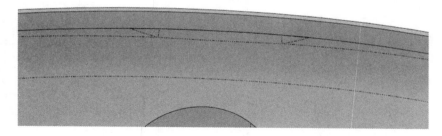

To fix the draft and the smaller faces, we'll add a face fillet. Select the "**Fillet**" command with the "Face fillet" option. For the "Face Set 1", select the inside of '*Boss-Extrude1*', and for "Face Set 2", select the rounded face inside. Enter a 0.25″ radius. The fillet blends both faces and eliminates all the faces between them.

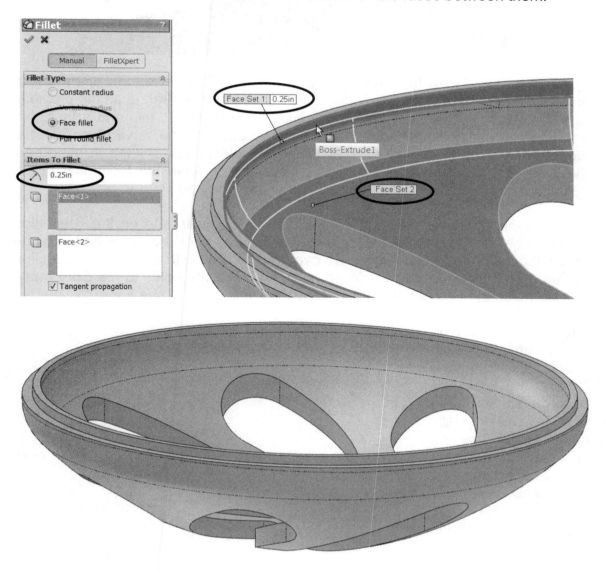

**487. –** Run the "Draft Analysis" tool again to reveal the remaining faces that need to be drafted using the same "Direction of Pull".

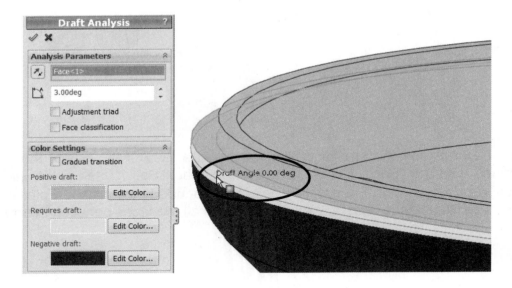

The only faces that need to be drafted are the ventilation holes and a small cylindrical face on the outside. This face cannot be drafted as the previous one using a face fillet. On the other hand, it's only 0.013″ tall, and a face that small can be easily machined with a draft or merged with the curved face. This is just another thing to consider. When designing plastic parts, keep in mind how they are going to be made, and if at all possible, involve the toolmaker in the design process. He'll be glad you did, and you will be, too. ☺

In this example, we'll ignore this face and concentrate on the ventilation holes which are more critical. One thing we need to decide is if the holes will be made in the Core or the Cavity so we can add the draft with the correct "Direction of Pull". To make our mold easier to build, we'll add the holes to the Core (male part) to make the Cavity part completely round inside (you'll see it in a few steps).

**488. –** If we turn on the "**Draft**" option in the 'Cut-Extrude1' feature, the holes will become smaller than what we originally intended because the cut feature starts in the face where the part was originally split, and adding a 3 deg. draft will shrink the hole too much as

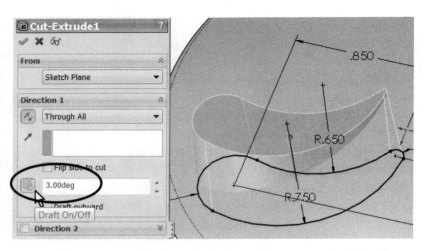

it moves forward. Cancel this change as this is not the result we are looking for.

**489. –** To add a draft to these cuts, we need to create a new plane to be used as a "Neutral Plane". Make an auxiliary plane parallel to the Right plane at a point at the top of the part, as indicated.

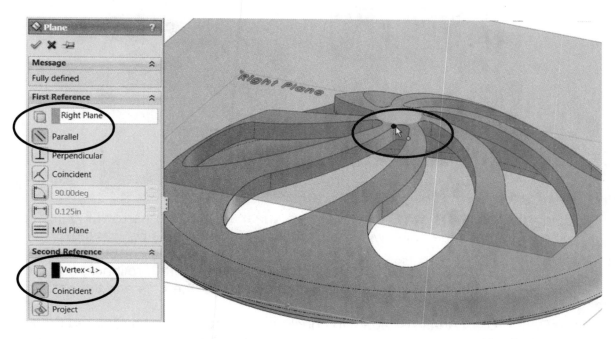

**490. –** Select the "**Draft**" command and use the plane we just created as the "Neutral Plane". Select the "Neutral Plane" option and enter a 3 degrees draft. The arrow indicating the "Direction of Pull" must be pointing into the part to make the draft so that we can build the holes with the core. Click on the "Reverse Direction" icon, if needed.

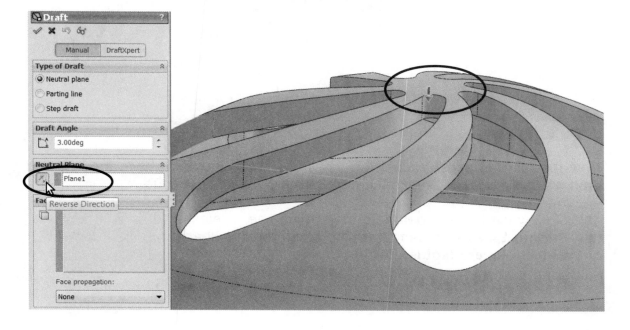

To select the "Faces to draft", right mouse click in one of the faces in a hole, and pick the option "**Select Tangency**". Repeat in all holes to select all the faces. Click OK to finish.

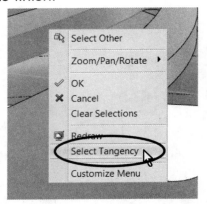
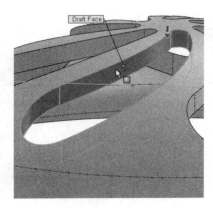

By doing the draft this way, the holes are wider inside and narrower outside, allowing us to make the holes with the Core side of the mold as we wanted.

 **CHALLENGE:** Instead of selecting all the holes to draft, rollback, add the plane, draft the first cut, edit the pattern to include the hole *and* the draft.

**491.** – Run a "Draft Analysis" again to check all the faces have the required draft.

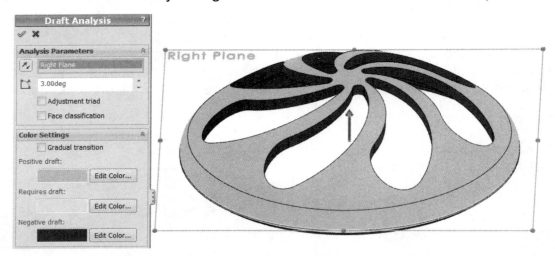

Now that all the faces (except the small one we're ignoring) have the required draft we can proceed to make the mold. Click Cancel to continue.

**492.** – Now we have to generate the parting line. Select the "**Parting Line**" command from the Mold Tools toolbar or the menu "**Insert, Molds, Parting Line**".

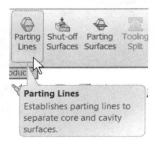

**Parting Lines**
Establishes parting lines to separate core and cavity surfaces.

Select the Right plane (or a flat face parallel to it) for the "Direction of Pull", enter 3 degrees as before, and click the "**Draft Analysis**" button. In this case the parting line edges are not automatically selected. The reason is because the small face without draft (which we ignored...) is at the parting line. Now we have to manually select the edges to define the parting line.

To define the parting line, select the edges along the bottom of the part where the red faces meet the yellow face. Notice the perimeter is made of multiple edges; be sure to manually select them all *or* right mouse click in the edge and use the "**Select Tangency**" option.

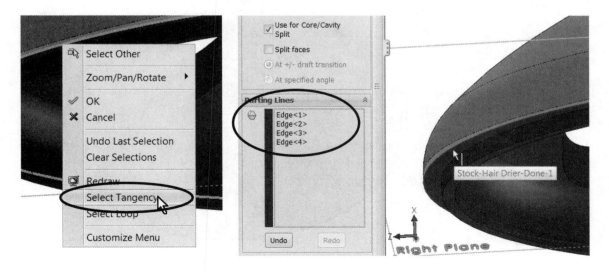

After selecting the parting line edges, the message at the top of the command (still in yellow background) says that the parting line is complete, but the mold cannot be separated into Core and Cavity, and we may need to create shut-off surfaces to close the holes. Click OK to complete the parting line.

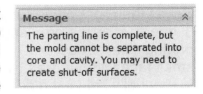

**493. –** Now we need to close the holes in the part to be able to split it into Core and Cavity. Select "**Shut-Off Surfaces**" from the Mold Tools toolbar or the menu "**Insert, Molds, Shut-Off Surfaces**".

After selecting the "**Shut-off Surfaces**" command, the open loops are automatically selected based on the "Direction of Pull". Be sure to leave the "**Knit**" option checked to have the new faces automatically merged with the rest of the Core and Cavity faces when we finish this command. By turning on the "Preview" option, we can see the resulting surfaces. The message at the top of the command (now with green background) says that now the mold can be separated into Core and Cavity. If a hole had not been automatically selected, we'd have to manually pick them. Click Ok to complete the command.

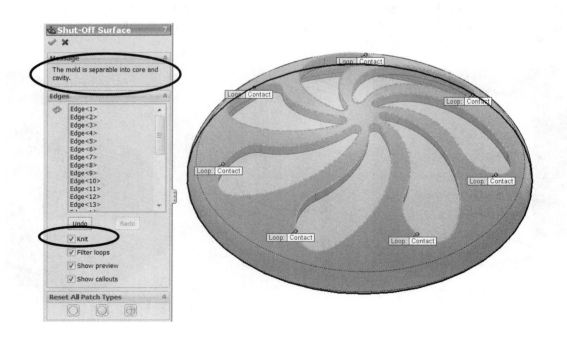

**494.** – The next step is to generate the parting surfaces to separate the mold. Select the "**Parting Surfaces**" command from the Mold Tools toolbar or the menu "**Insert, Molds, Parting Surfaces**". The option "Perpendicular to pull" option is automatically selected, as well as *Parting Line1*. Enter a value of **1″** for the "Parting Surface" distance and be sure the "Knit all surfaces" option is checked. Click OK to finish.

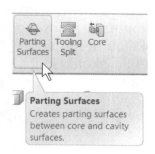

**Parting Surfaces**
Creates parting surfaces between core and cavity surfaces.

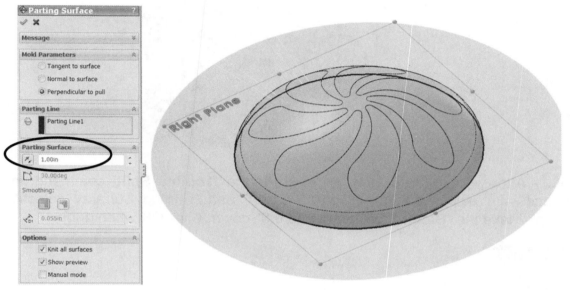

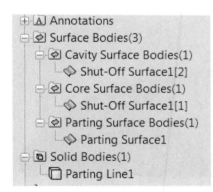

After completing the parting surface, we can see the "Core", "Cavity" and "Parting Surface" created and listed under the "Surface Bodies" folder in the corresponding mold sub-folders, and a single solid body. If we select the surfaces, they will become visible and remain visible until manually hidden. By making the surfaces visible, we can see them overlapping each other. In the holes we see the green and red surfaces overlap. Because the shut-off surfaces are knitted to both the Core and Cavity surfaces, the green and the part overlap in the Cavity side, and the red and the part overlap in the Core side.

**495. –** Now we are ready to make the core and cavity. Select the "**Tooling Split**" command from the Mold Tools toolbar. In this example we'll make the tooling sketch at the same time we make the tooling split. Select the parting surface to add a sketch in it. Use "**Convert Entities**" to project the surface's edge and exit the sketch as we did before.

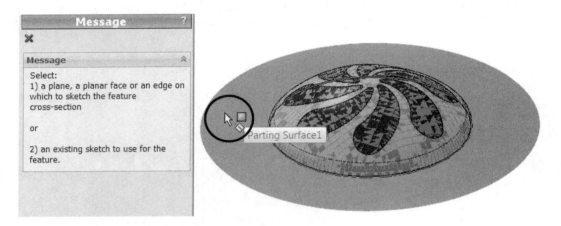

**496. –** After we exit the sketch, we return to the "**Tooling Split**" command; the surfaces are selected in the "Core", "Cavity" and "Parting Surface" selection boxes. Make the "**Block Size**" 1″ up and 0.5″ down. Click OK when done.

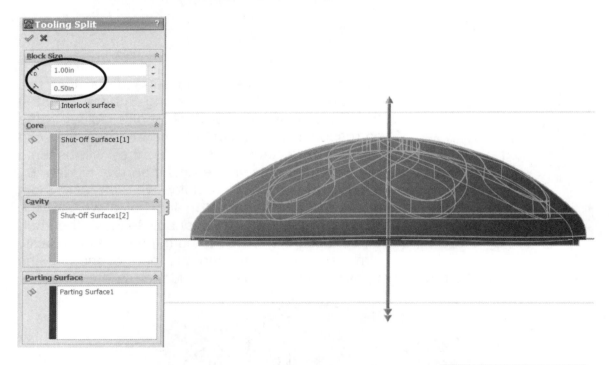

**497. –** To view the core, cavity and part bodies as an open mold, select the menu "**Insert, Features, Move/Copy…**". This command allows us to copy and/or move surfaces and solid bodies.

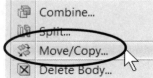

Select the top body (Cavity) and either enter a value to move it along the X direction, or drag the direction arrows in the graphics area, similar to exploding an assembly. Repeat the **Move/Copy** command to move the lower body (Core). Make sure the "Copy" option is not checked.

If needed, hide all the surfaces at the same time by selecting the "Surface Bodies" folder and picking "Hide".

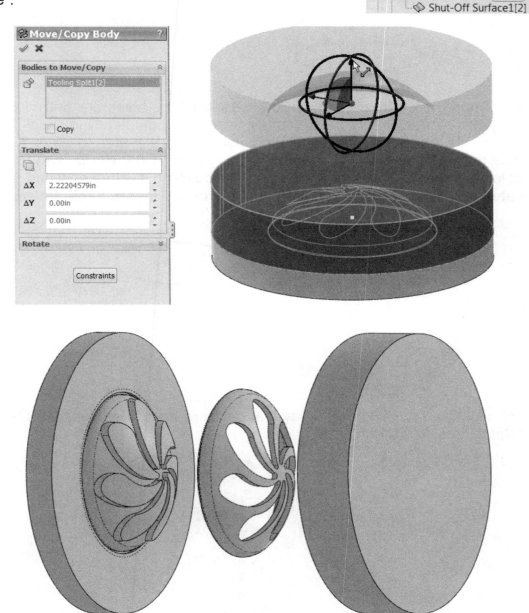

When we make multi body operations like combining bodies, it's often useful to make a copy of a body in the same location to subtract one from another, and retain the original bodies.

**498. –** The next step is to save each body to a separate file as we did with the previous part. Select the core and cavity bodies and save them to a file as '*Hair Drier Cover Core*' and '*Hair Drier Cover Cavity*'.

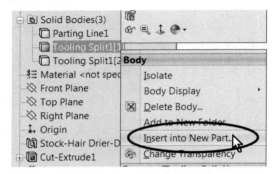

If we save the core and cavity bodies in a new part with a "Body-Move/Copy" command, they will be located in the position relative to the origin as they were after moving them.

**499. –** Open the cavity part. If we pay attention, the holes are outlined in the cavity part. A part like is usually made with a Computer Numerical Control (CNC) machine, and for manufacturing purposes it's better to have a single surface than a surface split in multiple areas like this. One way we can fix this is by deleting the faces from the solid body, and patching it with a new one. Select "**Delete Face**" from the Surfaces toolbar or the menu "**Insert, Face, Delete**".

Select all the faces inside the Cavity that outline a hole. Use the option "Delete and Patch" and click OK to finish.

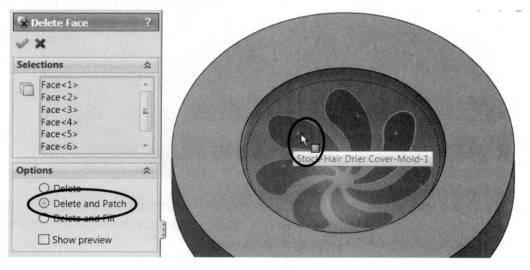

And now we have a single surface in the Cavity that can be easily machined with a CNC. Save and close the Cavity.

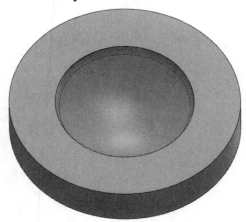

**500.** – Another common task is to add inserts to a mold. Opening the Core part, we see the protrusions that will make the holes in the cover extend past the top surface; these can be made from an insert in the core, or built in the same part as a single piece. The problem with a single piece mold is that it's harder to make, and if these protrusions wear out, it's more difficult and expensive to repair, whereas an insert can be replaced easier, cheaper and faster. We'll see how to cut an insert (if needed/wanted) from the Core by using a split feature. Make a new sketch <u>in the bottom of the part</u> and use "**Convert Entities**" to project the outlines of the inserts onto it (use "**Select Tangency**" to make selection easier).

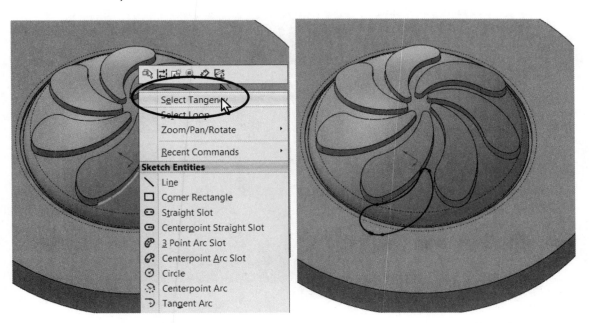

 We cannot select the top face and use "Convert Entities", because the surface at the top is smaller than it is at the base because of the draft we added to release from the mold.

**501. –** A different way to split a solid body is by using a surface. From the Surfaces toolbar select "**Extruded Surface**" or the menu "**Insert, Surface, Extrude**". Extrude the surface past the top of the Core. Click OK to finish.

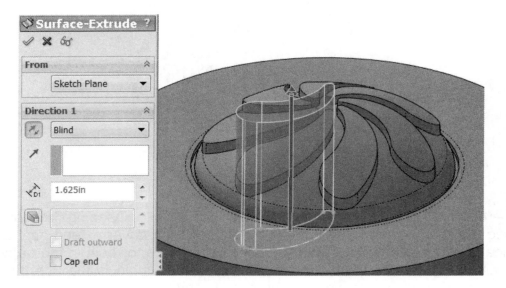

**502. –** Select the menu "**Insert, Features, Split**" and cut the part using the previous surface. Double click to give the insert's body a name and save it as *'Hair Drier Core Insert'*. Use the "Consume cut bodies" option. Click OK to finish and hide the surface used to split the part.

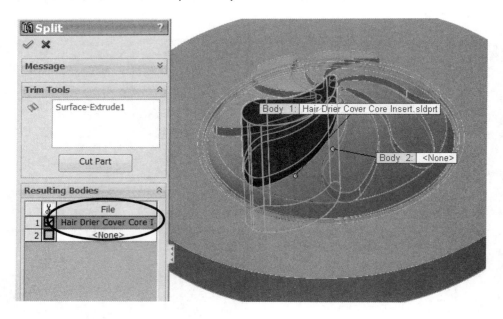

**503.** – To make the rest of the inserts, we'd follow the same procedure. In this part all the inserts are equal; we can make one insert and use a cut extrude feature to cut out the rest of the holes.

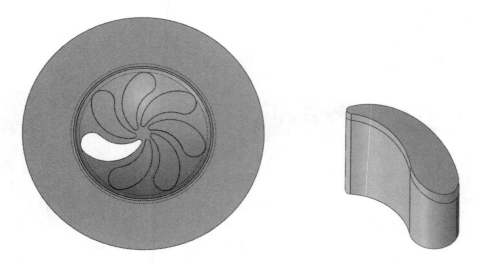

Save and close the all the parts.

**504.** – For the next exercise, we are going to use a part that will not automatically generate the correct parting line and we'll have to manually select it. Download *Hair Drier Mold Exercise* from www.mechanicad.com/download.html and open it.

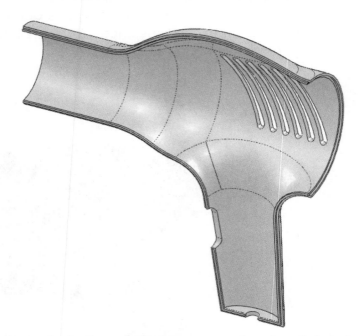

This part is complete, including vents, power cord and switch cutouts; drafts have been added to the necessary faces and external relations have been broken to prevent possible conflicts with user generated files.

**505. –** In this part we'll show a new option available when we make a draft analysis. Select the "**Draft Analysis**" command, pick the Front plane as the "Direction of Pull" and enter 3 degrees draft.

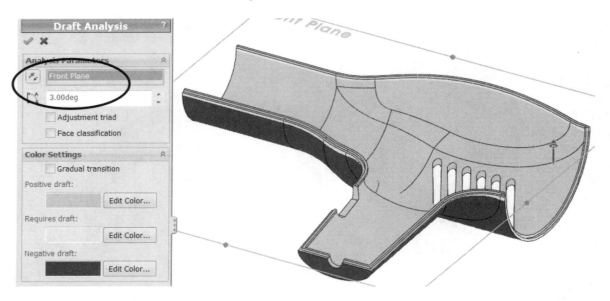

Under the "**Analysis Parameters**" options turn on the "**Face classification**" checkbox. This option will identify the model faces as "Positive", "Negative", "Requires draft" or "Straddle faces". "Straddle faces" refers to a face that has both positive and negative draft; this usually happens when a round face or a fillet crosses the parting line. An advantage of using this option is that we can turn on or off faces by clicking on the 'glasses' icon to easily identify them, and we also know the number of faces in each situation.

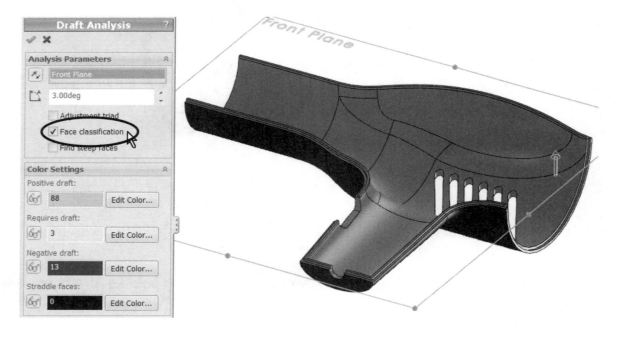

**506.** – Click in the 'glasses' icons next to the green and red boxes to turn off the "Positive" and "Negative" draft faces and identify the faces that require draft. Here we can see that only three faces do not have the three degrees draft required. At this time we'll proceed to make the core and cavity and ignore these faces. Click Cancel to continue.

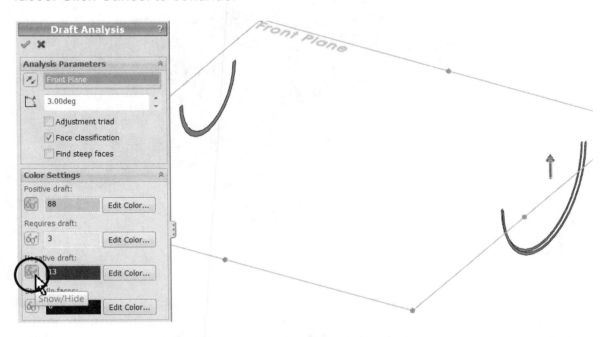

**507.** – To compensate for shrinkage in the mold when the plastic cools down, scale the part and make it 2% bigger. Select the "**Scale**" command; use the option "**Uniform Scaling**" about the "Centroid" and enter **1.02** as the scaling factor. Click OK to finish.

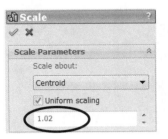

**508.** – Select the "**Parting Lines**" command; use the Front plane for the "Direction of Pull" and enter **3 degrees** for the draft angle. Press the "**Draft Analysis**" button when done. A parting line is automatically selected, but since we left three faces with no draft, we need to review and make sure the parting line is where we want it (experience helps in making these decisions).

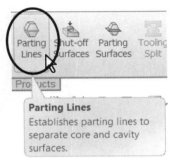

**Parting Lines**
Establishes parting lines to separate core and cavity surfaces.

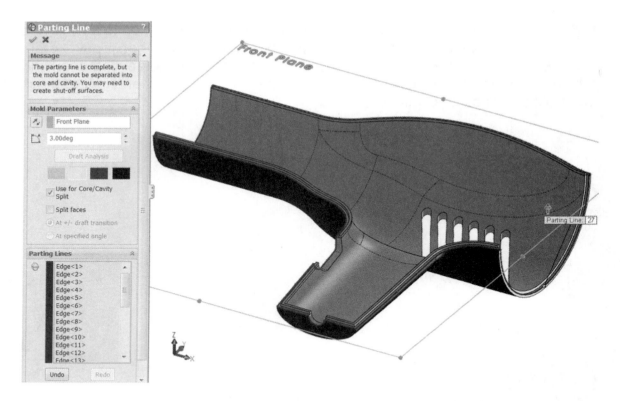

Upon closer examination, in the front and back of the hair drier we see small faces on one side of the parting line and a larger face on the other side; in this case it's more convenient to make both of these faces on the same side of the mold.  Unselect the edges between the green and yellow faces in the front and back of the part, and select the edge between the red and yellow faces. *(To show the Edge labels, they were selected in the Parting Lines selection box to enhance image visibility.)*

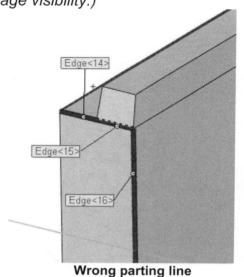

**Wrong parting line**

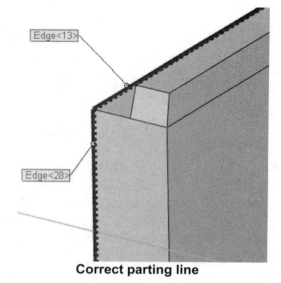

**Correct parting line**

Repeat for the other side on the front of the hair drier...

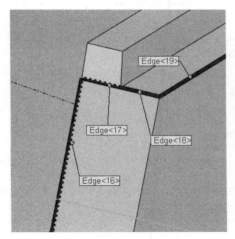

**Wrong parting line**

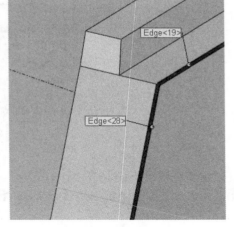

**Correct parting line**

...in one side of the back of the hair drier (where the cover goes)...

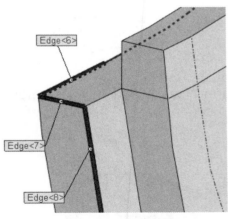

**Wrong parting line**

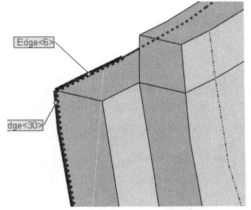

**Correct parting line**

... and the *other* side in the back of the hair drier.

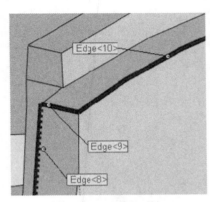

**Wrong parting line**

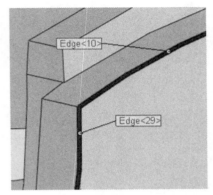

**Correct parting line**

The message in the "Parting Line" command is in yellow and says that the parting line is complete but we still need to create shut-off surfaces. Click OK to continue.

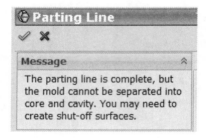

**509. –** Select the "**Shut-off Surfaces**" command from the Mold Tools toolbar or the menu "**Insert, Molds, Shut-off Surfaces**".

All the holes are automatically selected and closed, and now our mold can be separated into core and cavity. Click OK to continue.

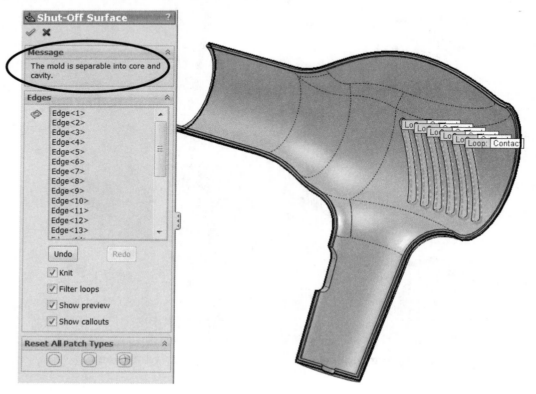

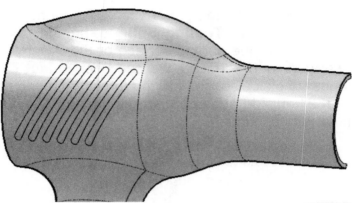

**510.** – The last step before creating the core and cavity is to select the **"Parting Surface"** command from the Mold Tools toolbar or the menu "**Insert, Molds, Parting Surface**". Use the option "Tangent to surface" and enter a surface distance of **0.75"**. Make sure the "Knit all surfaces" option is checked. Click OK to finish.

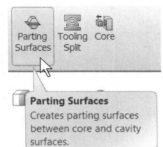

**Parting Surfaces**
Creates parting surfaces between core and cavity surfaces.

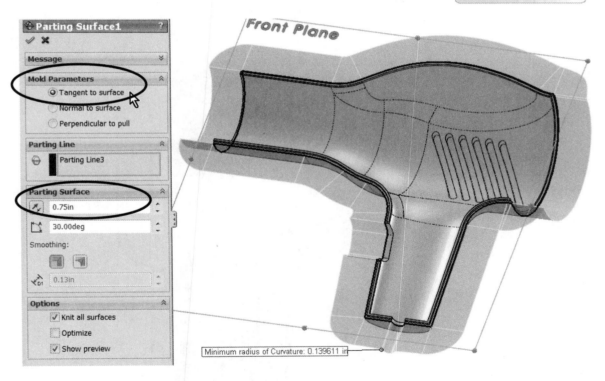

In this case, using the option "Perpendicular to pull" generates surfaces that are not desirable, and we would have to delete them, create new surfaces and knit them to complete the parting surface, and then move the knitted surface to the "Parting Surface Bodies" folder before we can make the tooling split.

**511. –** After completing the "Parting Surface" command, we can proceed to splitting the mold. Select the "**Tooling Split**" command from the Mold Tools toolbar; pick the flat face of the parting surface or the Front plane to add a new sketch. When we work with surfaces, we can use "**Select Open Loop**" (right mouse click an edge) to pick all edges around the surface and then use "**Convert Entities**" to project all outside edges of the parting surface into the sketch. Exit the sketch when done to continue.

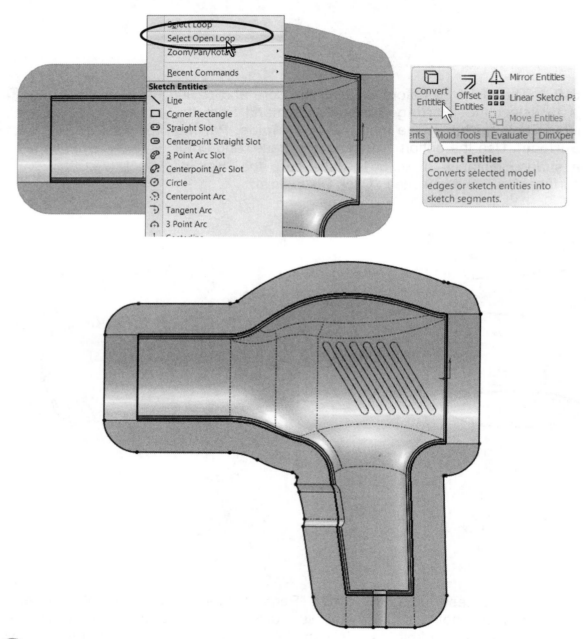

 The tooling sketch must be bigger than the parting line and as big or smaller than the parting surface.

**512. –** Back in the "**Tooling Split**" command make the "Block Size" big enough to fully enclose the part. Click OK to continue.

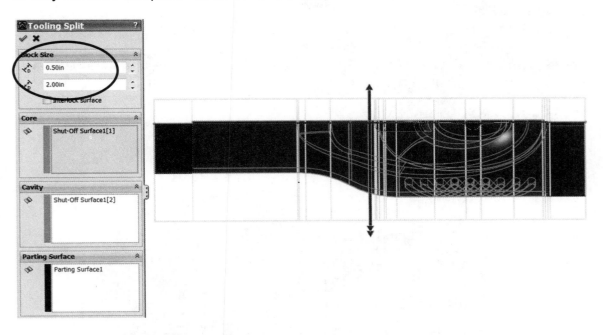

**513. –** Hide the 'Parting Line', and all 'Surface Bodies'.

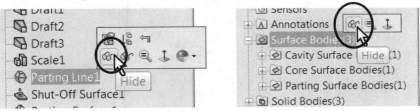

… and then hide the body at the top of the mold to see the cavity and the part. Optionally, change the color of the part's body (just the body's color) to make it easier to identify.

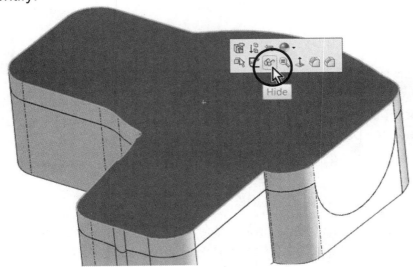

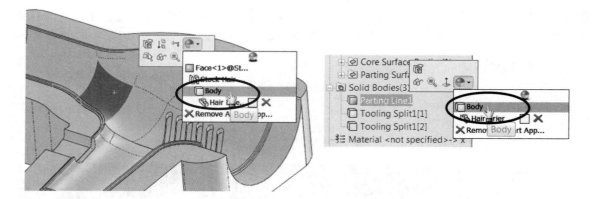

Save and close the file.

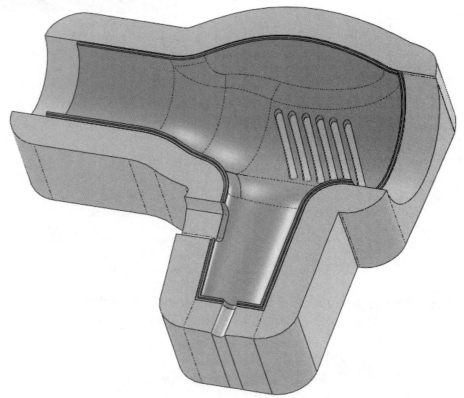

**CHALLENGE:** Insert the Core and Cavity bodies to a new part file.
- In the Cavity part, delete the vent holes markings and make a smooth surface (like we did with the back cover).
- In the Core part, cut an insert for the vent holes

**514. –** In the last mold exercise we'll learn how to make a "**Side Core**". Think of a side core as a part split from the core or cavity to help us make a feature that would otherwise not allow the part to be released from the mold, like a hole perpendicular to the "Direction of Pull", an undercut, or a negative draft face in the positive draft side of the part. Download the part *Bucket Mold* from www.mechanicad.com/download.html (or the bucket we made in the Surfacing lesson) and run a "Draft Analysis" with 3 degrees using the Top plane as "Direction of Pull". Use the "Face classification" option to show the "Straddle

faces" in and around the holes for the handle. The blue faces will not let the part release from the mold using a two part mold, and this is a good example of a situation where we need to make a side core. After a part is molded, the side core is pulled out from the mold first, then the mold is opened and the part is released. Cancel to continue.

**515. –** Add a 3 degree draft to the outside face at the top of the bucket in the negative draft direction (down). Use the "Along Tangent" face propagation option.

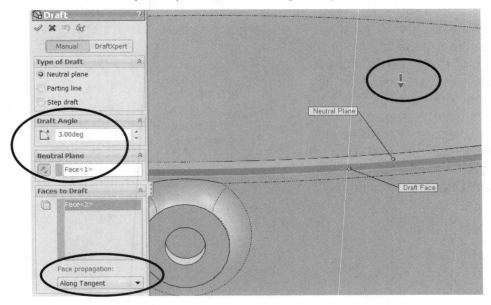

**516.** – The next step is to add a draft to the side cores, since they also need to have it in order to correctly release from the part, but in this case the "Direction of Pull" is along the boss' axis. Edit the 'Boss-Extrude1' feature and activate the "**Draft**" option with 3 degrees. Turn on the "**Draft outward**" option.

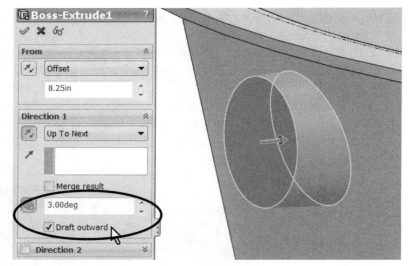

**517.** – Now edit the 'Cut-Extrude1' feature and also activate the "**Draft**" option with 2 degrees, but in this case the "Draft Outward" option is off.

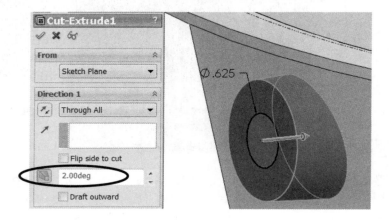

**518.** – Run a "Draft Analysis" using the flat face in the boss for "Direction of Pull" and 2 degrees. The boss and hole now have the draft angle needed for the side core to properly release. And since the boss on the other side is a mirror of the first one, it should also be correct. Cancel the "Draft Analysis" to continue.

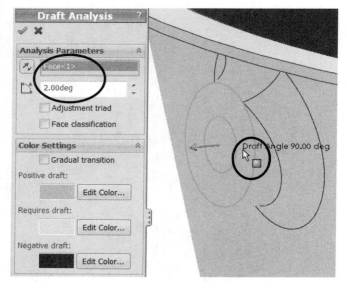

**519.** – Add a "**Parting Line**" using the Top plane or top face for "Direction of Pull".

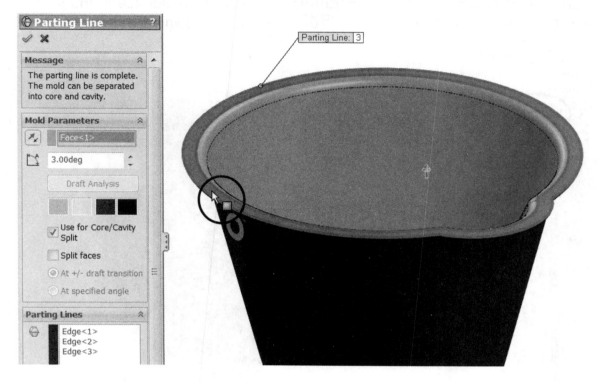

**520.** – Add a "**Parting Surface**". Make the surface 2 inches "Perpendicular to pull" using the "Smooth" option. This option smoothes the transition between adjacent surfaces, giving us a better result in certain situations like this.

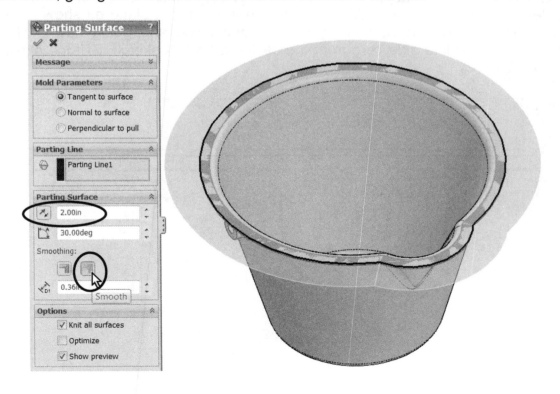

**521.** – Select the "**Tooling Split**" command, add the tooling split sketch in the parting surface and use "**Convert Entities**" to project the surface in the sketch. Exit the sketch and make the block size 1″ up and 13″ down as shown.

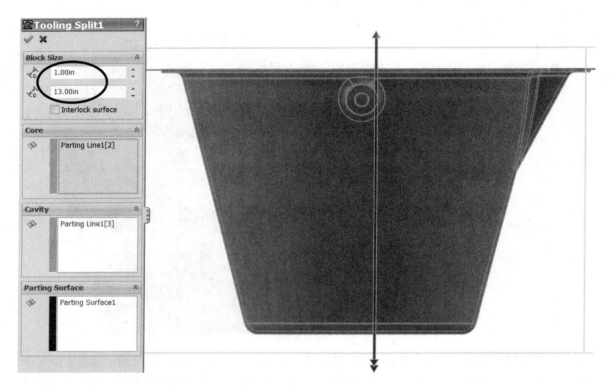

**522.** – Now we are ready to make the side cores. Switch to a Front view and hidden lines visible mode. Add a new sketch in the Front plane as shown. The sketch is a closed profile starting at the parting line and going down. The objective is to split a side core from the cavity using this sketch. Exit the sketch when done.

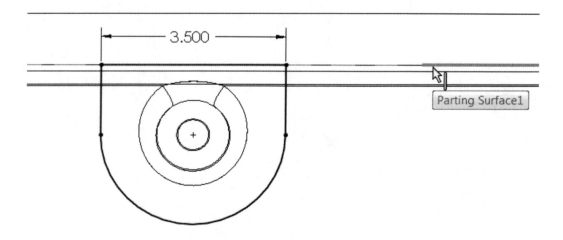

**523. –** Select the "**Core**" command from the Mold Tools toolbar or the menu "**Insert, Molds, Core**", and select the sketch we just made.

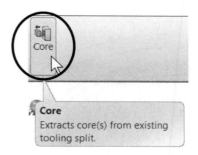

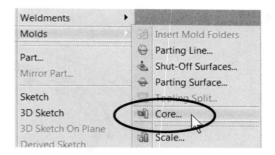

In the "Core" command, select the cavity's body, which is the one we want to make a core from, and in the "Parameters" options use the "Through All" end condition. The preview will show the core split from the cavity. Click OK to split the cores.

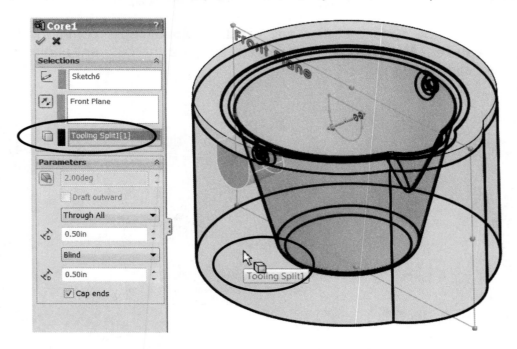

The core is added to a "Core bodies" subfolder in the "Solid Bodies" folder.

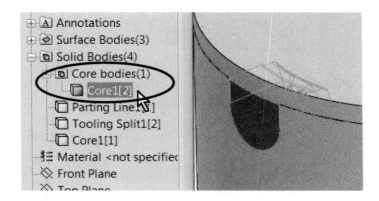

**~4. –** Make the same sketch again in the Front plane and make a second Core, now going in the other direction. Click OK to finish the second core.

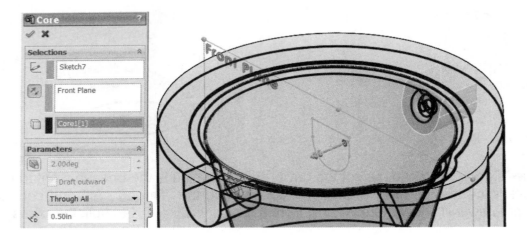

**525. –** Hide all the surface bodies and use the "**Move/Copy**" command (menu "**Insert, Features, Move/Copy**") to separate and see the different bodies of the mold including the side core.

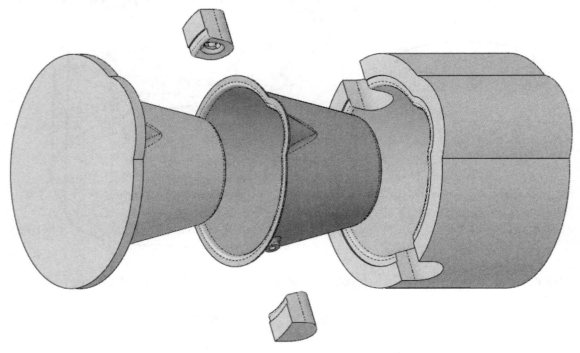

At this point the different bodies would be inserted into a new part to continue adding the mold specific features. Save the part and close.

**CHALLENGE:** Save the core, cavity and side cores to external files.

# *Final Comments*

After going through the exercises in the book, the reader will have acquired a good understanding of several topics including sheet metal, welded structures, 3D Sketching, Top Down design, Editing tools, Multi Body parts, Surfacing, Mold tools and a handful of tips and tricks that can help a designer work faster and more efficiently.

Even though most of the topics included in this book are usually considered advanced, they are presented using simple examples that break down the concepts and make them easy to understand. Topics covered explore the most commonly used options to enable a reader to use them efficiently for the different design tasks at hand.

The Sheet Metal, Mold tools and Welded structures topics fall within the scope of the individual manufacturing trades, each of which has very specific tools, techniques and 'fine details' that are (usually) learned after studying and by experience, like mold making, that includes most of the tools available in SolidWorks, going from the very basic to advanced surfacing, mold tools and more.

The amount of trade training that can be shown in a CAD oriented book is limited, since the objective of the book is to teach how to use SolidWorks and not a trade. If a reader has experience in one of these fields, he/she will quickly understand the purpose of specific tools, but we also tried our best to explain in a basic form trade terminology and processes so a *trade-untrained* reader can understand the purpose of a tool and the reason for certain operations.

We welcome all suggestions and ideas. This is the first edition of the *Level II* book and we are almost sure we may have missed a couple of details, or perhaps there are models that are easier to make or can show certain functionality easier. If you have any comments about this book, by all means please send it our way; we'll really appreciate it.

Please visit our website as we have other materials available that we are sure will be of interest to the reader.

Sincerely,

Alejandro Reyes,
*Certified SolidWorks Professional, Instructor and Support Technician.*

areyes@mechanicad.com
Mechanicad Inc.

# *Index*